Abroad in Japan

www.penguin.co.uk

Abroad in Japan

*Ten Years in the Land of
the Rising Sun*

CHRIS BROAD

PENGUIN BOOKS

TRANSWORLD PUBLISHERS
Penguin Random House, One Embassy Gardens,
8 Viaduct Gardens, London SW11 7BW
www.penguin.co.uk

Transworld is part of the Penguin Random House group of companies
whose addresses can be found at global.penguinrandomhouse.com

Penguin
Random House
UK

First published in Great Britain in 2023 by Bantam
an imprint of Transworld Publishers
Penguin paperback edition published 2024

A CIP catalogue record for this book
is available from the British Library.

ISBN
9781804992227

Typeset in Bembo Book MT Pro by Jouve (UK), Milton Keynes.
Printed and bound in Great Britain by Clays Ltd, Elcograf S.p.A.

The authorized representative in the EEA is Penguin Random House Ireland,
Morrison Chambers, 32 Nassau Street, Dublin D02 YH68.

Penguin Random House is committed to a sustainable future
for our business, our readers and our planet. This book is made
from Forest Stewardship Council® certified paper.

In dedication to the incredible Abroad in Japan community, who've joined me on this wild ride over the last decade.

Contents

Prologue: The Interview

JANUARY 2012

I was sitting in the corner of one of the cavernous rooms at the Japanese embassy in Mayfair, London. The room was impressive, with a golden chandelier dangling from the ceiling and a lavish red carpet, but it was practically empty, giving me nothing to distract me from my mounting nerves. The only furniture was a table, on top of which sat a clipboard holding the results of the English grammar test I'd just completed. It took all my self-control not to sneak a peek.

There are few things in life more nerve-racking than a job interview for a role you desperately want. After a five-minute eternity, the towering oak doors opposite me swung open and one of the embassy staff ushered me into an equally imposing room, motioning me towards a single chair facing a long table and two unimpressed interviewers.

I'd been anxiously awaiting this moment for three years, and in the next few minutes the polite but seemingly emotionless middle-aged Japanese man and a somewhat sterner-looking British guy – an alumnus of the programme I was hoping to gain a place on – would determine my fate. The whole set-up had something of a good-cop/bad-cop vibe, which didn't do much to quell my nerves.

In 1987, the Japanese government launched an initiative to place native English speakers in schools throughout the country in a bid to improve English-language proficiency and encourage grassroots internationalization. In the two decades since, the JET scheme had become the largest exchange teaching programme in the world, with over five thousand participants a year from fifty-seven countries.

For me, this was my sweet ticket to a spectacular adventure on the far side of the world. Now, having made it successfully through a rather lengthy written application process, all I had to do was overcome this final hurdle.

I'd obsessively researched the interviews online and discovered from past applicants that the secret to success was to be overly positive. The perfect foreign teacher should come across as *genki* (元気) at all times. This commonly used Japanese word means 'energetic' or 'lively', two words that have never been used to describe me, so it was with great difficulty that I forced a creaking smile for the duration of the thirty-minute interview.

'How is your Japanese?' asked the British alumnus, skimming his pen across my application form.

'No.' I replied, and instantly cringed at my awkward reply. 'Er, sorry . . . I mean, not no. But not good. I absolutely plan to learn if I'm lucky enough to get the job.'

Then the Japanese interviewer, who'd been flipping through his copy of my application, let out a chuckle when he arrived at the page with my preferred location choices.

'So, in your application for your preferred locations, you've written that you'd like to live either in the countryside or in Kobe. Could you explain why?'

It was common knowledge that the quickest way to fail a JET interview was to ask to be placed in Tokyo. There are very few positions in the scheme available in the densely populated capital, and unless you have a clear reason to be there it comes across as a lazy or ill-informed choice.

'The truth is, I'd be happy living anywhere in the countryside. I like the idea of playing a bigger part in a smaller community. You could put me in a cave in Hokkaido and I'd be delighted.'

The room fell silent, and I realized that my cave comment had been taken at face value. The interviewers exchanged puzzled looks before pressing on.

'But why Kobe?'

I had been quietly dreading being asked this question. The reasoning behind me choosing Kobe was pretty poor. I'd spent a few days exploring Japan on Google Maps and concluded that Kobe was perfectly positioned between Kyoto and Osaka, two cities that intrigued me, close to each other yet stark contrasts between traditional and modern. Beyond that, Kobe was home to the world-famous marbled Kobe beef. I'd foolishly assumed this legendary meat must be cheap and easily accessible to the residents of Kobe, and so, to me, it would make sense to live there.

'Well, honestly, the beef looks bloody good around there.'

Anticipating another wave of silence, I was relieved to hear both interviewers break into laughter.

'Good thinking!' said the Japanese interviewer. 'Kobe beef is very delicious indeed.'

I'd dodged a bullet, but I knew I wasn't off the hook just yet. There was one last thing I was dreading being called up on. On my application form I'd remarked that I'd read numerous books about Japan, citing one in particular, about wabi-sabi, a Buddhist philosophy and aesthetic that's notoriously difficult to define.

'Chris san, you say you've read about wabi-sabi. Would you be able to explain to us what it is?'

The best way to describe the concept of wabi-sabi (侘び寂び) is that it's about embracing imperfections and appreciating the beauty in the incomplete or the imperfect. Often the most sought-after hand-made pottery in Japan are pieces that appear asymmetrical, simplistic or modest. This is an ideology very much at the core of Japanese living.

That would have been a fantastic answer.

Instead, I looked at the floor and mumbled, 'Er . . . er . . . it's like . . . well . . .'

The Japanese interviewer peered over his glasses intensely, and I realized that this was a make-or-break question. This was my chance to prove that I had the communication skills expected of a teacher.

'Well, look, the thing about wabi-sabi is that it's something that can't simply be defined. It's more of a feeling or an emotion than a clear, definable concept.'

What a load of shit.

Fortunately for me, his sense of humour had kicked in again.

'Haha, yes. It certainly is a difficult thing to explain – I know what you mean!' He chortled for a moment, then said, 'Well then, that's all for now. Thank you.'

It was over.

Stumbling out of the imposing building and across the road to Green Park tube station, I knew in my heart there was no way on earth I'd get that job.

However, somewhere amidst my disastrous replies, something must have worked. Perhaps it was my evocative description of wabi-sabi, or the sheer desperation of offering to live in a cave in Hokkaido, but twelve weeks later, to my utter shock and delight, I received a letter informing me that I'd been accepted. My life was about to take a sharp turn nearly 10,000 kilometres east, to a country I knew little about, for a job I felt woefully underprepared for.

I.

The Sushi Revelation

To travel between London and Tokyo is one hell of a jarring transition, traversing no less than eight time zones and a cultural divide that nothing could have prepared me for.

As I said goodbye to my parents and hauled my bag-laden trolley into the departure lounge at Heathrow airport, I had no idea when I'd see them again or how many years I would be away. Any thoughts of sadness were suppressed by adrenaline and anxiety at the journey that was about to begin. The flight from Heathrow to Tokyo Narita airport would take around twelve hours, inflicting the worst possible jet lag just in time for my arrival.

I stared out the window and watched the London rooftops give way to the North Sea and the forests of Scandinavia, then all signs of civilization gradually faded, as almost all the flight time was spent 11,500 metres above expanses of remote Siberian tundra.

I attempted to get some sleep, but the girl beside me – a fellow participant in the JET scheme – had a snore so loud it put even the sound of the whirring jet engines to shame. As there was to be no excited chatter on this flight, I leafed through a cheap

Japanese phrasebook, eventually falling asleep while trying to memorize my self-introduction for my school speech.

Aged twenty-two and fresh out of university, I was still consumed with disbelief that my first graduate job was on the opposite side of the world in a country where I knew no one, with a language I had no real comprehension of.

While I'd always hoped to visit Japan, the idea of living there hadn't crossed my mind until, at the age of eighteen, I'd learned about the JET programme on a flight to France. I'd sat next to a sweet middle-aged couple whose daughter was currently teaching in Japan, and they were thrilled to hear that I hoped to travel the world and teach English after graduating. By the end of the flight they'd convinced me to enrol and had ignited a new passion in me.

Given this whole journey had kicked off from a conversation with strangers on a plane, it was unfortunate that today's far longer flight had yielded no such destiny-altering encounters. Just buzz-saw snoring and frustration.

After the twelve hours had passed, I awoke with a thud as the plane landed at Narita airport. As I looked out at the grim terminal building, it all felt rather anticlimactic. There were no *kawara* roof tiles or pagodas. A quick scan of the landscape offered no far-off view of a snow-capped Mount Fuji. There was almost nothing to indicate that we'd landed in Tokyo. And, to some extent, we hadn't.

It quickly transpired that Narita Airport wasn't so much in Tokyo as slapped down in some rice fields 70 kilometres east of the city.

As I stepped out of the terminal and into the oven-baked afternoon, I was appalled that the air could be so despicably humid; each breath was like inhaling a mouthful of steam. Fortunately, before my blood had the opportunity to evaporate, I was promptly bundled on to a waiting coach along with the other JETs, where I said a prayer to the gods for the absolute miracle that is air conditioning as we took off down the highway into Tokyo.

If Narita has one thing going for it, it allows you to appreciate the sheer, breathtaking scale of the world's biggest city. The journey begins on the endless plains of Chiba prefecture with clusters of traditional Japanese homes nestled between miles of rice fields. Gradually, towns emerged alongside the highway, the rice fields replaced by utilitarian apartment blocks and billboards with smiling men and women grasping must-have beauty products. I spotted a tacky love hotel built in the shape of a medieval castle with the awkward name 'Hotel Smile Love Time' emblazoned across its rooftop.

Thirty-seven million people call the greater Tokyo area home. That figure seems almost incomprehensible – over half the British population in just one city – but when your eyes first set upon the Tokyo skyline, it's a figure that quickly becomes believable.

In the space of just one hour all greenery had disappeared. As our coach crossed the Rainbow Bridge in Tokyo Bay we were surrounded by towering high-rises on all sides, the iconic Tokyo Tower – Japan's answer to the Eiffel Tower – protruding through the skyline. With my face pressed up against the window, I was in absolute awe that no matter where I looked there were more skyscrapers, more concrete, more chaos. In terms of sheer scale, it made an absolute mockery of London.

Snaking its way along ever more complicated highways and overpasses sandwiched between rows of buildings plastered in billboards of glamorous celebrities tempting us with Asahi beer and Suntory whisky, our coach took us deeper into the heart of Tokyo. The two-hour drive felt more like a theme-park ride, my stomach dropping as we were launched up and down a succession of highway ramps. But at last we arrived at the prestigious

Keio Plaza Hotel in Shinjuku's skyscraper district. Consisting of two towers and 1,400 rooms, it was one of the few spaces large enough to house the annual influx of JETs.

Herded off the coach, I got my first whiff of the Tokyo summer air: hot, humid and teeming with the pungent smell of sewage from the city's decaying system of pipes concealed beneath the utterly spotless streets.

Up until this point, having got on to the JET programme and feeling a great sense of pride, I'd deluded myself that I was special. But as I stood in the vast lobby of the Keio Plaza Hotel, just one in a thousand foreign faces, it dawned on me that I was merely a cog in a well-oiled machine.

As I reached the front of the queue, a Japanese man thrust me a key card to my room, which was up on the twenty-fifth storey. I was sharing a triple room with two sporty British lads called Colin and Michael. Crashing open the door, I found the two of them laughing and discussing rugby. My entrance seemed a bit of a distraction.

'Where are you guys headed to then?' I enquired, plonking my backpack down on the one bed clear of luggage, the one by the window.

'I'm off to Himeji, right next to Japan's most famous castle,' declared Michael with a smugness that implied he actually owned the castle.

'Yeah, and I'm off to Nagasaki, mate,' beamed Colin.

God damn it. Why didn't I get Nagasaki or Himeji?

'And where are you off to?' asked Michael, curious to see if I was about to trump his castle.

'I'm in Yamagata. It's in the north.'

'Oh yeah? Can't say I know it.' Michael threw me a victorious smirk, fully aware that he'd won JET placement Top Trumps.

I felt drained after the endless journey, but my fatigue was

4

outweighed by my restlessness. I left Colin and Michael discussing rugby and masculinity and snuck out of the room and into the dying light of Tokyo at dusk. The golden hour illuminated the top floors of the glimmering towers dotted through the skyscraper district. The twin peaks of the Tokyo Metropolitan Tower stood out to me, offering, according to my Japan guidebook, 'The best view of Tokyo – for free.'

As a weirdo who obsesses over observation decks, I'd clambered up numerous towers for views across a number of cities, from Shanghai and Seattle to Barcelona and Berlin. But as I stepped out of the lift of the Tokyo Metropolitan Tower and pressed my weary forehead against the glass windows at the top, I gazed out in amazement across a city with seemingly no end. From where I was standing, at the centre of the metropolis, to the hazy outline of the mountains surrounding the city, I saw only concrete. The view was both exhilarating and frightening.

I watched as in the space of twenty minutes darkness swept across the vista and millions of tiny lights in windows dotted across the skyline started popping on. The lights sparkled across the vast expanse, as mesmerizing as a firework display. Witnessing Tokyo at dusk for the first time felt somewhat momentous and I decided it demanded a celebration.

Propping myself up on a stool by the window in the over-priced observation-deck coffee shop, I tucked into a ludicrously expensive slice of chocolate cake and watched the sun set over 36 million people. By the last mouthful, I was so tired I'd collapsed on to the table and drifted off. I must have slept for almost half an hour before a waitress came over and gently tapped me on the shoulder, to kick me out.

What followed were two days of intense training and orientation sessions peppered with desperate attempts to try and bond with my new companions. The JET seminars were a hazy blur of jet lag and information overload. On my second day, instead of attending an important talk on what not to do in Japan, I spent the morning recovering in bed, eating a packet of underwhelming soy-sauce-flavoured crisps from 7-Eleven. I snuck into a workshop later that afternoon, on the dos and don'ts of working with Japanese teachers, and hoped no one had noticed my crisp-filled absence. An enthusiastic British girl called Amy who was on her second year of JET was running the workshop and posed a series of multiple-choice questions to the anxious audience.

'If a Japanese teacher makes an English mistake in front of the class, what should you do? A. Stop the class and point out the mistake. B. Continue the class and say something to the teacher quietly away from the students. C. Ignore the mistake and let the class carry on.'

There was momentary pause before an eager guy with a Southern US accent shouted, 'B!'

'Yes, you don't want to embarrass the teacher in front of the class and cause any friction with your colleague. Though when this occurs, it's always best to assess on a case-by-case basis, depending on the teacher.'

When this occurs. It dawned on me there and then that Japanese English teachers might not be so good at English after all. Up until this point, I'd envisioned taking the back seat in classes, being guided by a proficient superior. It hadn't occurred to me that I might be the most knowledgeable person in the room. Suddenly the responsibility of the role felt a lot heavier.

I'd been keeping my room mates, Colin and Michael, at arm's length, given our clear lack of common interests. Any attempts at small talk and bonding had so far been fruitless. Nevertheless, it was our third and final night in Tokyo, and seeing as we knew no one else in the city, we decided to venture out into Shinjuku's gritty red-light district. The JET programme organizers had warned everyone to stay away from Kabukicho, due to the danger of street touts luring unwitting tourists into shady bars run by local crime syndicates. Unsurprisingly, their warnings had the opposite effect. Now we *had* to go.

The entrance to Kabukicho was marked by a giant red illuminated gateway, with the road sloping down into a blinding array of billboards and neon promising food, sake, karaoke and love. One hoarding for a hostess club showed six young women in bikinis smiling and beckoning revellers with outstretched hands. Alongside it, a sign with the silhouette of a cow and the word 'Wagyu' alluded to a neighbouring steak restaurant tucked within a stack of buildings. To the right of the cow, there was an image of a pair of hands massaging a back beneath the English word 'Flamingo' and a list of prices, for example ninety minutes for 2,500 yen. Steam rose from a shack selling buns from a hole in the wall and the deafening sound of jingles and slogans being played simultaneously from advertising screens the size of buses blared out overhead. Overwhelmed and utterly naive, I had no idea what was going on.

Used to British shops and restaurants, which are typically on the ground floor, the thing that struck me in Tokyo was the sheer verticality of Japan's dining options. Restaurants and bars were stacked on top of one another, with neon signs indicating what could be found on each and every floor. While it gave the streets a futuristic, cyberpunk aesthetic, it also made picking a restaurant rather intimidating, given there was no way to see inside. We rode a lift up to the third floor of a building, the gaudy sign promising cocktails, and the doors opened up to a dingy interior with a crowded bar counter and a barman making an 'X' gesture with his arms. Either the bar was full or he didn't want us there. We promptly scurried away.

Eventually we settled for a sushi restaurant on street level where we could at least peer in through the glass windows. We were reassured by the sight of a bustling interior, complete with a team of chefs dressed in characteristic white aprons and hats passionately crafting *nigiri* sushi.

Walking into a Japanese restaurant for the first time, I was nearly knocked off my feet when everyone from the chefs to the waiting staff erupted with an '*Irashaimase!* Welcome!' It was a real chorus of tones, from the booming deep voice of the head chef to the high-pitched screech of a passing waitress delicately balancing two *hinoki* wooden plates.

Given it was evening rush hour and commuters were ducking and diving into restaurants for dinner, nearly every seat in the restaurant was taken, leaving only three stools at the counter. A young woman running between tables hurriedly approached us, holding up three fingers, indicating the size of our group. We nodded.

'*Hai, douzo!* This way please.' She steered us to the counter and placed a piping-hot cup of green tea before us, then disappeared off to a nearby table.

I'd only ever eaten sushi two or three times in the UK, and only ever from supermarket shelves. The experience of flavourless fish stuck atop a nugget of rock-hard rice hadn't exactly sold me on it. As I sat, bracing myself for the real thing, I became engrossed by the half a dozen chefs working rapidly in unison to serve up a cuisine that seemed closer to artwork than food.

Three chefs were slicing away at sumptuous fresh cuts of tuna and salmon, while two others moulded the rice in their hands into perfect balls. I noticed another chef with a small blowtorch methodically searing a slice of tuna resting on a ball of rice, turning the fish from pink to golden brown under the glow of the flame. The finished piece was carefully placed on a wooden plate alongside a variety of *nigiri* with an assortment of toppings, from salmon roe to a fluffy-looking omelette and cuts of white fish I'd

8

never seen before. The alluring, sweet scent of the seared fatty tuna met with the already overpowering smell of fresh fish, giving the room the feel of a coastal port rather than the middle of the world's biggest city.

While the menus were absent of English, fortunately they came with gloriously tempting photos of each piece of sushi. I pointed to a platter of tuna. The bountiful plate featured three cuts of tuna: *akami*, a dark red, meaty cut; *ootoro*, the fattiest of all, light pink in appearance; and *chutoro*, the medium fatty cut. These three cuts had been seared, shredded, sliced and wrapped to perfection, served up as *nigiri* hand-pressed sushi, *maki* rolls and a few slices of sashimi served on a bed of *daikon* radish, alongside a blob of wasabi. The twelve-piece platter of sushi came in at 2,700 yen ($24), which seemed much pricier than my supermarket meal deal.

I popped the first *chutoro nigiri* in my mouth.

The first thing I noticed was the *shari* – the rice itself. Perhaps the most underrated ingredient in sushi outside Japan, the rice is infused with vinegar, salt and sugar to give it a distinctly sharp, sweet flavour. It had a sticky yet firm texture that made it easy to pick up but it somehow effortlessly broke apart in my mouth. I'd never had anything like it. The 'sushi' I'd experienced in the UK felt like a hate crime compared to this.

And then there was the *chutoro* tuna itself. It had a buttery, melt-in-your-mouth consistency reminiscent of a good steak and was surprisingly free of almost any fishy taste. The balance of fat and meat gave it an incredibly satisfying bite, especially when complemented with a subtle kick of wasabi.

'Holy crap. So *this* is what sushi tastes like,' I observed.

'This puts British sushi to shame,' spluttered Colin, taking a breath before stuffing more sushi into his mouth.

When the tuna had first been brought to the table, I'd been worried that it wouldn't be enough. It all looked so delicate. But after my twelfth piece, I was about ready to explode. I'd underestimated how filling vinegared rice could be.

The meal took a turn for the worse, however, when Michael insisted on ordering us a dish to finish the meal off.

'My friend in Japan said I needed to try this when I went for sushi. It's called *shiokara*.'

None of us had heard of it, but I grew concerned when I caught the baffled expression etched on the face of a nearby sushi chef when he overheard our order.

A few moments later, we discovered that Michael had poor taste in friends.

Three small dishes were brought over by a waitress, and one was placed before each of us. It looked like somebody had gutted a fish and thrown the bloody entrails into a bowl.

Because they literally had.

It turned out *ike no shiokara* meant 'fermented squid guts'.

'A must-try dish, eh?' I remarked as I pushed my chopsticks into the brown, sloppy mess.

'Yes. Though I fear it's time I was leaving for Himeji castle . . .' A suddenly less smug Michael got up to leave.

The chef slicing his way through a fillet of tuna behind the counter laughed at our reactions.

'*Ganbatte ne!* Good luck!' he urged, comically clutching his fist as though bracing us for battle.

Not to disappoint my champion, I took a mouthful and instantly felt my tongue shrivel at the salty, bitter taste. I swiftly dived for my green tea.

Several chefs and customers at the bar squealed and cheered with glee.

I'd survived my first trip to a Japanese sushi restaurant and, fermented squid guts aside, it'd been nothing short of a revelation.

2.

The Japan Lottery

With the intense honeymoon period of the three-day Tokyo induction at an end, everyone I'd ever met or befriended was abruptly whisked away, never to be seen again.

Some were sent off on bullet trains to exotic cities like Osaka, Himeji and Kobe – presumably to eat the wagyu beef that I'd hoped to be eating. The less lucky ones were bundled on to coaches heading to Tokyo's less exotic neighbouring prefectures of Chiba and Saitama. As each semi-familiar face faded into the distance, any sense of security I'd felt faded too.

As for me, I was escorted on to a minibus to Haneda airport for a one-hour flight north to Yamagata. I was joined by just one other JET colleague, a shy but friendly guy from Colorado called Mark, and our Japanese minder, who would be hand-delivering us to our Japanese colleagues in what felt like some kind of glamorous prisoner exchange.

As our plane took off, I started to feel increasingly nervous. It wouldn't be long before I was standing in a school, trying to present myself as a teacher. To reassure myself, I dug into my pocket and pulled out my now tattered and torn employment letter. There was one line written by my Yamagata-based JET coordinator that I kept returning to.

'Congratulations, Chris, you've won the Japan location lottery.'

I gazed at the words with a growing sense of dread.

The odds that I was about to arrive somewhere exciting felt impossibly remote. In the anxiety-riddled days leading up to my journey to Japan, I'd frantically attempted to learn as much as I could about Yamagata, the rural prefecture I'd shortly be calling home for the next few years of my life.

A Wikipedia search on the region and its population of 500,000 inhabitants had yielded just one result: 'Yamagata is famous for its high yield of cherries.'

Outstanding.

There was no mention of landmarks, festivals or anything of cultural or historic value. But thank goodness there were cherries. They'd see me through.

I began to overanalyse the excessively positive tone of my letter. Perhaps it was little more than a ruse to sugarcoat the uncomfortable truth that I was off to Japan's worst region.

My concern growing, I distracted myself by peering out of the window. We were flying over the stunning Ou mountain range which runs like a spine down central Japan. The country's longest mountain range, at 500 kilometres, it would soon become the physical barrier between me and everyone I knew. The mountains were undeniably beautiful, with sharp, rocky peaks giving way to endless luscious forests. While most images synonymous with Japan are either Tokyo's urban sprawl or Kyoto's red-lacquered shrines, in reality, 70 per cent of Japan's surface area consists of mountains and forests. Its mountainous landscape is the reason so much of the country's population is crammed into the plains in between, giving rise to the concrete megacities of Tokyo, Nagoya and Osaka.

Our Japanese minder, who'd so far been almost silent, suddenly leaned forward and pointed out of the window.

'In the winter, these mountains, many snow,' he grinned, rather ominously.

I nodded in acknowledgement, unaware at the time that the paltry inches of snow I'd experienced back in the UK were nothing compared to what I'd be seeing later that year. I had no idea that the Ou mountains experience some of the highest snowfall on the planet from December to March, making escaping Yamagata all but impossible during the winter months.

As we made our final approach I looked out to see a 30-kilometre plain of verdant green rice fields criss-crossed with perfectly straight roads that lead to Mount Choukai, a volcano perched sinisterly on the horizon. Through the humid summer haze I could just about make out the 2,200-metre summit and I wondered if this towering peak would lead to my demise if it were to erupt. After all, in the UK, earthquakes and volcanic eruptions were events just glimpsed on the news or while scrolling through Wikipedia. To my relief, I soon learned that the volcano was more or less dormant, last caught puffing out a mediocre quantity of smoke in 1974. Rather than imparting dread, the sleeping giant of Mount Chokai would quickly become a daily reminder of how lucky I was to live in such a magnificently exotic landscape.

The Shonai plain was sandwiched between the Sea of Japan in the west and the Ou mountains in the east, making it quite the dramatic landscape. It couldn't have been more different to the chaotically carved-out fields and rolling hills of the British countryside.

Here, there was a sense of order, as if each field had been painstakingly measured out into rectangles, and the plain itself was perfectly flat, before abruptly giving way to towering mountains. The contrast between the turquoise sea, the vivid green rice fields and the hazy blue mountaintops was an incredible sight to witness for the first time. Though I'd never recommend visiting Japan in August unless you want to experience what it feels like to be a rotisserie chicken, there's no doubt it's at its most visually striking at the height of summer.

'Ladies and gentlemen, we will shortly be arriving at Shonai airport. Please fasten your seatbelts and prepare for landing.'

I stuffed the letter into my pocket and quickly did up my top button. I was dressed in smart work clothes, as I'd been warned I'd be taken directly from the airport to meet the school principal: effectively, it would be my first day on the job.

By this point, I was a dishevelled wreck. The nerves churning in my stomach combined with the jet lag to induce a brain fog that rendered me incapable of coherent speech. The idea of conversing with anyone of importance in English, let alone in broken Japanese, filled me with fear. I suspected I was about to become the most quickly fired English teacher in Japan's history.

As we approached the arrivals hall, Mark bent down to tie his shoelaces. I feebly hoped it was a sign of his own anxiety.

'You feeling nervous at all?' I asked, hoping to share in some kind of JET camaraderie.

'No. Not particularly,' he said, continuing to tie his laces without a hint of emotion.

Bastard.

After the noise and commotion of Haneda, Shonai airport felt pretty small. There'd barely been any passengers on the flight. It seemed the allure of the cherries had failed to reel in any Japanese tourists.

I began to wonder what I'd let myself in for but was quickly snapped out of my downward spiral. The moment of reckoning was here. We hauled our luggage through the arrival gates to meet our new work colleagues. The first test.

The door opened to reveal two waiting groups of Japanese teachers clutching placards bearing our names. A tall, middle-aged man with wire-framed glasses raised the one that read 'Chris Sensei' with a friendly smile.

He was standing between two colleagues who looked older, one a man with almost identical glasses, and a woman who was smiling and waving.

It was an encouraging start.

'Well, Mark, I guess this is it—' I turned to say goodbye, but Mark had already wandered off with his group. So much for life-long friends.

My handler gave a quick bow to my waiting colleagues, said, 'Nice to meet you,' then disappeared into thin air like an apparition. Finally, the training wheels were off and I was on my own with my three new colleagues.

I walked over, waving over-enthusiastically with both hands. '*Konnichiwa*, hello!' They all bowed. '*Konnichiwa*. Nice to meet you, Chris san.'

'Please, let me take this,' gestured the taller man, grabbing the trolley from me and placing the placard inside. 'Maybe you would like some coffee?'

'Yes, please. I feel dead from jet lag,' I joked awkwardly. They all nodded with a smile and ushered me over to the small café within the airport.

Once we'd ordered iced coffees and sat down at a table in the corner, I felt all eyes on me. My three colleagues were still smiling, as if their expressions had been frozen in place.

The older man broke the uncomfortable silence. 'So, Chris san, did you have a good flight?'

'The flight was decent, but good god, do I feel jet-lagged!

Tokyo was pretty intense, with the onslaught of training and whatnot. And it was so hot I barely slept a wink the whole time I was there,' I blurted out without pausing.

Silence followed, and I looked around at my three colleagues. Their expressions remained fixed, though they had nodded along politely.

No response. Maybe I had said something offensive or inappropriate. I took a long sip of iced coffee to fill the silence, praying someone would say something. The older man looked at his colleagues before speaking gently.

'Chris san. Maybe could you speak again, a little more slowly, please?'

Oh crap. They hadn't understood a word I'd said.

I'd later discover that of the eleven Japanese teachers I was to work with, only one had lived overseas longer than three months, and at least three couldn't speak or comprehend English at all. As pleasant as most of my colleagues would be, it seemed that being able to speak English wasn't necessarily a qualification required to become an English teacher in Japan. That might partly explain Japan's low ranking in English proficiency, placed fifty-third out of a hundred countries, far below China and South Korea.

The speed at which I spoke, combined with my British accent – American English is typically taught in Japan – meant that anything I said was pretty much indecipherable.

'The flight was good. But I'm very tired with jet lag. Tokyo is so hot!' My words came slowly and deliberately, and it worked. I could see that my usual sneering, sarcastic speech personality, packed full of metaphors and nonsensical British slang, was redundant here. My vocabulary was going to have to be dramatically simplified in order to communicate – which resulted in me coming across as even more boring than I already am. In time, hand gestures would also start to feature far more prominently in my interactions.

'Ah yes. Tokyo is so very hot in summer!' said the older man, and the other two nodded along in agreement.

It was at this point that they formally introduced themselves. The younger man was Nishiyama sensei. Uncharacteristically tall for a Japanese man, he was in his late thirties and had spent three months in Canada studying English. He spoke it slowly and methodically, clearly focusing very hard on not making any grammatical errors. This style of speech had an eerie, almost robotic quality to it, saved only by his warm, slightly unnatural smile.

Next was Kengo sensei, who I would find out was in his late fifties but looked like he was in his early forties. He was the most confident English speaker of the three and spoke with a mild American accent. He'd travelled the world and loved to play guitar, and had learned English through his love of music. He'd been part of the post-war peace movement in Japan, involved in protests against the military and atomic weapons. He was the most enthusiastic of the three and seemed obsessed with London, something I hoped would work in my favour.

Finally came Saitou sensei, who seemed to lack confidence in her speaking skills. 'My English, not so good!' she jokingly remarked, more or less leaving her introduction at that and retreating to down her coffee.

They were all very different to one another, but all friendly and welcoming in their own, slightly awkward way.

'Chris san, the principal is waiting for you. Shall we go?' Kengo said, wandering off to pay the bill.

I downed the last drops of iced coffee, and we stood up and headed to the nearby exit. Outside, I was met with the scorching heat and my first experience of the deafening sound of the cicadas which forms the soundtrack to the Japanese summer: imagine the sound of a million crickets sped up and played through festival speakers. The outside of Kengo sensei's car was so hot I could barely get the door open without grilling my fingers.

I needed to cool down fast. Looking like I'd just clambered out of a swimming pool was most certainly not the first impression I was aiming for with the school principal.

During the twenty-minute drive to the school, I slumped by the car window, trying to catch the breeze as we drove through endless rice fields sprinkled with hamlets, each with a bright red *torii* gate and traditional Japanese homes topped with *kawara* roof tiles. Mount Choukai loomed overhead, almost too perfectly, as though the region had been terraformed to create the quintessential video-game Japanese landscape. The view and the screeching of the cicadas brought it back to me that I was a long way from home. Nothing about this setting felt remotely normal to me.

Weirdly, the thing that threw me most was that I couldn't see a single patch of grass. Now that I've lived here a few years, I've realized that most people don't even notice this absence; in Japan, every patch of land is either a rice field, concrete or a forest-covered mountain. None of the houses we passed had lawns; instead, a mixture of gravel and carefully curated trees adorned the tiny gardens of each home. Even the local parks were predominantly comprised of gravel and sand.

I would later learn that less than 1 per cent of schools in Japan had playgrounds featuring grass, and in feudal times only lords would have lawns, and these were ornamental, a visual feast for the eyes.

Unfortunately, my time pondering the ins and outs of grass was almost up, as we arrived in the town I'd call home for the next three years of my life.

Sakata (酒田) literally, 'sake, rice field', was an unremarkable-looking town. In fact, if it were a British town, it would most likely be referred to as run-down. At the mouth of the Mogami river, in the past Sakata had been a bustling merchant shipping town, but its glory days were long since over.

For hundreds of years, merchants had shipped the lucrative safflower plant, used, among other things, to produce dye for clothes and pigment for luxury lipstick, from Yamagata down the river to Sakata and then along Japan's west coast to Kyoto and Osaka, a trade that had generated immense riches for Sakata and the Shonai plain. So much money was made in this quiet backwater that the local Honma clan became the largest landholders in Japan, leaving a legacy of estates behind. However, given the not so prosperous appearance of modern-day Sakata, there were few indications that such glorious wealth had ever existed here.

The twentieth century hadn't been as kind to the region, with a tragic fire in 1976 at the local cinema burning down most of the town's prized historic architecture and clearing an area of 22 hectares in the town centre.

The old buildings had been replaced with generic, utilitarian apartment blocks and buildings devoid of any discernible character. The one saving grace for Sakata was the waterfront, lined with trees and with huge, rustic rice warehouses built from wood giving on to a canal with bobbing fishing boats. These warehouses with their immaculately tiled roofs were a great source of pride for the town and were showcased in every mention of Sakata online.

As our car meandered through the maze-like streets, there seemed to be a troubling number of empty or abandoned shops and houses, albeit neatly boarded up, which made me wonder if I'd just been posted to Japan's most decrepit city. But each time this feeling of disappointment arose it was immediately washed away by the sight of an immaculately curated bonsai tree, a bright red *torii* nestled in front of a shrine or a trendy-looking *izakaya* restaurant branded with striking kanji characters.

I felt restless, wanting to hop out of the car and explore, just as I had during the endless seminars in Tokyo. Like in an open-world video game, I wanted to unleash myself and discover my new surroundings. The issue was, I'd been on work hours from the moment I landed in the country.

As we made our way through downtown Sakata, I noticed more derelict shops, their shutters pulled down and their windows boarded up. The ghost-town atmosphere pointed to one of rural Japan's biggest problems: rapid depopulation.

Japan's population peaked at 128 million in 2010. By the time I arrived, in 2012, it had declined by almost 1 million, and it is predicted to drop below 100 million by 2050. And it was rural Japan that had borne the brunt of it, as younger generations fled to nearby cities such as Sendai or Tokyo to partners and work opportunities that didn't involve farming.

In rural towns such as Sakata schools frequently closed or combined with other schools. The school I was about to work at was the culmination of three separate schools merging into a brand-new mega school, the largest senior high in north Japan. As we turned the corner, Sakata Senior High appeared before us, its white exterior beaming in the afternoon sun and the new school gym towering nearby, big enough to house a space shuttle. It was perhaps the most impressive modern building I'd witnessed on our drive through the town.

'Welcome, Chris sensei, to Sakata Senior High School,' beamed Nishiyama sensei as he drove us through the gates and into the car park. We bundled out of the car and stood in the shadow of the gigantic gymnasium, which gleamed in the burning afternoon sun. Heat radiated off the tarmac, to the point where I'm confident we could have fried a full English in seconds.

To call Sakata Senior High a school would be a massive understatement. It was a huge complex comprising three newly built school buildings with classrooms, a gym, a hall large enough to house an aircraft fleet – or, at the very least, 1,200 students and 120 teachers – and a sprawling playground covered in (you guessed it) dirt.

It was an intimidating sight but, to my relief just then, it felt as much of a ghost town as the town centre had. As it was August, the students were off school for the summer holiday, save for a few who were doing clubs and activities. As we walked up to the entrance, three girls dressed in sportswear scurried passed, bowing and greeting us cheerfully.

We all nodded back and I replied with an upbeat '*Konnichiwa!*' The girls hurried off, looking back furtively to catch a glimpse of their new, dishevelled English teacher. I could only imagine their disappointment.

As we headed inside I was struck by a clear difference between Japanese schools and British schools: rows and rows of shoe racks. Every single person who sets foot in the building has to remove their outdoor shoes, place them on a rack and switch to a pair of indoor-only trainers. This was my first experience of Japan's forbidden-footwear culture. You must always remove your shoes before entering a Japanese home and even before entering some public spaces. God help you if you step on a tatami straw-mat floor in your trainers. One of the few times I've truly seen a Japanese person snap was when a friend wandered into a public bathhouse without removing his shoes, only for the elderly woman at the reception desk to spring up out of her chair and forcibly push him back out of the door.

Given it was my first time, it felt undeniably odd as a grown adult to be standing in my socks at the entrance to my new workplace. But I would soon adapt to this way of thinking. Today, years later, I feel like I've committed a criminal act if I wear shoes indoors.

As it was my first day and I hadn't yet invested in an indoor pair of shoes, Kengo sensei handed me some slippers, saying, 'Don't worry, Chris san, we'll buy some shoes tomorrow.'

Nishiyama led me into the cavernous building, and we passed two giggling schoolgirls sitting on a bench who blurted out, 'Hello!'

I smiled and gave a quick nod. 'Good afternoon!'

'*Kakkoii!*' one of them replied, and they both laughed. I had no idea what it meant, so I gave a thumbs-up and hoped they hadn't just called me a twat.

When we were a few steps away Nishiyama sensei turned gleefully to me with a chuckle, and said, 'They said you are cool.'

Phew.

Kengo and Saitou sensei trailed behind us, grinning all the while, like my own beaming private entourage.

The inside of the school was ridiculously hot, the heat amplifying the smell of the freshly polished floors. In the summer months, instead of using air conditioning, the school just opened the windows, which did almost nothing to lower the sauna-like temperatures.

My shoes squeaking on the immaculate floors, I strolled past walls covered in student artwork depicting local scenery and a huge blue poster of an angry manga policewoman holding up a hand beneath the English words 'No! Drug!' I assumed it was trying to dissuade students from taking drugs, but the slipshod syntax almost made it seem as though the officer was encouraging the students to stop what they were doing and take drugs immediately.

Just as I'd started to feel at ease wandering through the empty school, we arrived at the doors to the staffroom and Nishiyama turned to me with his characteristic glee.

'OK, Chris sensei, before we meet the principal, you can introduce yourself to the staff.' He presented this news as if he was offering me an all-expenses-paid trip to Disneyland.

Oh god.

'Er, like, right now?'

'We should do it now.'

'Oh, I'm just so jet-lagged!' I joked half-heartedly, hoping to escape the abject terror of addressing dozens of colleagues.

'It's OK. Just a short introduction.'

Nishiyama slid the door open to reveal a sprawling rectangular office filled with dozens of desks piled high with books, paper and laptops. On a typical workday, around 120 teachers would be in the staffroom, marking, typing, napping or disciplining students who had misbehaved.

Luckily for me, as it was the summer holidays, only about thirty teachers were present. If the room had been full, I think I would have cried. Around the room, a few teachers glanced over to suss out the new guy.

I knew I needed to make a good first impression, and for that to happen I'd have to at least try to introduce myself in Japanese. I'd successfully memorized five key sentences from the induction but suspected that I'd quickly come undone when attempting to deliver them in front of everyone.

I was escorted across the room to a long table where no less than three vice-principals sat facing me, like investigators on a government commission.

All three stood and greeted me with a bow and a *Yoroshiku onegaishimasu*, a Japanese greeting that literally means 'Please have favour upon me in our future dealings' and is used in the same way we'd say 'Nice to meet you' in English. They were all men in their fifties or sixties, their seniority clearly reflected in their slick businessman suits and their huge desks at the head of the room, facing the rest of the staffroom in an intimidating Orwellian fashion.

One of the three, but only one, seemed genuinely delighted by my presence. It quickly became clear why when he started speaking in rapid English.

'Welcome, Chris sensei, I'm Saitou. It's my pleasure to meet you.'

'Thank you. Oh, er, Saitou?'

I turned to Mrs Saitou, who'd accompanied me from the airport.

They both shook their heads with a laugh, waving their arms furiously.

'Oh, no, no!' Saitou chuckled. 'Many people in Sakata are Saitou. Too many Saitou.'

I'd noticed that Saitou had been speaking in whispers as he ushered me towards the window. I sensed he was reluctant for his colleagues to know that he was secretly fluent in English. He hid it as if his very life depended on concealing his sneaky English proficiency. I soon discovered that the dozen or so teachers who spoke English but didn't teach English were also reluctant to show off their skills, in case they found themselves having to take on more responsibility or being asked to help out in the absence of the English teachers.

'How was your flight? You must be very sleepy?'

'Haha, yes, I'm still quite jet-lagged.'

'Are you ready for your *jiko shoukai*? Your introductory greeting?'

'Yes, I'm ready.'

I wasn't.

He turned to face the staffroom, his voice struggling to compete with the noise of a dozen electric fans turned on in a desperate attempt to cool the room down.

'*Minnasan!* Everyone, could I have one moment, please!'

The teachers stopped what they were doing and promptly turned their attention to us. One teacher had clearly just woken up from his afternoon nap, his head emerging from a pile of textbooks.

'I would like to introduce our new foreign English teacher, who comes from London. Please, Chris sensei.' He gestured for me to step up and give my introduction.

Ah, crap.

'*Minnasan, konnichiwa.*' I gave a gentle bow. In unison, the teachers said hello and bowed back.

In my nervous, dream-like state, I mumbled on in Japanese.

'Er. How do you do? My name is Chris. I'm from London in the UK. This is my first time in Japan. Er . . . my hobby is photography. My Japanese isn't very good. I'm still studying . . . er . . . nice to meet you.'

Having delivered my powerful state-of-the-nation speech, I gave a deep bow and arose to applause and a chorus of '*Yoroshiku onegaishimasu!*' Then, as quickly as the teachers had snapped to attention, they continued on with their day. The napping teacher lowered his head on to his pile of books once more.

Before I had a chance to be relieved, I was ushered out of the room. Nishiyama took me to meet the *kouchou sensei*, the school principal. He was in his late sixties with steel-grey hair, square glasses and a stern expression. Suzuki sensei was just two years from retirement and his intimidatingly large office was filled with indecipherable awards.

'Oh! *Konnichiwa!*' In a booming voice he encouraged us to sit on one of the couches surrounding his lavish coffee table. Like clockwork, his assistant brought in three cups of green tea and vanished before we could even say thank you.

We exchanged pleasantries and Nishiyama told me that Kouchou sensei's daughter had studied at Cambridge University.

'Oh wow, did you go to England?' I asked Kouchou sensei, hoping his trip to England hadn't left any negative impressions of my home country.

He said something and turned to Nishiyama to translate. 'Yes, he went one time and tried fish and chips. They were very delicious.' Ah yes, fish and chips. England's gift to the world.

After a few moments of polite small talk, something I'd never experienced before happened. Both Kouchou sensei and Nishiyama sensei went completely silent. I'm not talking about a momentary awkward silence. I'm talking about a deafening silence that went on for ever. It was as if we'd initiated some kind of impromptu meditation session. It might sound trivial, but it was phenomenally uncomfortable and genuinely concerning. Had I said something wrong? No one even looked around or out of the window. Nishiyama and the principal sat motionlessly, staring at the green tea, as if they'd been powered down.

I coughed in an attempt to jolt people back into the conversation, but there was no response. I cast my eyes over the vacuum that was the office and pretended to read the plaques and trophies. I couldn't tell if we had been there for twenty seconds or two hours.

A few agonizing moments later and completely without warning, Nishiyama rebooted, looked up and said, 'Well, I think we should let the principal get back to work.'

'Yes, definitely,' I said, and stood up abruptly, immensely relieved that the experience was over.

'Good luck!' The principal bellowed, catching me off guard with his English, and we left the room with a series of bows.

Once we were out of earshot, I turned to my new colleague.

'Er, Nishiyama sensei, did that go well?' I felt slightly deflated after that rather frosty first meeting. Had I committed some unspeakable offence?

'Yes, Chris sensei, I think he liked you very much.' His reply seemed sincere. But what on earth had just happened?

I'd later learn that in Japanese culture these long periods of silence, *chinmoku* (沈黙), were commonplace. It has its roots in Zen Buddhism, where silence is said to hold the secrets of existence. The Japanese proverb 'It is better to leave many things unsaid' captures the essence of *chinmoku*. Far from being awkward, in Japan silence is a natural part of daily interactions. However, on this first day at the school, I had yet to discover this, and left the principal's office wondering just how long I'd last here. I had an awful lot to learn.

My accommodation was a ten-minute drive from the school, in a four-storey concrete apartment block owned by the local government. The exterior looked more like a prison in the former Soviet Union, but it had optimistically been painted pink to try and cover up what was essentially a travesty of architecture. The overall effect was probably more depressing than if they'd not bothered at all. Nishiyama sensei showed me to my room on the first floor and swung open the door to reveal a tiny apartment with a comically small kitchen. There was zero counter space for cooking. Just a sink and a gas hob, with a rice cooker stacked on top of the microwave, which itself was stacked on top of the fridge.

The air conditioning clearly hadn't been on for a while so we stepped into a blast of heat. I noticed the pungent smell of the fresh tatami mats that had been fitted just before my arrival. It's not an easy smell to describe to someone who's never smelled tatami before. While in Japan it's a nostalgic smell, beloved by adults, reminding them of their childhood, to me it smelled more like a farmyard. Imagine a bale of hay mixed with freshly cut grass with undertones of mouldy socks. I couldn't say I was a fan.

Walking a whole two steps through the luxurious kitchen, we opened the sliding door to reveal a small living area kitted out with a black leather couch at the far end, a *kotatsu* table, a reclining chair sitting on a cheap rug, and finally, in the corner, what may have been Japan's tiniest television. For a country renowned for its tech prowess, I was a little underwhelmed by my decidedly retro apartment. My main concern was how on earth I was going to stay warm in the winter months given the absence of radiators and the paper-thin walls. The *kotatsu*, essentially a table with a heater underneath to keep your legs and feet warm, seemed like a nice idea, but in practicality, it was no substitute for the twenty-first-century heating that was so sorely missing.

I noticed the absence of a bedroom and asked Nishiyama where I would sleep.

'Ah yes, your futon is here!' He opened the large, creaking wardrobe, and a poorly folded futon burst out, as if clamouring to escape. Clearly the previous owner had jammed it in hastily before leaving.

Looking around the room, I couldn't help but feel that an apartment this small would be illegal in the UK. The one saving grace was that it was dirt cheap, at about $110 a month. It also had a tiny balcony, adorned with two severely rusted chairs that looked like a first-class ticket to tetanus. Bonus.

'Thank you for your good work today, Chris sensei. Please get rest. Tomorrow I will pick you up for work at 8 a.m.'

I thanked Nishiyama sensei as he walked out the door, leaving me to luxuriate in my palatial residence. I flopped on to the leather couch. It was surprisingly comfortable.

During the last, intense four days, since the moment I'd arrived at Heathrow airport, I'd been on a carefully choreographed journey, seemingly exercising no free will of my own. Now, alone at last, the reality of the situation dawned on me. After all those years of hoping, here I was, alone in a room in north Japan, wondering what the hell I'd got myself into.

3.

Sweat and Sand

AUGUST 2012

'Chris sensei, won't you join me on Monday morning for some special event?'

I'd taken a liking to the softly spoken, music-loving Kengo sensei, who'd helped me immensely since I'd arrived in Sakata. And so without questioning what the event was, I'd blindly said yes to his vague invitation as we left work on Friday afternoon.

'Very good! I will pick you up at 7 a.m. and we will go before work.'

It had been a brutal first week of relentless travel, introductions and jet lag. With the students away, I'd spent my first few days in a nervous stupor, rearranging the papers on my desk while trying not to break anything or offend anyone.

But at last I was a free man about to embark on my first weekend alone in Japan. I'd resolved to explore my new surroundings.

I was rudely awoken on Saturday morning by the sound of a screeching mountain hawk who liked to perch majestically on a neighbouring apartment-block roof. Unable to get back to sleep, I stumbled bleary-eyed out of my apartment at 9 a.m. into the already scorching sun with only a paper map and the distant outline of Mount Chokai as a rough guide. I hadn't yet got my hands on a mobile phone, so I was going to have to do things the old-fashioned way.

My first port of call was the local Family Mart convenience store. The moment the doors swung open I was met with a loud *Irashaimase!* that nearly knocked me off my feet. Still uncertain as to how to react to the welcome chants one receives when walking into a Japanese store or restaurant, I gave a half-hearted nod and a smile and began bumbling down the aisles in search of recognizable food and drink.

A staple of Japanese life, there's an impressive sense of clockwork discipline to the convenience store. Every customer who enters is faced with the exact same welcome. Regardless of what burdens the staff are facing, be it the hectic lunchtime rush, a till malfunction or the end of the world itself, they would never hesitate to shout '*Irashaimase!*' the moment the doors swing open. To ensure they don't miss a single customer, each chain of shops has its own jingle that plays when you enter the store, with Family Mart's iconic eleven notes the most famous and well known. Technically, Family Mart doesn't own the jingle – it comes from a Panasonic-made doorbell – but, regardless, in just five minutes in the store I'd heard the jingle play at least twenty times. It's a testament to the Japanese work ethic that staff can endure the jingle over a thousand times on a single shift and still maintain any degree of sanity.

Compared to a British corner shop, Japanese *conbini* are light years ahead in terms of the sheer breadth of services they provide. The big three brands are 7-Eleven, Family Mart and Lawson, and as well as being open twenty-four hours a day, 365 days a year, absolutely without fail, each store is fully stocked with an ATM, a photocopier/printer, washrooms and a computer you can use to pay for everything from flights to Disneyland tickets. You can even pay your bills at the till. And that's not even mentioning the extensive range of food, drinks, ready meals and an area where you can prepare them, complete with microwave, coffee machines and a kettle. Simply put, living off just a single Japanese *conbini* is frighteningly easy. The only inconvenience is deciding which one to go to. Even out here in the middle of nowhere, I had no less than four stores within a five-minute radius to choose from.

Perusing the drinks refrigerator, I noticed a few familiar brands, such as Coca-Cola and Tropicana, but for the most part I was confronted by a selection of colourful, alien-looking products, the names of which, to my surprise, were all written in English. A striking yellow bottle labelled 'CC Lemon' caught my attention, a carbonated soft drink that proudly boasted '33 lemons' worth of vitamin C'. Next to it on the shelf sat the questionable-sounding Pocari Sweat, a popular isotonic beverage, and next to that an equally questionable drink named 'Salt and Fruit'. Feeling bold, I grabbed a bottle of Pocari Sweat and tried not to think about the connotations.

Shelf after shelf was filled with perfect crustless sandwiches and *onigiri* riceballs filled with everything from tuna mayo to pickled plum. Each came wrapped in dark green, crispy *nori* seaweed and they were presented in a variety of shapes and sizes, the most common being triangles, which sat upright, as if they were patiently waiting to be snatched up by a customer in a hurry. On the top shelf of the *onigiri* fridge, I noticed a bright pink plastic wrapper with the concerning words 'Baked Sand' slapped on it. Clearly Japanese cuisine was more complex than I'd imagined. Fortunately, on further inspection, it became clear the item was a sandwich wrap, as opposed to some groundbreaking form of edible sand. *Sando* is short for 'sandwich' in Japanese, and it appeared not even that was short enough for the Baked Sand branding team.

Navigating the aisles filled with sweat and sand, I soon became aware of a young boy in a baseball cap following me around the store. He popped in and out of sight at the end of each aisle, making little effort to conceal his surprise at the presence of the baffled Englishman carefully examining random food items. After a couple of minutes of this intense surveillance, his mother dragged him away. '*Okaasan! Gaijin!*' he exclaimed, alerting his mortified mother to the foreigner in their midst. Her eyes darted sheepishly between me and the floor as she apologized with a *Sumimasen!* and gave a speedy bow, before disappearing into the heat with her cheeky son.

I knew this sort of interaction was going to be inevitable out here in rural Japan. With so few non-Japanese residents, I was something of an unwilling celebrity. I'd been told that, including me, there were less than ten Westerners living in an area with a population of 100,000 people. Even so, my first experience felt both bemusing and slightly awkward. I felt self-conscious for the rest of the day, painfully aware of all the drivers staring at me as I trudged down the roads armed with my Pocari Sweat and my first ever *onigiri*.

Following the map, I headed into downtown Sakata. I withdrew the rice ball from my bag and unwrapped it. Half expecting a chewy lump of dry rice, I was impressed by how moist and fresh it tasted, like it had just popped out of a rice cooker. The lightly salted rice complemented the creamy mayonnaise and chopped tuna in the centre, and the nori exterior added a deliciously satisfying crunch to every bite. I quickly saw the appeal of Japan's most popular fast food; it seemed infinitely superior to the crumb-laden mess of the depressing sandwiches back home, and I resolved to buy another one at the next convenience store I saw.

Sakata's practically empty streets made it feel like the Wild West. Pedestrians were a rare sight and over half the stores on the main shopping streets were closed, rusted metal shutters sealing them off. I almost expected to see tumbleweed rolling along the pavement, but the only things rolling around were the OAPs on *mamachari* bicycles (literally, 'Mum's bicycles') bursting out from the side streets before disappearing into alleyways.

The *mamachari* is the most common bicycle in Japan, and the best way to describe it is to imagine a bike stripped down to its bare bones: a seat with a basket and a bell and, typically, only one gear. The bike was manufactured after the Second World War to be affordable and appealing to busy mothers who needed to get around with groceries and children. The low frame and centre of gravity make it a safe, stable ride and, with the simplest bikes costing just 10,000 yen, they're often treated as disposable, left around like an old umbrella. It was a hideous-looking bike. And I wanted one.

I was still very much in a state of culture shock, and Sakata's street corners seemed full of surprises. I left the shuttered main street, dodging the occasional *mamachari* darting along the road, and came to a hill leading up to the town's only park. As I turned the corner I came face to face with a gigantic blue *hentai* drawing of a naked woman, her breasts on show and a faux shocked expression on her face as she gazed down at passers-by. Her thighs were adorned with the text 'Hair Salon Kaji'. *Hentai* characters are typically overtly sexualized and the preserve of manga comics read behind closed doors.

I stared in disbelief for a good few seconds, wondering how something so crude could possibly exist in Japan's sleepiest town, in a culture that is often considered incredibly conservative. Such abrasive *hentai* artwork looming freely over Sakata's main street, next door to a bakery that sold cat-shaped buns and across from a children's playground, was certainly a bold move. What did parents tell their kids when they caught sight of it on the walk to school?

As I stood laughing on the corner, an elderly woman hobbled innocently beneath the artwork. It was the perfect juxtaposition of Japanese extremes and an image I knew I wouldn't forget in a hurry.

Astonishingly, the *hentai* girl would remain visible for at least half a decade longer, before it was hastily covered up by a town map days before the emperor was due to visit the town as part of a tour of north Japan. After all, I suppose art is subjective.

I continued on, sweating profusely as I clambered up the hill. I reluctantly decided it was time to crack open the bottle of Pocari Sweat and prayed it didn't taste like its name. To my relief, I was treated to a sweet, citrusy beverage packed full of salts, which helped replenish the bucket of sweat I'd lost in the previous ten minutes.

At the top of the hill, I escaped the glaring sun by ducking into the shade of a small forest. As I pressed further in, the sound of the cicadas grew more and more deafening. I came across a striking *torii* leading to an immaculate wooden temple surrounded by trees and dense foliage. It's a cliché to describe Japan as a land of stark contrasts, but going from a poster of a naked woman to an ancient temple in the space of five minutes, it was certainly delivering.

A gentle breeze carried the sweet scent of half a dozen incense sticks burning in a large cauldron in the temple yard. The temple had a magnificent roof caked in *kawara*, and sitting on the ridge was a small statue of a demon, or *onigawara*, said to exorcise evil demons and prevent fires. The roof was so large it enshrouded the interior shrine room in darkness, even in full daylight. There was a notable absence of stone, the structure supported by aged wooden pillars, many of which appeared weathered and chipped. Standing before the temple, I felt an instant serenity, something I'd never experienced in the grounds of a Christian church surrounded by crumbling gravestones. Japanese temples tend to be walled in, with a stone path overlooked by *komainu* guardian lions and a small *temi-zuya* fountain, or tap, where worshippers cleanse their hands with cool water before prayer. In this case, there was also a small stand – closed today – where worshippers could purchase *omikuji* paper fortunes; you tie the bad ones to a piece of string, so as not to take the bad luck home with you.

A lone middle-aged man stood facing the shrine. He tossed a coin into a donation box and gave two deep bows, before clapping twice and closing his eyes in silent prayer. After a few moments of peaceful contemplation he gave one more deep bow and turned, jumping in surprise at the sight of the sweaty British guy clutching a bottle of Pocari Sweat for dear life.

He smiled with a warm *Konnichiwa!* And, seeing my bottle, chuckled. '*Atsui, desu ne!*' ('It's hot, isn't it!'). I nodded and replied in poor Japanese, 'Yes, it certainly is hot!' Sensing that I couldn't speak the language, the man promptly ended the conversation and gave a friendly nod before disappearing off into the forest. I'd noticed that Japanese strangers tended to flee the moment they realized I couldn't communicate in Japanese. I got the impression that the idea of escaping was far more appealing than deploying any English knowledge. Or perhaps folks out here really didn't know any English? I still wasn't sure.

I was tempted to pray myself, but having already forgotten the complicated clapping ritual, I carried on, strolling beyond the temple.

When I emerged on a ridge at the edge of the forest with sweeping views over Sakata, I could see fishing boats bobbing in the distant port and the afternoon sun shimmering off thousands of dark grey *kawara* on the traditional Japanese houses. Off into the distance, a lone cloud perched perfectly above the hazy outline of Mount Chokai.

I drained the last, salty drops of Pocari Sweat and tried to take it all in, vowing to explore the rest of the town and the distant mountains the moment I got my hands on a car. I made a mental note to visit this temple again once I'd mastered the art of Japanese prayer. Little did I know, just two days later, I'd be back again.

Come Monday morning, Kengo sensei arrived dead on 7 a.m., and we drove off across town, retracing the route I'd taken over the weekend. Heading in the direction of the port, I wondered if we were off to see the catch of the day or do some early-morning fishing. I couldn't have been more wrong.

Ten minutes later, we pulled up at the edge of the forest where I'd stumbled across the temple.

'We're here, Chris san. The service will begin in about ten minutes. Do you know today's date?' he asked rather cryptically.

I looked down at my watch: Monday, 6 August.

The penny dropped. As a member of the post-war peace movement, Kengo sensei had spent my first week telling me about the demonstrations he'd joined as a teenager, to call for Japan's demilitarization.

'Am I right in thinking this is a memorial service for the Hiro-shima bombing?'

'Yes, you guessed correctly, Chris san. On this day in 1945, a most terrible tragedy occurred. At eight fifteen in the morning, thousands of people were killed instantly. I feel I need to honour their spirits in some small way.'

Having grown up amid the chaos of the post-war era and the peace movement it inspired, Kengo sensei was looking beyond the politics of war. I hadn't heard him debate the events of the Second World War, nor seen him show any feelings of anger or hostility towards the West or those who dropped the bomb. He simply felt that it was essential to acknowledge the horrors of war and ensure that such a thing never happened again. Especially the use of nuclear weapons.

As I stood before the temple that morning with Kengo sensei and three locals who'd also come to commemorate the anniversary, it felt strange to be viewing the Second World War from the other side. The priest struck the great bronze *bonsho* bell, by pulling a rope attached to a stick the size of a battering ram. I bowed my head and reflected on the estimated 100,000 people – many of them civilians – who'd had their lives cut short that morning of 6 August 1945. As the echo of the bell reverberated through the forest and the temple grounds, eerily on cue the heavens opened and the pale morning sky began to rain down upon us.

My role as an assistant language teacher (ALT) meant that I'd be paired with one of ten Japanese teachers of English in each of the classes I taught, so forming good relationships with my colleagues was important. To kick things off, I faced the daunting task of trying to memorize everyone's name – not just the teachers in the English department, but in the whole school.

I'd never been good with names in English, let alone in another language. Given that the Japanese use names far more frequently when talking to someone than an English person would (the word 'you' is considered almost rude in Japanese), it was going to be quite a challenge.

Fortunately, I'd been given a booklet with names and profile photos of each one of the 110 teachers. Aided by a book on memorization techniques I'd snapped up at Heathrow airport, I used word association to force the names into my head.

Asami Shinya
I visualized someone knocking over a cup of *Assam* tea with their *shin*.

Natsuki Yoshiro
The video-game character *Yoshi*, *skiing* down a mountain
of *nuts*.

Shotaro Saito
A web*site* dedicated to *shot arrows*.

So I sat at my desk, going through the staff photos and making notes as curious colleagues and onlookers bustled past. I wondered if I'd lost my mind only eight days into the job. And my task wasn't made any easier by the fact that at least ten teachers shared the surnames Sato or Saitou – as common here as Smith is in England.

However, to my complete shock, in the space of just seven hours using this technique, by the end of the day I'd memorized all the names. I even asked Nishiyama sensei to test me at lunchtime, by covering the names and pointing at the photo.

After I had successfully conjured up two dozen names, Nishiyama slammed down the school booklet and congratulated me. 'You have a very good memory, Chris sensei!' he chuckled.

In my second week a procession of teachers – whose names and faces I now recognized – made the pilgrimage to my desk at the far end of the staffroom to welcome me to the school.

The friendliest teacher was Umetsu sensei, who taught business studies and spoke fluent English. A middle-aged woman with round glasses and a shiny black bob, she was delighted to have a new British colleague with whom she could discuss her obsession with George Michael. 'He has the very best face!' she exclaimed, handing me a box of premium matcha green tea. I accepted the generous gift and agreed wholeheartedly. I too liked George Michael's face.

The most bizarre conversation I had was with a colleague

from the English department called Komako sensei, an elderly woman on the cusp of retirement who came to my desk bearing a fistful of KitKats.

Komako sensei probably had the best English knowledge in the department, but she spoke very slowly and methodically, as if someone had turned the playback speed down to 50 per cent. While most other teachers came over and initiated small talk that would last around five minutes, Komako sensei turned each of our interactions into an extended interrogation about the world outside Japan, frequently demanding my views on the cultural intricacies of life in the UK.

'Chris sensei, I hear you eat fish and chips every day in the United Kingdom. Is this true?'

'Well, not quite every day. Closer to once a month, I'd say.'

'Oh, really!' She nodded slowly with her mouth wide open, as if she'd had a game-changing revelation.

'But Chris sensei, everybody must love the royal family, surely?'

'Well, not everyone. But many.'

'Oh, really! Not everyone!'

This was my first encounter with Komako sensei, and after our twenty-minute chat she headed back satisfied to her desk at the other end of the room, only to return an hour later with yet more KitKats. It was almost as if the KitKats were a bartering tool in exchange for which I would offer her the gift of knowledge about Britain. But nothing could have prepared me for her next series of questions.

I was enjoying a cup of Umetsu sensei's matcha at my desk when Komako reappeared and abruptly asked, 'Chris sensei, what do you think of Osama bin Laden's girlfriend?'

I choked on my tea, wondering if I'd heard her correctly. This wasn't quite the conversation I thought I'd be having in my second week in Japan.

'Honestly, Komako sensei, I'm not really sure,' I spluttered, wiping the green tea from my mouth. Bin Laden had been assassinated the year before, and for some reason his love life had made its way into Japanese newspapers. It seemed that Komako sensei had seen a picture of his girlfriend in the paper and thought she was 'very cute!' and rather out of his league.

The seriousness of her tone made the conversation all the more ridiculous. I couldn't believe I'd moved to the other side of the planet to discuss the details of a mass murderer's love life.

I could tell that teaching alongside Komako sensei in the coming weeks and months would be an interesting experience.

4.

Hot Springs and Tiny Cars

AUGUST 2012

With the students' imminent return to school after the summer holidays and my anxiety levels rising at the thought of standing in front of a class of forty Japanese teenagers, James, a veteran JET who'd lived in Yamagata for two years, suggested that Colorado Mark and I go with him to an *onsen*, a hot spring, for an afternoon of relaxation.

An affable New Jersey native, James had a mop of curly hair that often obscured his freckly face, and he spoke with the air of a wise professor. It was he who'd written the letter congratulating me on winning the Japan lottery and, with two years under his belt, he'd explored Yamagata from top to bottom in his trusty Kei car.

Despite the popularity of Japan's *keijidousha* (軽自動車), literally, 'light automobiles', which make up 30 per cent of all vehicles on the road in Japan, somehow I'd never heard of them until the morning James drove up to the front of my apartment in his faded blue Suzuki Wagon.

These cars resemble a regular hatchback – if it had been driven into an industrial car crusher and been squeezed to half its size and the roof forced upwards. The end result is a cosy contraption that can fit four passengers, with no physical space between the driver and the passenger up front. Not even for cup holders. Quite simply, it's the most intimate car ever made.

Toss in a 660cc engine and some tax incentives and it's not hard to see the appeal when driving along Japan's cramped city roads on a budget.

'Morning, man! Hop in!' James gestured enthusiastically through the open window.

My first thought was whether anyone could possibly survive a car crash in a Kei. One incident and the passengers would be transformed into human pancakes.

'They're surprisingly safe!' James reassured me. 'They have airbags.'

I was unconvinced.

We arrived at the *onsen* at the base of Mount Chokai to find a cheerful Mark parked up in his own Kei. We'd only been in Japan a couple of weeks, yet his colleagues had already hooked him up with a car, while mine had only hooked me up with KitKats. I felt ever so slightly envious.

As one of the most seismically active countries on earth, Japan is one big geothermal wonderland, with over three thousand registered hot springs around the country. While traditional inns, or *ryokan*, now house most, this one was a public bathhouse where locals would stop by for an afternoon dip at the weekend or come to unwind after a hard day's work for the reasonable price of just 500 yen.

The main difference between *onsen* and other hot springs you might have experienced elsewhere is that everyone gets completely naked. In an effort to keep the baths clean and get the full benefits of the mineral-rich water, everyone enters as naked as the day they were born. Even though our excursion had been motivated by a desire to relax, visiting a hot spring in Japan for the first time felt anything but relaxing. As three white Westerners in a very rural area, we were stared at from the moment we entered the prémises by the many families relaxing on the communal tatami mats in the lobby. Had a local black bear wandered in off the street, it would have elicited less of a response.

Now, if there are only ever two Japanese kanji you master, let them be male (男) and female (女). In many Japanese bathhouses, the toilets and changing rooms have no English signs, so learn these, lest you wander into the wrong one and get deported. Thankfully, when it comes to hot springs, the male and female changing areas have a *noren* curtain draped over the top half of each changing room, blue for male and red for female, so as long as you know your basic gender stereotypes, you can avoid making the ultimate faux pas.

Coming from the UK, where the idea of being naked in public fills most people with a nightmarish horror, it can be quite the culture shock entering a Japanese bathhouse or hot spring. As the three of us stood in the cramped changing room, surrounded by half a dozen middle-aged and elderly Japanese men in varying degrees of undress, I felt ever so slightly uncomfortable, knowing that this was the first time in my life that I was going to be naked in public.

To my relief – and dare I say glee – I could sense that Mark shared my dismay. We sheepishly removed our underwear and stuffed it into a basket on the shelf, pretending that this was a normal thing to do.

Fortunately, James came to our aid, handing us each a 'modesty towel', essentially a flannel to cover our private parts as we entered through a glass door into a room so steamy it felt like the gateway to hell.

Through the clouds of smoke, I saw a dozen or so figures

immersed in two large pools, most of them motionless with their eyes closed, and each with their blinding-white modesty towels folded neatly upon their heads, creating almost a halo effect. One man was lying on his back on the edge between the two pools, his full figure unashamedly on display. I could tell that none of the Japanese were at all anxious about being naked, but that didn't stop me desperately manoeuvring the cloth below my waist as we walked over to the showers.

The first rule in an *onsen* is to clean yourself thoroughly before you go into the bath. To skip this step would be a cardinal sin and viewed with a fair amount of distaste by any onlookers. James gestured to a stool in front of the shower, and I sat down and started scrubbing myself with soap and working shampoo into my hair. I sensed that I was being studied by the locals watching from the pool, and I made an extra-special effort to scrub myself raw, drenching myself in the complimentary shampoo. I discovered that I rather enjoyed showering in this methodical way, sitting down, and by the time I headed towards the pool I felt as if I'd completed some kind of ritual.

The three of us moved towards the main bath, with light brown water at a temperature of 46°C. I tested the temperature with my foot and instantly retracted it from the scorching water. Suddenly I was struggling to see the appeal of climbing into the world's hottest bath on an already formidably hot summer's day. But standing awkwardly by the side of the pool grasping on to my loincloth for dear life, I realized I had no choice but to descend the steps, and gritted my teeth.

James, the *onsen* veteran, had long since got in and was now fully immersed, his flannel-topped head resting on the side of the pool.

'This is it, boys. This is heaven,' he muttered as he sunk deeper still.

Onsen are said to have healing properties, from improving blood pressure and blood flow to exfoliating the skin. Some even believe they're a reason why the Japanese are one of longest-lived populations on earth.

But as I submerged myself, boiling alive like a frog and feeling my heart palpitate out of my chest, I began to suspect I wasn't reaping the full health benefits of the hot spring.

After twenty-five minutes alternating between the indoor pool and the slightly cooler *rotenburo* outdoor pool, where the afternoon breeze offered some respite, I escaped and left the guys to it. For some reason, they seemed to like boiling alive.

At a Japanese public bath, you will generally find vending machines in the rest area stocked with different-flavoured milks, chocolate and coffee the most popular choices. When public bathhouses exploded in popularity in the 1950s, a milk company had the genius idea of sticking refrigerators in the changing or waiting areas so that bathers could rehydrate after a steamy bath. So ubiquitous are these vending machines, they have effectively become synonymous with bathing culture.

As I slumped down on to the tatami mats in the rest area, my skin so red raw from the blood pumping through my veins and feeling I could practically pop corn with my bare hands, I took a sip of the cool, creamy coffee milk and instantly saw the appeal. The best thing about tatami mats is that you're able to truly relax on them and, sprawling out across the floor as though as I'd just fought in a medieval battle, I vowed never to go to an *onsen* again in the height of summer.

I'd barely been lying down for two minutes, my eyes closed, when an elderly man walked in my direction, clutching a basket of cherries.

'*Sumimasen. Sakuranbo suki desu ka?*'

I opened my eyes and was startled to see a man in his seventies with a friendly, crescent-moon grin on his face. Sitting up, I nodded and replied in my poor Japanese, 'Yes, I do like cherries!'

'*Douzo!*'

He handed me the basket, which was filled to the brim with the juiciest, freshest-looking cherries I'd ever seen, so flawless and so perfect they reminded me of the plastic sample foods that are commonly displayed outside Japanese restaurants.

'Oh wow! Er, really? *Daijoubu desu ka?*'

I had no idea what the etiquette was when it came to randomly accepting cherries from a stranger. He gestured at me to try the cherries and disappeared as quickly as he'd appeared.

It was the sort of kind gesture I'd read about in stories of travellers visiting Japan. Nobody in the UK had ever popped up and given me a basket of fresh fruit, especially not a basket of immaculate, pricey cherries. I realized that the man must have seen me lying on the floor and bought the cherries specially from the gift store.

I popped one into my mouth, and as I did so I looked up and saw the man sitting on a bench in the distance watching my response. Luckily for me, I didn't need to pretend to enjoy the fruit. The sweet, juicy cherry was easily the best I'd ever had. It now made sense that the only thing under 'Yamagata' on the internet was cherries. I mouthed, 'Wow,' and gave him a thumbs-up, and he seemed very pleased.

The Yamagata cherries were so amazing that, in my greed, I made sure to devour the whole basket long before my American friends wandered out of the changing rooms. Sharing was simply out of the question.

5.

Mr Dick

It was the point of no return.

I watched as morning chaos filled the staffroom before the school bell rang – the iconic Big Ben chime made famous in Japan by thousands of anime series. Students scurried to their classrooms while teachers grabbed textbooks from their desks and dashed down the corridor to begin the first class of the day.

Kengo sensei swept across the room and arrived at my desk, balancing a mountain of pink exercise books in his hands.

'Chris sensei, are you ready for your first class?'

Being referred to as *Sensei* for the first time feels awkward. One common misconception is to assume that *Sensei* means 'schoolteacher', when in fact it means 'instructor', or 'master', more generally. If you're a schoolteacher, a doctor or a lawyer, you've earned the honorific of *Sensei*. The two kanji in the word (先生), 'before' and 'life', allude to this, conjuring up images of a wizened traveller.

To suddenly be assigned a position of authority and respect made me feel like a complete charlatan when I'd done so little to deserve the title. My only skill was that I spoke my native

49

tongue – hardly an achievement that made me worthy of being called a 'master'.

'Let's go, Kengo sensei! You bet I'm ready.'

I definitely wasn't.

Japanese classes are typically larger than those in British or American schools. While in the UK we might have thirty students in a class, in Japan they somehow pack in forty.

As we entered the classroom – my heart rate rising rapidly – students were hurrying back to their seats, having just finished morning roll call. Their laughter and talking immediately died out, replaced with a scraping of chairs as all the students stood up to greet us in their pristine navy uniforms, the boys in trousers, the girls in skirts.

'Good morning, everyone!' yelled Kengo sensei, grabbing the attention of the few straddlers at the back who were still talking among themselves.

'Good morn—' The class tailed off at the end of the phrase, the 'ing' practically inaudible. I wasn't sure if they were uncertain how to end the phrase or if they felt intimidated by the presence of a native English speaker.

'Please sit!' gestured Kengo, and the students gave the customary bow before sitting down. I was impressed by the sense of order abruptly brought to the room. Commanding a class of forty students suddenly felt feasible.

'Today we have some special guest for you from England . . .'

I gave a nod and a smile as my eyes swept across the room. The entire class was transfixed by me, their faces wearing a mixture of expressions. A few students looked nervous, as if a snarling Rottweiler had just been unleashed into the classroom, but thankfully most were smiling in anticipation. Two enamoured girls near the front of the class fluttered their eyelids at me comically and shouted, '*Ikemen!*' the Japanese word for 'handsome'.

'They say you are very cool!' said Kengo sensei reassuringly.

'Er, yes.' I blushed and clumsily gave a thumbs-up, which was fast becoming my trademark physical response to confusing daily interactions.

For my first class, the plan was to do the customary *jikoshoukai* introduction – mercifully in English this time – and get the students to ask questions so they could ascertain the sort of fool they'd be dealing with.

'Good morning, everyone! My name is Chris, and I'm from England.'

As someone who always hated sitting in a classroom listening to someone talk endlessly, I'd planned to make the ordeal as interactive as possible, getting the students to guess the answers to my questions. What could go wrong?

'First, how old do you think I am?'

I wrote four potential ages on the chalkboard – 22, 28, 36 and 41 – pointing at each number in turn and asking the students to raise their hands if they thought that was my age.

When I pointed the chalk to the number 36, nearly every hand in the room went up.

'Oh dear. I'm twenty-two.'

The class laughed out loud as I pondered how my physical appearance could have deteriorated so catastrophically so early into my twenties. Any smug satisfaction I'd previously derived from being called handsome had now evaporated.

In an effort to move on from this mortification, I tried something else.

Two Truths, One Lie was a game I'd stolen from the JET teaching handbook. It was an excellent listening exercise wrapped up in a game, and I'd tried to choose three very different examples to put their English skills to the test.

'Number one: I've hiked along the Great Wall of China.

Number two: I've had tea with the queen. And number three: I crashed a moped in Rome last year.'

I wrote the three options on the chalkboard and pointed at each one, asking them to guess the lie. I thought it was a no-brainer, but to my surprise, as I pointed the chalk at number one, most of the hands went up.

'Sorry, guys. The right answer is that I've never met the queen!'

The students were incredulous. There was an assumption that, being British, I *must* have met the queen.

I then put a photo up on the projector of me bumbling along the Great Wall of China in a tank top and one of me riding the shattered remnants of a red Italian Vespa in front of the Colosseum. As the image with the motorbike came up, I wondered if a story involving me almost being mown down by a Fiat in Rome was setting the best example for a class of innocent sixteen-year-olds.

However, as we reached the Q&A section after my underwhelming introduction I found I'd overestimated their innocence.

'OK. Do you guys have some questions for Chris sensei?'

At first no hands went up, as students turned to their neighbours to discuss potential options. After a few moments of muttering, one of the cheeky girls from earlier shot her hand up and asked the inevitable.

'Do you have a girlfriend?' she giggled, as the classroom erupted into laughter. While I stood there sheepishly, not quite knowing what to say, Kengo sensei, who I'd hoped would rescue me, encouraged me to divulge my deepest secrets to the classroom.

'Yes. So many girlfriends,' I beamed, giving yet another thumbs-up.

Everyone burst into cheers and applause, as if I'd won some sort of prize; it seemed they were oblivious to my obvious lie. In reality, my love life was an utter shitshow, but describing the sensation of abject loneliness and despair to a class of Japanese teenagers seemed one step too far for our first encounter.

Meanwhile, at the back of the room, a group of four tough-looking lads with shaved heads were sniggering uncontrollably. One of them put their hand up and asked, 'Are you so very big dick?'

The laughter grew even more raucous, and Kengo sensei looked displeased but unsurprised at the direction the disastrous Q&A was heading. I smiled and waved it off, realizing that in all honesty, it was the sort of shitty question we would use to bully the language assistant when I was at school. The journey had truly come full circle.

In total, I had about thirty classes with students aged between sixteen and eighteen, and over the course of two weeks, I'd taken every one, dispensing, I hoped, invaluable English language knowledge.

Over the roughly sixteen classes I taught in my first week, I discovered I could quickly get a sense of how screwed I was the moment I entered each classroom. The best classes would instantaneously burst into applause and whooping. They knew that the presence of the goofy foreigner meant the lesson would be light-hearted fun – a welcome deviation from the dreary English textbooks that dominated most of their lessons. On the other end of the spectrum, some classes would remain completely silent when I entered. It was as if the air had left the room, save for the cool breeze blowing whenever I tried to start a conversation. These were the classes I actively dreaded, where students zipped up and sat in stunned silence for the full lesson. You could ask the simplest question and not a single hand would go up. It was as if to interact with me was to court death.

It wasn't just the students who could sway the mood. Which teacher I was paired with had a huge effect on how enjoyable the classes were, for the students and for me. After my first few weeks of teaching I became aware of the chasm in teaching styles between Japan and what I'd experienced in the UK.

Japanese classes involved far less debate or discussion, typically revolving around a teacher dictating, lecture style, for most of the fifty minutes. It wasn't uncommon to see students asleep at their desks and, providing they didn't snore, often the teachers would do nothing about it.

There was also a far greater emphasis on group dynamics over the individual. If I asked a question and called on a specific student to answer, nine times out of ten they'd freeze up. Yet before they had time to answer, the teacher would encourage their neighbouring classmates for help and they would chime in with the answer. This made sense from a Japanese perspective. One popular proverb I'd come across exemplified this: 'A single arrow is easily broken, but not ten in a bundle.' The Japanese emphasize working together as a collective. Coming from the UK, I saw this method of teaching less as a team-building exercise and more as a great way to rob the students of any individual empowerment, and this was something I grew to notice more and more during my time working in the Japanese education system. Schools churned out model citizens who followed the rules and rarely questioned authority, but robbed students of any rule-breaking, entrepreneurial spirit.

My favourite teacher was Kengo sensei. He was a rare breed of English teacher, both fluent in the language and thrilled with his role in teaching it. This made him a joy to work with, and it soon became clear that he was a ray of light in the English department.

Teaching with Komako sensei, with whom I exchanged state

secrets for KitKats, was a different kettle of fish. I soon discovered that she was not only disliked by the students but that she harboured a similar dislike for them. Perhaps forty years of teaching had worn her down, or maybe the students just didn't share her fascination with Osama bin Laden's love life.

Whatever the case, when we walked into classes together, chaos reigned supreme. No matter how loud she screamed, her attempts to control the class were useless. The students would just talk over her, ignoring her attempts to teach. My classes with Komako sensei usually involved me standing in the corner watching the madness unfold.

Classes with Saitou sensei were slightly more bearable, but it was apparent from our first class that she couldn't speak English. I ended up spending more time teaching her English than the students themselves. It seemed that, back in her day, the bar for becoming an English teacher in Japan wasn't so much low as practically non-existent, requiring only a handful of written exams and no practical speaking ability.

In one of our first lessons together, she wrote 'Chris is a London' on the board, and I had to hastily correct it before the students copied it into their books. Fortunately, she welcomed interventions like this and they never led to the awkward teacher–assistant dynamic I'd been warned about at the Tokyo orientation. I was grateful for Saitou sensei's willingness to be corrected but wondered just how much these students would learn in her classes.

Still, even if the teacher's language skills weren't up to scratch, the classes could still be a ton of fun.

One of the more wild-card teachers was Sasaki sensei, a shy middle-aged man who spent his time in between classes smoking like a chimney and whose tinted spectacles and mop of greying hair made him appear older than he was. His clumsy, slapstick demeanour made him Japan's answer to Mr Bean. Like Saitou sensei, he was painfully aware that his English language skills were a disaster. He knew it. His students knew it. And within thirty seconds of my first lesson with him, I knew it.

Embarrassed by his atrocious English, he would speak to me exclusively in mumbles. He sounded like he had an invisible hand stuffed in his mouth. Our baffling exchanges en route to the classroom usually hit a dead end very fast.

'So, Sasaki sensei, did you have a good weekend?'

He would nod enthusiastically. 'Yes, I really like weekend.'

'Did you do anything interesting?' I would ask, desperately hoping to extend our conversation at least until we reached classroom.

'Yes. Interesting weekend!' he would say with a smile, and turn to look the other way, promptly bringing an end to our insightful small talk.

Yet, despite his poor English, both the students and I really enjoyed his classes. They would quickly descend into an unhinged comedy performance. Nearly every time we walked into the classroom he'd manage to drop at least one item on the floor, from chalk to books to his glasses, to the great amusement of the class. As far as I could tell, it was never on purpose. On this occasion, he'd dropped his car keys and, amid sniggers from the students, fumbled around on the floor trying to pick them up. And this was just the start of fifty minutes of physical comedy.

'Right! Now! This. It's a Chris sensei!'

He flailed his hands in my general direction and the class applauded and cheered in delight.

'OK. Chapter Two! Reading. Now!'

He grabbed the English textbook, flapping it around frantically. I have to admit, even I found him captivating.

'Chris sensei! Reading. You do! Let's go!' That was my cue.

I read the chapter aloud like a human tape recorder. It was a bizarre passage about a man placing items around his bedroom, meant to teach prepositions such as 'over', 'in' and 'under'. At the end of the chapter, Sasaki sensei wanted us to demonstrate this concept in real life using two questionable props: his desk – and me.

He would yell, 'Where is Chris sensei!?' and the whole class had to shout back where I was in relation to the desk. It was thrilling stuff.

At first I hid under the desk. Easy enough.

'Where is Chris sensei?'

'UNDER the desk!' the class shouted.

Next he gestured for me to climb inside the tiny cupboard beneath his desk and squeezed the doors shut after me, as if he was hastily trying to conceal a corpse.

'Where is Chris sensei?'

'INSIDE the desk!' the class shouted.

He opened the doors and I rolled out on to the floor, wondering how on earth £30,000 of university fees had led to this.

Next, he told me to stand on top of the flimsy desk, which seemed like a terrible idea.

'Is this OK, Sasaki sensei?' I asked as I kneeled precariously on the table.

'Yes, yes! You go up now!'

I slowly stood up and the wooden desk wobbled and creaked under 80 kilograms of British man – a weight it had not been built to bear – I started to worry about the health-and-safety implications if the desk collapsed.

Like a surfer rising from the waves, eventually I was upright, towering over the classroom to a cheering audience. I could already imagine the next answer.

'Where is Chris sensei now?'

'*In the fucking hospital.*'

One of my favourite teachers was also one of the most awk-ward. Naoko sensei spoke English so well, with a subtle American accent, thanks to spending a few years in the States. A petite woman in her late forties, she wore striking purple lipstick that matched her restless, chaotic energy. She aways seemed like she'd slammed back a triple shot of espresso before kicking off each class.

In one of our first classes together she initiated a needlessly humiliating situation that made me want to run out of the classroom. She came bouncing over to my desk with a pile of books.

'Come on, Chris sensei, let's go!' Oddly, despite her excellent English skills, she had a propensity to misinterpret everything I said, as though she only ever listened to the last word of every sentence.

'Did you get up to something fun at the weekend, Chris sensei?' she asked as we headed to class.

'This weekend I was looking for a place to rent a car, as I really need to get one soon.'

'Wow! That sounds like fun! And so where did you drive to?'

'Er . . .'

In the class, we were teaching students how to talk about their future dreams in life with simple sentences such as: 'When I graduate, I want to be a firefighter.'

Naturally, many students hadn't a clue what they wanted to become, so to encourage them to use their imagination Naoko asked me to present what I had wanted to become when I was a kid. This was easy. As a big fan of *Muppet Treasure Island*, I'd always wanted to be a swashbuckling pirate. To this day, it's a goal I continue to strive towards.

'Well, Naoko sensei, when I grew up, I wanted to become a

pirate!' Given the popularity of the manga series *One Piece*, I figured this would go down well with the class.

But I'd barely finished speaking when Naoko sensei shot me a dirty look, as if I'd uttered a swear word in front of the class.

'Oh my goodness! A pirate? But, Chris sensei, why would you want to *kill* and *rape* people!'

'Er . . . well . . .' I felt like I'd been slapped in the face.

I swung around to look at the class. Forty pairs of eyes were gazing at me. I stood aghast, my mouth wide open, not quite knowing how to defend myself against such salacious allegations. I don't know what version of *Treasure Island* she'd been watching, but things had taken a dark turn very fast.

Thank god, I thought, as I realized the class hadn't a clue what Naoko sensei had just said. Now all I had to do was defend my motives.

'Well, Naoko sensei, I like to have adventures and travel the world, searching for treasure.'

She paused for a moment and her shocked expression faded into a smile and a nod of approval.

'Oh, I see! Now, that sounds like fun.'

And, just like that, she went back to her normal bubbly self and it was never mentioned again.

From that day on, I never brought up the subject of pirates in the classroom again. Especially when Naoko sensei was around.

6.

Sake, onegaishimasu!

OCTOBER 2012

While my American colleague, Mark, had been riding around the rice fields in his swanky new Kei for almost two months, I still hadn't got my hands on my own set of wheels. The situation wasn't helped by the fact that I'd come to Japan with an indebted credit card and a mountain of student debt that hung over me like the sword of Damocles.

To buy even the most reasonably priced car seemed unthinkable: even a cheap Kei would cost around 400,000 yen, two months' salary. Luckily, I'd been thrown a lifeline.

I wasn't the only foreign teacher working at Sakata Senior High School – the number of students was so large they needed two foreign English teachers to handle the workload.

A New Zealander three years my senior, Roy looked like a handsome version of the DC comic-book character Bane. He'd called Sakata home for four long years and, with the JET programme's five-year limit, was set to leave in a year's time. His parting gift to me would be his beloved Toyota Starlet – a dark green, rickety car that had hit the road in 1996 and was somehow still going. The optional extras included broken air conditioning, windows that could be wound down but not up and seats peppered with cigarette burns. It was by no means my dream car, but it was free. How could I refuse?

It was in this car that Roy would drive us to work every morning, puffing away on a Melvius cigarette, steering wheel in one hand and a can of cheap vending-machine coffee in the other: a fine daily breakfast.

It had taken me a while to get to know my fellow JET. At the end of my first week at school, I'd been sitting at my desk when a New Zealander randomly appeared in the room. Having struggled through the entire week without seeing another foreign face, I wondered if he'd been trapped in a cupboard somewhere. (It turned out he'd been on a trip to Tokyo.) But we'd got along well, bonding over British TV and nerdy film quotes and celebrating our first encounter with a six-pack of Asahi beer back at my apartment.

When I started to mention Roy at JET gatherings on weekends, I discovered he was something of an enigma, as he had remained hell-bent on avoiding other foreigners in the JET community throughout his time in Japan. He spent most of his evenings at an *izakaya* across town, downing endless beers amid a thick cloud of cigarette smoke. He claimed it wasn't that he hated other JETs, although he definitely did, but more to do with the fact that having spent four years in Yamagata he'd watched the revolving door of foreign teachers coming and going and didn't see the point in befriending colleagues who'd soon be gone.

Despite his lone-wolf persona, Roy was seen as something of a legend throughout the Yamagata JET community for successfully passing a formidable Japanese test, Kanji Kentei, for which you have to memorize over three thousand kanji. He was one of only a handful of non-Japanese to ever pass the test nationally. With over 2,200 kanji characters typically used in everyday life, he'd gone one step further to learn the ones that mostly remained in textbooks. It had become a game to him. And so impossible was the test, even most native Japanese didn't dare try it. Having passed, he was the pride of the school and was sought out by those in the foreign community who obsessed over mastering Japanese. They wanted to know his secrets. He just wanted to smoke and drink Asahi.

Working with Roy had its ups and downs. It was great to have a mentor who could show me the ropes, but his fluency put me to shame. While I could scarcely say 'I like cats', there he was, running classes solo in Japanese. Many of the teachers saw him as an equal. His roguish demeanour masked a man who was good at his job and very well respected.

Despite working in his shadow, having a fellow foreigner around made life in a Japanese school far less daunting – even if his strong New Zealand accent meant he was about as decipherable as his Japanese counterparts. During school assemblies in the gym, as I stood surrounded by 1,200 Japanese students and teachers, I felt uncomfortably visible at times, the only non-Japanese face in the school. Seeing Roy's cheeky face pop up when he returned from a smoking break was reassuring.

My first winter in Japan was approaching and I braced myself for the horrific snowfall I'd been warned about. With no other friends and little else to do, I'd started to fall into some nasty habits with Roy. While driving us home after work, most weekdays he'd shoot me a cheeky look on the way home.

'Mar?' he'd ask.

I never hesitated. 'Let's go.'

Roy had found the cure for spending a day in front of two hundred teenagers reading from poorly written textbooks. It was a cure that many Japanese salarymen embraced in a climate of insane working conditions where the concept of a work–life balance was frighteningly absent.

Alcohol.

It's estimated that Tokyo has 120,000 bars and restaurants – more than any city in the world – so it's fair to say that Japan has a thriving drinking culture. It's very common to head out after work to an *izakaya* to eat, drink and smoke oneself to oblivion before crawling home in the early hours of the morning.

While working as an ALT wasn't gruelling, it wasn't the most dynamic job either, so having something to look forward to certainly helped you through the day. For us, that something was a neighbourhood *izakaya* called Mar.

Izakaya (居酒屋), literally 'reside, sake, shop' are one the greatest joys of living in Japan. They are often cramped holes-in-the-wall, so you find yourself elbow to elbow with strangers who more often you'll end up sharing a pint with by the end of the night. The first thing you notice about an *izakaya* is that often there are no windows or any means of seeing inside from the street. While this might suggest something more like a cult than a pub, given the drunken antics within, it's only natural to conceal the patrons from the prying eyes of passers-by. Behind these walls folk let their hair down after a day of uncompromising rigid politeness.

Fortunately for us, our local *izakaya* happened to be one of the best in town, with cheap, delicious food. To set foot inside was to be transported into a hedonistic bubble. The glow of the golden lights never failed to draw us in from the bitter winds that swept through Sakata in the run-up to winter. With its wooden counters and its paraffin heater puffing away at the entrance, Mar had an incredibly cozy atmosphere that encouraged you to stay and eviscerate your paycheck.

Walking through the sliding door, we'd be greeted by the staff and dispatched into one of two areas: a tatami-floored room on the right big enough for four low tables; or, to the left, a counter with six seats facing the narrow kitchen. When possible, we always chose the counter, where we'd huddle side by side and eat an endless procession of food chosen by Roy, by virtue of the fact that only he could read the damn menu.

I quickly learned that regardless of what you *want* to drink in Japan, everyone, without fail, starts with *namabiiru* – draught beer. It's an unwritten rule of Japanese etiquette. It doesn't matter what brand, just as long as it's a draught beer. Whether it's a work party or with friends, it's extremely rare for anyone to choose anything else, and the reason behind it is to not complicate the first order and to swiftly get drinks into everyone's hands. Even though I wasn't a fan of Asahi, I toed the line and forced myself to love it. While, in the UK, we scoff down pub snacks like peanuts and crisps, the standard accompaniment to beer in Japan is *edamame* soybeans sprinkled with salt. A somewhat healthier alternative, it's just as crunchy and delicious but without the greasy-fingered guilt of Western pub snacks.

This health benefit was somewhat cancelled out, however, by Japan's smoking culture. Given smoking was allowed indoors – to Roy's delight – as we munched our way through the French- and Italian-inspired menu of fish, pizza and pasta, he could make short work of his second pack of cigarettes. The clouds of smoke gave the interior a glamorous haze, ruined only by the putrid stench of tobacco. Smoking is so entrenched in Japanese culture that on occasion sales staff from cigarette companies would enter the *izakaya* with new menthol flavours and go from table to table offering free packs to try. It was bonkers; in a world that was retreating from the tobacco industry, Japan still fully embraced it.

Unfortunately for me, I soon started to join in. I knew my end-of-year health report would be an atrocity after spending half my week eating, drinking and smoking in a Japanese pub, but for three or four hours straight I did a fantastic job of deluding myself that it was all for 'educational purposes'. Immersion is the best way to learn, after all.

Roy was a walking, talking, smoking encyclopaedia of all things Japan and, sitting at the counter chatting with him and the two men who ran the *izakaya* and were now his friends, I soon began to pick up some key Japanese phrases.

Best of all, I'd found eating out in Japan to be relatively cheap, especially given the absence of tipping culture. In Japan, it's considered almost rude to tip. The Japanese believe that service staff should *always* be giving their absolute best all of the time, and if you tried to leave money, you'd likely find yourself chased down the street by a waiter brandishing your change. Japan offers some of the best service on the planet, and it's a shame you can't reward the bar and restaurant staff for it.

However, to help mitigate this, most Japanese bars and restaurants have a seating charge disguised as a starter dish called an *otoshi*. It's a quick nibble that's served the moment you arrive, typically adding 400–500 yen to your bill. At cheaper eateries, it can make up for the absence of a tip.

During my evenings propping up the bar, it was fascinating to see Japanese locals truly being themselves. Alcohol is nothing short of a magic wonder potion in Japan. The moment a customer has so much as sipped their first mouthful of draught beer, they instantly loosen up, expressing the thoughts and opinions they have held at bay throughout the workday. Some refer to it as *nommunication*, cheekily blending 'communication' with the Japanese verb *nomu* (飲む), to drink.

Japan has such a strict social structure and such rigid hierarchies in the workplace that when company employees head out for a drink it's their opportunity to tell their boss what they *really* think. That terrible idea your supervisor forced upon you in the office is fair game for debate after you've chugged back three beers. Alcohol is the social lubricant that unleashes it all, which is why *nomikai* (飲み会), or work parties, are so actively encouraged. This is something I would soon experience first hand.

Customers sitting alongside me at the counter often provided excellent opportunities to practise the Japanese phrases I'd been learning. The only problem was, two beers down, most Japanese people crack out any English language ability they do have, after concealing it all day, so I barely needed to use Japanese.

On one of my first outings to Mar, a couple of guys were celebrating finally reaching Japan's legal drinking age of twenty. Seeing a guy from England in their quiet town, they immediately struck up a conversation in broken English. By this point, I'd grown used to the fact that, as a rare foreigner, I was often the centre of attention in a room full of Japanese people. Foreigners in Japan often refer to this as 'foreigner rock star status' and, although there were days when I'd have paid anything for some anonymity, it did have its plus sides.

'Do you like Japanese sake?' one of the guys asked eagerly.

I shook my head. I'd briefly tasted sake in the UK, but I'd never had a proper swig.

'Wow – you must try! *Sake onegaishimasu!*' He gestured to the waiter.

Within moments a white ceramic beaker of sake was brought over, along with three square wooden *ochocko* cups. To the untrained eye, the contents of the beaker could easily have been water.

'Mate, you want to be careful of this stuff,' chuckled Roy as he took a sip of his Asahi. The man drank like a fish, but rarely deviated from beer. I was about to learn why.

My new friend poured the sake into the polished wooden cup and, after a brief '*Kanpai!*' we all took a sip. Expecting the worst, I was pleasantly surprised by the delicate flavour. If you've never had sake, it tastes like a mildly sweet white wine and leaves a pleasant kick at the back of your throat, similar to vodka or gin. Though it's not as strong as vodka or gin, generally around 14 per cent, it's dangerously easy to drink.

I'd barely placed the *ochocko* down when my jovial benefactor poured me a second cup.

'*Dou?* Good taste?'

'Beautiful!' I beamed, taking a hearty swig.

In just three minutes the beaker was empty and a second pay-load was inbound. Having never properly encountered sake before, I made short work of the next bottle, assuming it'd be impossible to get drunk from what essentially tasted like flavoured water.

After twenty-five minutes of drinking and chatting about British culture, which in Japan invariably means Harry Potter, I turned to Roy and felt the room begin to spin.

'Oh, crap.'

'I warned you, mate!' laughed Roy, as I dropped my head into my hands.

Meanwhile, one of the young Japanese guys, who'd tried valiantly to keep up with the high-stakes sake brinkmanship, had dashed for the toilet. I didn't need to be a seasoned sake drinker to know that something spectacularly bad was about to happen. His friend sat quietly in his chair, gazing at the kitchen counter and swaying gently from side to side. Had a gust of wind come through the door, it would have knocked him off his seat.

'Game over. I think it's time we left, mate.' Roy chuckled again, helped me up, and we stumbled out. As I passed the toilet door I heard the horrendous soundtrack of violent retching. My new friend had certainly come of drinking age in style.

7.

When Teaching Goes Wrong

One morning at school I received a random email from a Japanese woman called Noriko. She claimed to run an *eikaiwa*, an English conversation class, that took place every Monday. Each week a dozen or so adults would gather at the community centre to practise their English, and it turned out, with my predecessor at Sakata Senior High long gone, that I was now the heir to the *eikaiwa* throne. It was the tradition for Sakata's JETs to run these sessions and, in return, they'd be invited sporadically to dinner parties hosted by the students.

Although the JET programme encourages teachers to get stuck into their local community, undertaking paid side jobs is forbidden. This *eikaiwa* job seemed a decent substitute. I'd offer my time to the local community, and the occasional dinner party and the thrill of teaching adults who actually wanted to learn English would be my reward.

I told Noriko I'd be happy to run classes every Monday at 7 p.m., and so one Monday in the middle of September I stepped out of my apartment to find her waiting to drive me to class in her bright pink Suzuki Wagon.

Noriko looked to be in her fifties and had strikingly short black hair and bright purple glasses. With a warm motherly smile and a wave, she welcomed me into the car. As I hopped into the car of a complete stranger, I wondered what I'd got myself into.

It was a five-minute ride to where the class was held, which was just enough time for Noriko to interrogate me on my background.

'Oh wow, England! Our last teacher was from Canada and, before him, Australia. So many countries!' She licked her lips with glee, as if she'd stuffed my predecessors in a pot and boiled them alive and the same fate awaited me.

I got the impression that Noriko loved to talk, as she dominated the conversation for most of the journey, filling me in on just how wonderful the previous teachers had been. Apparently, one of them, Aidan, used to bring his guitar to classes and serenade the students.

'We all loved Aidan. He was a very special one.'

Fantastic. I hadn't even set foot in the classroom and already the bar had been set ludicrously high by some prick with a guitar. Still, I could beatbox. I'd one-up Aidan.

The *eikaiwa* took place at a village hall on the outskirts of town. Standing next to the local ice-skating rink, it was a bland grey building that would have been completely devoid of character if it weren't for the *kawara* on the roof. Walking in, I was hit by the strong, musty odour of a hundred shoes, followed by the bitter scent of matcha tea.

Sure enough, as we made our way down the corridor, I caught sight of a tea-ceremony club pouring hot green tea in one of the crowded communal rooms.

At the end of the corridor Noriko led me into a far emptier room, where ten adults ranging in age from twenties to seventies were talking quietly among themselves, sitting at a U-shape of desks around a large whiteboard.

As we arrived, the talking stopped instantly and I felt the familiar sensation of being under a spotlight as everyone eyed me up and down. I noticed that in the whole group, there were only two guys. This checked out with what I'd noticed at the school: English classes were always far more popular with girls than guys. I've never understood why this is, but I suspected that Japanese men feel less comfortable making fools of themselves when attempting to speak a new language. Not only that, but English is often seen as a soft, almost girly subject. Boys were expected to throw baseballs and chop wood, not learn a useless language spoken by a billion people. This glaringly antiquated gender norm is still very prevalent in Japanese society.

'*Konbanwa!* Good evening!' they cheered, bowing in unison.

'Nice to meet you, everyone!' I was relieved at the warm reception.

'Good evening, everyone! This is Chris sensei. He is our new teacher from England!'

A few of the female students waved.

'So, Chris sensei, *why* did you move to Japan?' Noriko kicked off my first class teaching adults with a Q&A. At least these questions would be more mature than the ones my high-school students had asked.

'Maybe you like Japanese girls?'

Or maybe not. At least they didn't ask me if I was so very big dick.

It's important to point out that if you ever spend time in Japan you're condemning yourself to the fate of answering the same question every single day. *Why did you come to Japan?*

I hated this question. There are usually two acceptable answers: 'I'm into karate' and 'Anime and manga are my favourite things.' These simple, predictable answers will satisfy anyone, from curious students to nosey old ladies.

I had no easy answer. How could I explain that a chance meeting with a middle-aged couple on an aeroplane had set me on a life-changing course of events?

As I stood before my quiet audience in the musty village hall, I mustered up an acceptable answer.

'I love *The Last Samurai*.'

'Oh, Tom Cruise and Watanabe Ken!' cheered Noriko. 'Very handsome men.'

Most of the ladies nodded in agreement.

But one of the guys wasn't satisfied with my answer.

'Maybe you do some kind of martial arts?'

All eyes fell on me once again.

'Not yet. But I'd like to do aikido.'

That did the trick. He gave an approving nod. Thank god, I'd live to see another day . . .

And so it was that every Monday after school I'd teach a motley crew of adults who may well have been the only townsfolk with a degree of fluency in the English language.

The guy who'd been keen to probe further into my interest in Japan soon became my favourite student. Tall, athletic and in his forties, Shotaro worked for an IT hardware company, often travelling between Tokyo and Sakata. His presence often gave me a degree of sanity when I was dealing with the older members of the group, particularly when I tried to confront their outdated ideas about the world.

On one occasion, while discussing the Fukushima exclusion zone, where a spate of robberies had taken place in the empty homes of evacuees, the older members of the group declared that it must be 'the Chinese or Koreans', as if Japanese people could never commit a crime.

Shotaro shot me a solemn look and shook his head, clearly used to these sorts of comments. (One pair caught burgling were two Japanese men from Hiroshima.)

One evening, as a creative exercise, I got the class to create and brand a type of coffee to be sold in convenience stores.

The usually stoic Shotaro threw himself into the activity, spending far longer than his classmates on conjuring up a poster for his brand, which he then presented to the group with an infectious enthusiasm.

'This is my premium coffee brand, Luxpresso. It has the very best taste of convenience-store coffee.' The class was in awe, as was I.

Every month, the highlight of the *eikaiwa* would be the house parties hosted by Naoko or one of the older members of the group. Everyone would come and bring home-made cakes and snacks for us all to tuck into. As well as being a far better backdrop than the sterile town hall, spending time in the homes of classmates made me feel more integrated into the local community. I was suddenly less like a ghostly foreign figure, wandering the streets alone, and more like a member of the community.

And the *eikaiwa* crowd wasn't entirely free of drama. Occasionally, one of the members of the group, an elderly woman called Reina, would invite me to a 'secret' house party to which Naoko was purposely not invited.

'She treats that *eikawa* as her personal fiefdom,' lamented Reina. 'Why is she the boss?'

I'd sit there, nodding along in a non-committal manner, my face stuffed with chocolate cake.

English is a tragically unpopular subject in Japan. I'd heard at the JET seminar that only 40 per cent of students enjoyed English; it's regarded as very difficult and ultimately useless. I faced an especially uphill battle in the countryside, where the odds of needing to speak or know English were negligible. I could see my students wondering why on earth they'd ever need these skills.

The adults at my *eikaiwa* class were the exceptions. Many of them had travelled frequently outside Japan, others were looking for a new hobby, having more time on their hands now that they had retired, and they approached the subject with excitement and vigour.

Teaching a subject to keen learners every Monday night helped to keep me sane and gave me renewed energy to battle with my more apathetic teenagers. Back at Sakata Senior High, I was starting to get to grips with my routine. I had spent my first month going from room to room, redelivering my *jikoshoukai* over and over and being teased about my age every time, but by autumn it was finally time to move on to actually teaching. Thankfully, I no longer feared walking into a room and having forty students captivated by me. Dare I say, I may have even gone mad with power.

While discipline is pretty good in Japanese classrooms, every class has its troublemakers and, as the weeks drew on, I began to get more creative with my disciplining.

I once lost my patience with a boy who never seemed to stop talking. One day I tossed my textbook aside in front of the startled class and scribbled 'Supercalifragilisticexpialidocious' on the board. Turning back to my bewildered students, I summoned the troublesome student to the front of the classroom, and rapidly said the phrase out loud. The boy looked baffled when I shouted, 'Your turn!'

British-style punishment at its finest.

I leaned back on my desk, prepared to watch him squirm. I mentally patted myself on the back for my novel approach to discipline. But just as I thought I'd got the better of him, the cheeky student repeated the word perfectly, doing a great impression of me as he did so. This caused the class to roar with laughter and break into applause. I hate to admit it, but I joined in.

He returned to his seat a triumphant hero.

Though I thought I'd been caught out, that my quick thinking had fallen flat in the classroom, I seemed to have earned some respect that day. From then on, the troublesome boy, a kendo prodigy called Keita, never misbehaved in my presence again, and we became good friends. He even began to seek me out in the staffroom to chat and practise his English.

Never underestimate the power of Mary Poppins.

These breakthrough moments were few and far between, however. For the most part, I was battling against the dull curriculum and the uninspiring resources I was provided with. As the weeks passed, I came to understand exactly why English was so unpopular. The Japanese–English textbooks were nothing short of an atrocity and often used very poorly by the teachers I worked with.

Nearly every chapter carried a strong anti-war message which, while heartening, was devoid of any practical everyday English. One of the first stories I read out to the class was about Mosha, an elephant in Myanmar that had stepped on a landmine and had its leg blown off. As I recounted the harrowing tale of how the doctors had amputated the elephant's leg and replaced it with a prosthetic, I looked out across the room of dozing sixteen-year-olds and wondered how often they'd need the term 'prosthetic leg' if they ever happened to take a trip to an English-speaking country.

Niche stories aside, because the textbooks had been written by Japanese English teachers, there were numerous mistakes in them. One chapter ridiculously titled 'Soccer Balls to Afghanistan' told the tale of a school in Japan that had worked tirelessly to stitch together five hundred soccer balls to send over there. No doubt, this was the one thing that the war-ravaged towns of Afghanistan were crying out for.

The story reached its climax when the children of Afghanistan were given the five hundred balls. In front of forty students, I read out the line, 'And when we showed the children, their eyes lit up. It was LIKE A MAGIC.'

Like a magic.

I burst out laughing, and the whole class tittered, although they were unsure why I was laughing.

It was a bit awkward, but I later complained to Kengo sensei about the quality of the textbooks.

'Actually, Chris san, my friends and I write many of these books.'

Oh crap.

All of a sudden, the stories made sense. Kengo's anti-war background had worked its way into the books. But as well intentioned as these sentiments were, it's a shame they hadn't been proofread by a native speaker.

But it wasn't just the textbooks that were awful. The teachers themselves could contribute to how ineffective the classes were.

In one lesson, Komako sensei thought it would be 'fun' to have me act out the English vocabulary charades style. The students would then shout out what they thought the word was in Japanese. I failed to see how this would improve their English comprehension but didn't want to overturn her grand plans in front of the students. Things started off well enough, with me acting out verbs such as 'chatting' and 'shuddering'. Then we got to words like 'posterity' and 'rebuttal' and things came to a grinding halt. I barely had a clue how to define the words in English, let alone through mime.

'Come on, Chris sensei. Please try harder,' said Komako sensei.

The forty exasperated students shouted out practically every word in the dictionary trying to guess while I wondered what the point of it all was.

I became increasingly frustrated by the restrictiveness of the Japanese education system, spending my free time trying to figure out creative ways to get the kids to engage. Naoko sensei was one of the few teachers who gave me a degree of autonomy. She let me do anything I wanted – just as long as it involved playing a song by her beloved Beatles.

And so, for one class, I turned the absolute mindfuck of a song 'I am the Walrus' into a listening exercise that nearly broke the students' minds. I'd printed out the lyrics, removed key words and asked them to fill in the blanks.

I could hear their little brains imploding, and Naoko sensei wasn't too impressed either.

'Chris sensei, what is the egg man? Who are the egg men?'

'He is the walrus,' I insisted.

'I don't understand.' She stomped her feet in frustration and insisted from that day forth we stick to her officially sanctioned list of Beatles songs.

Still, playing 'Hey Jude' was far more fun than getting students to repeat 'Chris wants to eat the chicken' over and over.

As I became more comfortable in the role and slowly gained confidence, I grew to appreciate my students, befriending many of them, particularly the ones who enjoyed English. One girl, Rina, would often leave presents on my desk. After I jokingly mentioned in class that I'd wanted to be James Bond as a child but had never achieved my dream, a few days later a poster for *Skyfall* appeared on my desk.

'Don't give up your dream. To never forget – Rina.'

I laughed as I read her note. It was a wonderful moment: a Japanese schoolgirl encouraging her teacher to become a British spy. I hope to make her proud someday.

Despite my occasional successes, the gaping language barrier between the students and me became a constant source of frustration. The majority of students found me intimidating and avoided talking to me, fully aware that my inability to speak Japanese put pressure on them to speak English.

In many ways, that was the aim of the JET programme. The plan never was to send in the finest English teachers the world had ever seen (clearly: I'd somehow found my way in). It was simply to give the students an opportunity to practise the language with a native speaker.

And though I did my best to make classes entertaining, once in a while things backfired spectacularly.

During a class with Naoko sensei, I'd been teaching students about British culture and the widely reviled topic that is UK cuisine.

I'd printed out photos of twenty popular British meals and desserts, from toad in the hole and bangers and mash to a full English and treacle tart. The goal was for the students to match the photos up to the names of the dishes.

Arranging the forty students into ten groups of four, the race was on to see which team could finish the fastest and claim the grand prize, a box of Cadbury's chocolates.

It was all going well at first. The allure of foreign chocolate never failed to push the class into making an effort – though I did make one fatal error by including the British pudding spotted dick. While the steamed pudding, filled with dried fruit and served with custard, was a delicious treat for millions in the UK, my students in Japan saw only one word. Before long the classroom was filled with sniggering.

A team of four girls won and I awarded them the chocolates to screams of delight.

But there was still a bonus prize to be won – a Hershey's

chocolate bar I'd picked up at the foreign goods store. The class cheered as I held it up in the air as if it were the Holy Grail.

One of the other desserts on my list was the tall ice-cream sundae Knickerbocker Glory. For many teams, it was the last one they guessed, given that the name of the dessert didn't exactly give students much to work with. For this final challenge, I'd asked for a brave volunteer to come up to the chalkboard and spell 'Knickerbocker Glory' from memory.

No fewer than seven students stood up to spell the word. Each tried and failed, to the tune of uproarious laughter.

Our final challenger, a shy bespectacled boy who'd barely spoken a word during my many visits, stood up to audible gasps and grabbed the chalk. Naoko sensei looked more surprised than anyone as the boy gave it his best shot, pausing pensively in between letters. You could cut the tension with a knife.

At last, after the longest minute ever, the boy stepped back to reveal the phrase:

'Knicker Poker G.'

The class knew instantly that he'd got it wrong and erupted once again into giggles.

I joined in, pointing out that 'Knicker Poker G' sounded like a nickname for the world's greatest poker player. 'I think it'd be an amazing name!'

Suddenly, there was a loud bang that instantly shut us all up.

The boy had smashed his textbooks into his desk, sending his stationary flying and startling both myself and Naoko sensei, as we dodged the flying pencils.

It seems the student hadn't taken kindly to being mocked by the whole class.

'*Sensei! Urusai!* They need to shut up!' he yelled, banging his books a second time.

Never had I felt the atmosphere change so fast in a classroom.

The smiles evaporated and all eyes were on Naoko and me, anxious to see how we'd react.

Naoko sensei put her hands together almost as if in prayer, the Japanese hand gesture for 'sorry'.

'*Sumimasen*,' she apologized in a sincere tone, and I followed suit. The shy student had clearly been affected by the laughter of the class.

The boy continued to look down at his desk, seething with anger.

I had mixed feelings about the situation. On the one hand, it highlighted the immense pressure students were under. Making mistakes is an essential part of language learning, and if the result of this means you're openly ridiculed, why bother trying at all?

Making mistakes in the classroom meant exposing oneself to mockery, and in the fragile collectivist dynamic of a Japanese classroom, standing out and being made fun of could lead to being a target of long-term bullying, as I would soon find out.

It was easy to see why the vast majority of students were reluctant to raise their hands in the classroom.

On the other hand, 'Knicker Poker G' was bloody hilarious.

It's a shame the boy hadn't been able to laugh at his own mistake. The previous students had tried and failed. They too had been teased but had taken it in their stride. From that day I vowed to become more mindful of how I reacted to classroom ridicule. I wanted my students to be emboldened by my classes, not pushed further into their shells.

Above all, though, I finally had a killer username for my online poker profile.

8.

Many Fucking Snow

With Japan's formidable winter months inbound, I was getting increasingly desperate to get a car. The thought of trudging through five feet of snow filled me with terror. Thankfully, in October, Kengo sensei came to my aid, connecting me with a friend who rented out used cars.

Soon I was the proud owner of a clunky Nissan Micra, which set me back an eyewatering 40,000 yen a month – almost a quarter of my net salary. Nevertheless, the prospect of freedom and the chance to break loose of Roy's tobacco- and coffee-fuelled carpool made eviscerating my wallet seem worthwhile.

To celebrate, I planned to make a video about driving in Japan for the YouTube channel I'd just set up. So far, I'd posted two videos on Abroad in Japan, the moniker a cheeky pun on my family name.

In the days leading up to my move to Japan I'd scoured You-Tube for any videos I could find on north Japan and the area I would soon call home. Finding only a handful of Tokyo-based YouTubers who offered little more than footage of themselves fawning over Family Mart strawberry sandwiches, I had a feeling I could do better. I decided that I'd try to make my own videos. It would be a great way to document my experiences but also offered an unexpected opportunity to pursue something that had always felt like my calling in life.

In 1951, while working at the British embassy in Jakarta, Indonesia, my grandad David was accidentally locked in a vault by a dopey colleague.

Though he was eventually found, the experience of being sealed in a tiny, impenetrable room for hours on end left him with acute claustrophobia that plagued him for the rest of his life. This meant that after years of travelling around the world as an embassy consul, he could never bring himself to fly in an aeroplane again.

Forty-six years later, when his youngest daughter – my Aunt Kate – got married in Vancouver, he sadly wasn't able to attend in person. That's when I, at the age of seven, was handed a top-of-the-range camera and tasked with capturing the event on his behalf.

This triggered a lifelong love of cameras and filmmaking. At the age of fourteen I wanted to be a film director, by eighteen I was one of the top students in my A-level film class and by nineteen I'd tossed all my filmmaking dreams in the bin when I realized the odds of me getting into the film industry were practically non-existent. I lacked both confidence and contacts.

But now, fifteen years after being handed my first video camera, I was finally about to unleash my filmmaking hobby upon the world. I'd produced a dreadful video of myself walking around my tiny Japanese apartment and, to my surprise, despite my monotonous voice, shoddy camerawork and a demeanour so inanimate I looked like I had rigor mortis, it was an instant hit, with a groundbreaking 250 views. Given I only had nine friends, it felt like a real achievement. I couldn't believe there were strangers out there that wanted to watch a guy moping around on a tatami floor.

My second video, on culture shock, did even better, with an astonishing three hundred views. I suspected the increase in views was due to the video thumbnail that featured the provocative *hentai* poster of the naked woman I'd seen on my first walk in downtown Sakata.

Unsurprisingly, the click-through rate, the number of people who click on a video when they come across it, was much higher. Unfortunately, viewers were furious to discover an absence of *hentai* when they clicked on the video. Instead, they'd been baited into watching a grumpy British guy sitting on the floor of his apartment eating a chocolate bar and complaining about Japanese TV. Oscar-worthy entertainment.

And now my third masterpiece was going to be on driving in Japan. Fortunately for me, as the Japanese drive on the same side of the road as the British, getting a Japanese licence only involved a few simple questions, while my American counterparts had to battle it out around a driving course. God bless right-hand drive. This is one of the long-lasting benefits of the British helping Japan to build their infrastructure and train lines back in the nineteenth century.

One of the most curious aspects of driving in Japan was reconciling the unrelenting drinking culture with being able to get home, especially in more rural areas, where there is little public transport. While in England you can have a pint and still get behind the wheel with a 0.08 per cent BAC (blood alcohol concentration), Japan is far stricter, with a limit of 0.04 per cent BAC. A mere sniff of alcohol rules you out of driving. It's probably for the best, too, as the Japanese population tends to be more susceptible to the effects of alcohol – at least from what I've seen.

Given the vital role alcohol plays in Japanese culture, where office staff typically have to sit for hours on end impressing their boss over a bucket of Asahi, it's no wonder that finding their way home afterwards presents an issue.

With a public outcry against drink driving after high-profile incidents in the 90s and 2000s, Japan reduced the number of drunk-driving incidents dramatically within a decade by taking a two-step approach, instigating harsh penalties and encouraging viable solutions, one of which was an ingenious and highly popular service known as *daikou*.

My first experience of the unique *daikou* service was on a work night when Kengo sensei and I were out for a drink at a local *izakaya*.

Kengo sensei had kindly been helping me practise my spoken Japanese with some basic conversation practice and we'd worked out that I'd be more willing to speak under the influence of alcohol.

When he offered to drive us both to dinner, I'd naturally assumed he'd be staying away from alcohol himself. This assumption went out the window the moment we sat down on the tatami and he ordered himself a draught beer.

My next assumption was that he intended to leave his car at the *izakaya* overnight and head home in a taxi when the night was over.

Three hours later, having eaten a platter of fresh, buttery tuna sashimi, consumed a barrel of beer and with me having spoken in halting Japanese in between courses, it was time to head home.

To my confusion, Kengo turned to me and asked, 'Chris san, would you like a ride home?'

I looked down at a table covered in empty beer glasses and spilt soy sauce and wondered if someone was about to lose their job.

'Are you sure it's OK to drive?'

'*Daijoubu!* No problem!' He laughed, waving his hands as if to allay my concerns.

He turned to a waitress who was waiting in the wings and shouted, '*Daikou onegaishimasu!*'

'*Hai!*' She headed over to the phone.

We'd been sitting by the window at the front of the *izakaya*, and when a grotty-looking Kei pulled up fifteen minutes later with a placard on the roof, I assumed we were about to take a taxi after all. Curiously, though, where the placard would normally read 'Taxi', it read, *Daikou*, and instead of a single driver there were two men in the front of the car wearing red baseball caps. The man in the passenger seat hopped out and entered the *izakaya*, and the waitress pointed out Kengo sensei and me.

He walked over, gave a friendly bow and muttered, 'Your key, please, sir!' as an inebriated Kengo jammed his hands into his trouser pockets searching for it.

I had no idea what was going on. Kengo finally extricated his key from his pocket and gave a brief description of his car and where he'd parked it. The man disappeared into the night, while I wondered if Kengo had just been part of the world's most courteous car robbery.

As we paid the bill, Kengo's Toyota appeared, being driven by the man in the red cap.

'Are you ready, Chris san? Let's go,' said Kengo. He steered me out of the restaurant and into the back seat of his car. Before long we were making our way through the streets of Sakata, a complete stranger at the wheel. It all felt a bit *Grand Theft Auto*. Puzzled as I was, Kengo seemed remarkably calm, so I assumed this was a normal situation.

In my somewhat drunken stupor I looked behind to find that the *daikou* taxi I'd first seen was now following along behind. The driver gave me a friendly wave and I gave a nod of approval, even though I had no idea what was going on.

'Well, here we are, Chris san! Have a nice rest, and see you tomorrow.'

I stepped out of the back seat, none the wiser, and turned to look at the stranger commandeering Kengo's car.

'Uh. Are you going to be OK getting home, Kengo sensei?'

'Oh yes, don't worry! The *daikou* will drive me home. See you tomorrow.'

And with that I slammed the door shut and watched the convoy disappear off down the road.

To my amazement, I later learned that, despite the *daikou* service requiring two drivers, it was only scarcely more expensive than a taxi. This was because, while taxi drivers needed a licensed vehicle to operate, *daikou* used the customer's own vehicle and so saved on licence fees, petrol and maintenance.

While in most countries the idea of letting a stranger drive your vehicle as you lie drunkenly on the back seat seems bizarre at best and dangerous at worst, in Japan there's a level of societal trust that makes honour-based systems like this work. *Daikou* seemed like a uniquely Japanese solution, and during the snowy winter months it was a service I would come to depend upon.

In December 2005 a Japan Railways East train travelling southbound from Akita to Niigata was passing through Yamagata when a powerful gust of wind launched it off the track and into a snow-covered roadside hut. Five passengers were killed and thirty-three injured. This accident was testament to the sheer power of the Siberian winds that blow across the Sea of Japan and crash into the western coastline. Combined with the highest snowfall on the planet, it's clear to see why winter in Japan isn't to be taken lightly.

I'd been warned of what was to come by Roy but had arrogantly laughed it off.

'Mate, I think I know what snow is.'

Reader, I did not.

One weekday morning in early December I awoke at seven o'clock and slid back my *shoji* screen doors. My window usually overlooked a busy car park, but this morning the usual two dozen cars had disappeared beneath a mound of snow. In the space of one night it had snowed almost two feet.

Before long, the car park had turned into an excavation site. It was like a scene from *Raiders of the Lost Ark*, except instead of searching for the Ark of the Covenant, the diggers were seeking Toyotas.

I ran outside to discover that, thankfully, the apartment had half a dozen communal shovels on hand for this very purpose. I took one and flung aside the powdery snow, astonished by just how much had fallen overnight. The voice of the Japanese minder who'd delivered me to Yamagata months previously echoed in my mind.

In the winter, these mountains, many snow.

Many fucking snow indeed.

After almost half an hour of steadfast digging, the Nissan was finally uncovered and the tyres freed to move. I'd removed enough snow from the roof of my car to build not just a single snowman but an entire infantry unit. As I was finishing up, Roy appeared around the corner smoking his usual morning cigarette.

'I warned you!' he chuckled smugly.

'Yeah, yeah. Good luck cleaning *your* car, mate.' At least I could watch him dig his way out with a degree of *Schadenfreude*.

But it was not to be.

Roy dusted off his driver door and a patch of windscreen directly in front of the steering wheel, swung open the door and slid in. He powered up the car and reversed aggressively out of the heap of snow that had buried his Toyota Starlet.

In the space of five seconds he'd managed what had taken me an age, and with a cheeky grin and a puff of smoke he hit the accelerator and shot out of the car park to victory.

What an absolute bastard.

It shouldn't have surprised me how bad the snow was. If I'd done my homework, I would have discovered that two of Japan's northernmost cities, Aomori and Sapporo, hold the world record for the highest levels of annual snowfall.

Aomori city, which was just 250 kilometres north of Sakata, received a terrifying 8 metres of snow in a single winter. The good news is, unlike bad weather causing the clusterfuck of train cancellations I was used to in the UK, Japan was prepared for it. As I drove to school that morning, I witnessed no less than a dozen snowploughs methodically working their way through the neighbourhood. With many farmers and agricultural workers out of work in the winter months, Japan had the genius idea of enlisting them as snowplough operators, so despite the aggressive snowfall, an army of farmers was able to turn the tide and keep society functioning.

I, personally, however, felt like I was losing the battle. Over the next few weeks, going outdoors turned into a constant struggle in the face of blizzards and shovelling. Shovelling the car. Shovelling the apartment doorway. Shovelling myself into a hole so deep I could hibernate all winter.

No matter how many times I excavated my car, the next morning it was gone.

It wasn't uncommon for the temperature to drop so rapidly that the windscreen wipers froze to the windscreen while they were in use. The biggest snowflakes I'd ever seen clumped around the wipers and rendered them inoperable, forcing me to frequently stop the car, dash out and dust it off.

It all came to a head one December morning as I drove my

Nissan up the hill to work. The tyres got stuck in a pothole covered with snow and ice, causing the car to falter and skid to a halt in the perfect position to block the approach to Sakata Senior High.

While I'd made the switch to snow tyres several weeks earlier in anticipation, unlike many of the local's cars, the Nissan wasn't a 4x4. As the tyres spun and I felt the car sink further into the snow, I felt utterly hopeless. Not only was I going to be late for work, but so was half the faculty, stuck in the increasingly lengthy queue behind me.

I was absolutely mortified to realize that I was on full display, as all my students were walking alongside the car on the pavement, fighting their own way through the blizzard. Some politely pretended not to see me, but one particular group of boys pointed and laughed obnoxiously before scurrying off into the warm. I made a note of their stupid faces; revenge would be swift and brutal when marking their end-of-term exams.

The driver in the car behind me appeared to be a severe-looking middle-aged man.

Brilliant. I'm sure he's going to love helping the dopey foreigner who is making him late.

I opened my car door and stepped out into the piercing cold, giving an uneasy thumbs-down to the driver, but to my relief he hopped out of his car without a second thought and trudged through the snow to start pushing.

'*Sumimasen, sumimasen!* I'm so sorry!' I yelled, over the sound of the running car and the winds that were whipping around us.

'*Iie, iie!* No, not at all!' he called back, and moved to the rear of the Nissan and began to push.

Moments later, another man joined him, followed by a female office worker from the school.

Giving a solemn bow to my team of supporters, I hopped

back into the driver's seat to try and manoeuvre myself out of the literal hole I'd got myself in.

On the count of four they pushed and I hit the throttle.

'*Ichi, ni, san, SHI!*' they cried, all pushing in unison. As I felt the tyre grip the road and the vehicle lurched forward to victory, I gave a triumphant wave back through the window to the cheering crowd. I'd survived my first real run-in with Japan's brutal snowfall.

'You're late today, bro,' said Roy as I collapsed into my seat in the teacher's office.

'Yeah, somebody's car got stuck on the hill,' I muttered under my breath.

After that day, I was so scared of reliving the situation that I avoided driving to work almost the entire winter.

Ironically, the car I'd so badly longed for spent most weekdays stuck in the apartment car park being transformed into a giant snowman. The experience had been so traumatizing that I'd sooner plod through the blizzard for twenty-five minutes than risk it happening again. Whenever Roy or Nishiyama asked why on earth I was walking in sub-zero weather, I'd proclaim it was for 'health and fitness reasons'.

With the outdoors becoming more inhospitable by the day, I started to spend more of my free time in the apartment, buried under my *kotatsu* heated table with a blanket draped over my lower half. Though there was barely any room to walk around in my apartment, the tiny surface area meant that it was wonderfully cosy.

Traditional Japanese homes and apartments are notoriously inadequate when it comes to insulation and heating. Who'd have thought it, but paper sliding doors don't do the best job holding back freezing temperatures. Unlike in the UK, where most homes come installed with radiators, Japanese homes often rely on kerosene heaters and *kotatsu*, and apartments like mine use air-conditioning units switched to heating mode, blowing out dry, hot air that turns each room into a desert.

But sitting on the soft tatami mat, hunched over my desk under a warm blanket, I made the most of every single hour. Hibernating like a bear, locked away in my apartment, there wasn't a second to waste. I'd set myself the goal of being able to converse in Japanese by the following spring and, with each passing day, I was coming to appreciate the sheer scale of the task before me.

9.

The Impossible Language

Two thousand kanji.

Three writing systems.

Three thousand basic everyday words to memorize.

I'd begun to realize how screwed I was as I embarked on my journey to learn one of the world's hardest languages. Even setting aside the sheer amount there was to put to memory, the grammar structure was so alien I suspected that the Japanese language had been specially designed to cripple an English speaker's brain.

Having studied both German and Spanish in school and failed miserably at both, I'd pessimistically told myself that my brain just wasn't wired to handle a second language. Any thought of mastering a foreign language seemed ludicrous.

You didn't have to be fluent in Japanese to apply for the JET programme – the whole reason you were there was to talk English, after all – and roughly 50 per cent of the foreign teachers I'd met appeared to have no experience of the language whatsoever. Some had no intention of learning it either, with the plan being to live in Japan for a year or two then head off home.

Even though I didn't anticipate that I'd stay in Japan beyond three years, I'd always intended to study the language and give it my best shot. The idea of living and working in a foreign country for an extended period and not making an effort to embrace the culture and the language seemed disrespectful, even if it wasn't expected.

Beyond that, it was a chance to prove to myself that I wasn't a complete failure. Learning Japanese would be the ultimate self-help course and finally help me to do something about my abysmal memory. This was a problem that had plagued me all my life. But while these things were what had motivated me in the run-up to moving to Japan, several months in I was finding the crushing sensation of being unable to function in everyday life a far more powerful motivator.

In the school corridor, students would run over and shout in Japanese, 'Chris sensei! ★★★★★ ★★★★★ ★★★★ ★★★.' I'd stand there, fumbling awkwardly, pretending to know what they were saying by making an occasional nod. Many teachers continued to avoid me, diving into side doors when I appeared. The thought of having to use their English was simply too much for them.

Unable to communicate with students and colleagues and struggling to undertake basic tasks like banking, paying my phone bill or even using my microwave, I felt paralysed and robbed of my independence. I was hopelessly dependent on friends like Roy or Kengo sensei, but every time I asked for their help I felt a growing sense of guilt for the burden I'd become.

Worst of all, my lack of Japanese had inadvertently led me to breaking the law.

A recent road trip to witness snow monkeys moping around the hot springs of Nagano took me to the mountains of central Japan. I'd endured the long six-hour drive down the east coast using Japan's formidably expensive highways.

With an estimated 10,000 road tunnels, Japan has more than any other nation on Earth, second only to China. In a land of relentless mountains and outrageous levels of snow, these highway tunnels are crucial for traversing the country and had shaved two hours off my journey time.

Emerging from the last infinitely long tunnel of the journey, I pulled up to the toll booth, where to my horror I realized I'd accidentally pulled into the wrong exit.

I'd driven into the exit exclusively for cars using a chip system called ETC, allowing seamless transition on and off the highway using a wireless transmitter on the dashboard. That was a luxury I'd failed to attain.

As I pulled up to a firmly shut barrier with no means to pay with cash, a long line of cars started piling up behind me. I was trapped. I poked my head out of the window, flailing around in distress amidst the backdrop of incessant honking. To my relief a man working at one of the cash only toll booths ran over. My savior had arrived.

'*Genki desu ka?*' He asked if I was okay, anxiously looking back at the long line of traffic.

'Er . . . yeah *genki*!' I gave a resilient thumbs up.

'*Hai, douzo!*' He gestured towards the barrier, which suddenly lifted, leading to freedom.

'*Arigatou gozaimasu!*' I cheered, as I drove full throttle down the ramp. Amid my relief at escaping, I realized that the man had let me off paying the toll entirely. It was an incredible twist of good fortune.

That was, until two months later.

One day as I was working my way through a new list of Japanese vocabulary, I discovered that the word for cash in Japanese was *genkin*.

I cast my mind back to the highway toll incident. The man

hadn't been asking if I was *genki*. He'd been asking if I had bloody *genkin!* Cash.

'Do you have cash?' the man had asked.

When I replied with a positive thumbs-up the man had assumed I did and had gestured to a place where I could pull over and hand it over.

I, however, had rocketed off down the motorway, leaving the dismayed toll-booth man standing in a cloud of exhaust fumes.

My stupidity might have saved me a few thousand yen, but it didn't exactly portray foreign residents in the greatest light. To absolve myself of my sins I promptly donated the unpaid money to a local Tohoku disaster charity.

Born out of my fears of becoming a petty criminal and continuing to be a burden on my colleagues, I felt a level of resolve I'd never experienced before.

On the war path, I threw my energy into mastering Japanese and built a ruthless daily regime to make it seem achievable. Cue the rocky montage.

At 7 a.m. I'd wake up with an hour to go before I needed to head to school. I'd sit on the floor of my apartment, hunched over the table, coffee in one hand, pencil in the other, writing out twenty-five kanji. At the rate of twenty-five a day, I'd calculated I'd be able to work my way through the 2,200 basic characters in three months.

Arguably the biggest hurdle in mastering the language, Japanese kanji are adapted from Chinese characters, and at first they seem like a rather large flaw in the system. After all, it can take a Japanese student nine to ten years of continuous study to memorize the reading and writing of their own mother tongue. You can pretty much learn the English alphabet in a day and be up and running.

But the logographic nature of kanji allows a single character to mean a whole word or concept, so they take up less space.

Where we have to laboriously write out the word 'water', the Japanese draw this beautiful little character 水.

Intuitively, and confusingly, similar words often share the same strokes. 'Ice' for example is 氷. It's practically identical to the character for 'water', with an additional flick to the left.

I found this captivating, and it was daily discoveries like these that fuelled my excitement at learning a new language. With each new character I mastered, I took a step closer to comprehending my surroundings. One morning after memorizing the character 茶 for 'tea', I wandered past a vending machine on my way to school and instantly recognized it on some of the bottles inside. In celebration, I snapped up a bottle of hot malty wheat tea and drank it on the walk to work.

Continuing my commute to school, I walked by a traditional wooden liquor store built into the ground floor of an elderly couple's house selling every type of sake known to man. Having committed to memory the kanji for sake (酒) early on, given it was in the town name of Sakata itself (酒田), as I bumbled past the shop each morning I loved to peer into the steamed-up windows and gaze at the sea of colourful bottles, each with 酒 emblazoned on it. This single recognizable kanji sat alongside a series of indecipherable characters. I longed for the day when the contents of the bottles were no longer a mystery.

One morning, I struck upon twenty-five new kanji focused on the theme of alcohol. After spending my usual hour at my desk with a pencil, scribbling each one down ten times, I downed the last drops of my coffee and headed out into the bitter blizzard once more.

As I reached the sake shop and took my regular look through the glass, my eyes swept across the bottles and the words magically popped into my head: 梅酒 – plum wine; 甘酒 – sweet sake; にごり酒 – cloudy sake.

No, I wasn't turning into an alcoholic. I could finally read!

At long last, the sake shop made sense.

In celebration, I burst into the store and bought a bottle of sweet, crisp plum wine to swig on my way into school.

If only.

These moments of triumph, though seemingly small, were now happening daily. This slow unravelling of my once incomprehensible surroundings felt increasingly empowering and rewarding. The hours of relentless study were paying off. I'd grown to love my meditative-style mornings on my apartment floor, writing out characters in silence over and over. It certainly beat rushing into work, inhaling a cloud of Roy's second-hand cigarette smoke.

Still, though I'd reached a point where I was able to lick my lips with glee while poring over the menu at a bar, when it came to shouting out to the waiter and ordering in Japanese, that was a whole different ball game.

Before I could start speaking, I needed to somehow stuff three thousand words of basic Japanese vocabulary into my head. I did this by using digital flashcards whenever I had free time in between classes, often testing them out with colleagues in the staffroom. I often felt a little guilty for bothering the teachers during their free time, but there was always one teacher who would help me out more than any other during my three years at school.

Arguably the craziest man in the staffroom, Chounan sensei was a science teacher who'd somehow become fluent in English over a lifetime of many adventures. With a raspy voice that had experienced the smoke of a thousand cigarettes daily for the last thirty years, if he wasn't out on a smoking break with Roy, he was perched next to me, causing mayhem between classes.

For most of the day, the staffroom resembled a library –

peaceful, calm and so quiet that there was usually more than one teacher asleep on their desk. That all ended the moment Chounan sensei stepped into the room.

The life and soul of the staffroom, with a chaotic wavy hairstyle that looked like he'd just stumbled out of a wind tunnel, you'd always hear Chounan long before you'd see him, his guffaws bouncing off the corners the room, often to the visible irritation of the other teachers. He was never even laughing at anything in particular.

'HAHA, Chris sensei! Good afternoon!'

'Afternoon, Chounan sensei! What does *muzukashii* mean?'

'Ah! *Muzuakashii ne!* It means "difficult". So, for me, stopping smoking is kind of *muzukashii*, HAHA!' he bellowed, collapsing into a neighbouring chair.

For at least twenty-five minutes every day without fail, we'd teach each other English and Japanese phrases, while he awkwardly tried to set me up with the young, attractive school nurse who sat at the desk on my left.

'She's single, you're single. You should date! HAHA,' he joked.

As the school nurse blushed and I shrank down into my chair, I recalled Roy's story about how my JET predecessor had caused an HR firestorm after chatting up a previous school nurse and sending controversial text messages. While dating among Japanese teachers was common, dating between JETs and Japanese teachers was forbidden. This was an unspoken rule that I intended to adhere to.

Back home at around 5 p.m., after a dinner of cheese omelette or pan-fried chicken, the only two dishes I could cook with any degree of skill, I'd put on an audio tape and practise my listening skills. When half of Siberia hadn't been dumped on Japan's west coast, I'd wander the streets at night, exploring the town and playing a list of vocabulary on a loop.

My day would end with watching Japanese TV or anime with subtitles then a bath at 10 p.m. I'd never been into anime before, but I'd become addicted to an absurd series called *GTO: Great Teacher Onizuka* that had been adapted from a hugely popular nineties manga series.

The plot revolved around Onizuka, a twenty-two-year-old who used to be a member of a biker gang and becomes a teacher with the sole intent of dating the attractive mothers of his students. With his dubious motives and a second-rate teaching diploma, he becomes the homeroom teacher of Tokyo's most misbehaved students and uses his unorthodox methods to solve school disputes, usually by punching someone in the face. Tongue in cheek and scandalous to the point where I'm sure the series wouldn't be shown outside Japan, *GTO* was especially fun to watch as the plotlines echoed my real-life experience, though with rather less punching. Watching Onizuka deal with school bullies and clumsy teachers made me wish we had our own rogue rule-breaking teacher at Sakata Senior High.

From scribbling kanji in the morning and memorizing vocabulary throughout the day to listening closely to Onizuka's outrageous classroom monologues, slowly but surely the Japanese language was seeping into my brain. The best analogy would be a sand timer constantly pouring in the words, grammar and characters every day, the language was slowly building up in my subconscious.

To really put these new skills to the test, I needed to throw myself in at the deep end and demonstrate to my colleagues that I was making progress. And what better place to test it all out than during the chaos and utter shitshow that would be my first official work party.

While *enkai* (宴会) simply means 'work party', *Bonenkai* (忘年会) means 'forgetting the year party', and it was the biggest and baddest of them all, an annual event held at workplaces throughout Japan in early December, as the year draws to a close. While Japan doesn't celebrate Christmas, though it does acknowledge the season in its own special way, the New Year holiday, or *Shogatsu*, is a major occasion, with the country more or less shut down from 1 to 3 January. The idea of the party is to forget the difficulties and troubles you've faced in the year so you can start the new year afresh.

At long last, the *Bonenkai* had arrived. And, ironically for a party celebrating forgetting, the night would be incredibly memorable.

10.

Party Time

Over the years, we've been taught through movies that if you want to extract the truth from a target, a syringe of sodium pentathol is all it takes to loosen them up and have them unleashing their deepest, darkest secrets.

In Japan, all it takes is two pints of beer.

'I think Nishiyama is kind of a fucking stupid man.'

'Oh, er, really?'

An English teacher I worked with who'd kept his thoughts to himself for the last four months was opening up about how he hated everyone else in the department. It was as if we were inside a church confession box and I was the priest. Standing in the corner of an expansive banquet room filled with a hundred drunken teaching colleagues clutching bottles of Asahi, I scanned around to make sure no one could hear Suzuki sensei's rant.

'He seems kind of lazy. I don't know why he runs the English department. He's kind of a fucking idiot.'

'Uh, I see.' I was trying to avoid phrases that seemed like tacit agreement.

Bloody hell, why on earth was this teacher telling me all of this?

The answer lay in the pint of beer in his hand and his bright red complexion. He looked like he'd plunged his face into a bucket of ketchup. Together they betrayed his insobriety.

He hadn't been the first teacher to ambush me in the circus that was the *Bonenkai*.

A group of four PE teachers in their late twenties had wandered over to my table early in the evening to practise their English and humiliate one of their group.

'Chris sensei, my English not so good! But Sasaki sensei, he has no girlfriend,' jeered Arashiyama sensei, and the whole group laughed at Sasaki's expense. Sasaki laughed uncomfortably, looking mildly offended but going along with the joke.

'He's so fucking bad man!' declared Sasaki, in triumphant rebuttal, while I stood there, gobsmacked, at the unravelling of my colleagues' composure. Meanwhile, teachers who'd avoided me like the plague in the corridors were coming over to pour me a glass of beer, treating me as if I were a celebrity.

I found the whole thing baffling. The free-flowing alcohol was turning my stern, rigid colleagues into pantomime characters.

The *Bonenkai* was taking place in the banquet room of the Sakata Landmark Hotel, the tallest building in town and easily the most ghastly. Unfortunately, it was one of only a few local venues big enough to handle the sheer scale of Sakata Senior High's workforce.

In the huge room, I was seated at one of the ten round tables alongside a dozen teachers, many of whom I'd never spoken to before. The only teacher I really knew was Suzuki sensei, who happened to be the one English teacher I'd never really bonded with.

He was middle-aged with short, spiky hair and his English

skills were among the best in the department. But he seemed reluctant to use them around me, as if making a mistake in front of me would lead to some sort of catastrophe. Consequently, throughout my whole first term at Sakata Senior High, every time our scheduled lessons came around, I'd look up from my desk to see him rise from his seat, grab a pile of textbooks and head for the door, while furiously avoiding eye contact with me. He seemed keen to avoid teaching classes with me and, rather than call him out, I just went along with it. I didn't want to feel like I was intruding in his classes. Besides, it meant more free time for me to pursue my Japanese studies at my desk.

Now, as we sat shoulder to shoulder, in his usual uncertain tone, stuttering and repeating himself, Suzuki sensei seemed to uncomfortably acknowledge the situation.

'Chris sensei, I think . . . I think my students would like to see you in class! Wouldn't you . . . I mean, won't you come along?'

'Sure, Suzuki sensei. I'd love to join you.'

'How can I say . . . you know. That's so great!'

I couldn't work out if he was being polite or extending an olive branch. Perhaps this whole time he had thought *I* was the one avoiding *him*.

The seating plan that had been designed to encourage teachers from different departments to converse appeared at first to have failed. Early on, as I looked around the table, most colleagues were shifting in their seats in silence, and I felt like I was looking down the barrel of a long, dull evening from hell.

While we waited for the headmaster to arrive and give the opening speech, I fled the awkward silence under the guise of needing the bathroom. In reality, the moment I shut myself in the toilet cubicle, I withdrew the sneakily concealed Japanese phrasebook from where I'd been hiding it inside my suit jacket and rehearsed phrases as though I were preparing for a last-minute exam.

'*Dono kamoku wo oshite imasu ka?*' Which subject do you teach?

It was to be my opening salvo in a conversation with my colleagues at my table. But the damn word *kamoku*, 'subject', kept eluding me.

Kamoku. Sounds like *cam mock* . . . Imagine mocking someone's bad camera.

That did the trick. God bless word association.

Alas, I needn't have bothered.

As the headmaster wrapped up his speech and everyone at the table held up their glass of freshly poured beer, the room shouted out the loudest 'KANPAI!' I'd ever heard and downed their drink in one.

Like Popeye after munching a tin of spinach, the people in the room transformed instantly.

To my amazement, everyone at the table burst into conversation. Not only that, everyone magically started speaking English.

'Chris sensei, so good to meet you! I'm Kumiko!' The timid calligraphy teacher to my left introduced herself in fluent English.

'How do you like Japan so far, Chris sensei?' shouted the hulking kendo teacher from across the table.

It was as if a switch had been flipped.

It soon became clear that there are only two rules at a Japanese *enkai*.

Number one was speak your mind.

As I'd discovered from Suzuki sensei and other colleagues, who were all having heated conversations around the room, the drunken antics of the *Bonenkai* provide the perfect backdrop for unleashing the thoughts and opinions kept bottled up throughout the year. Given it was the forgetting-the-year party, it seemed especially important to unburden oneself.

Rule number two was never, ever pour your own drink.

Whether it's beer, sake or wine, to pick up the bottle and pour for yourself is a big no-no.

Hearing this, naturally, you may be concerned that at some point in the evening you'll find your glass unfilled. But during the first hour of the party, no matter how much Asahi I drank, a neighbouring colleague would spring up to fill my glass up again.

Usually, it wasn't entirely altruistic either; I soon noticed that every time Suzuki sensei had finished pouring me a glass, he'd sheepishly look over to his own glass, which was invariably empty.

'Sorry, Suzuki sensei, let me fill your glass.' I grabbed a bottle from the centre of the round table and emptied it into his glass for the tenth time in five minutes.

'Oh wow! Thank you, thank you, Chris sensei.'

With the laid-back atmosphere and the sound of laughter and clinking glasses around the room, I was enjoying the *enkai* far more than I'd anticipated. It felt like an early Christmas miracle, seeing colleagues open up for the very first time – even if there were some things I'd rather forget.

At one point, deputy headmaster Saitou pulled out a CD player and started playing a song by Japan's biggest pop group, AKB48. They were both literally and metaphorically Japan's biggest pop group, with over forty-eight performers. He blared out the song 'Heavy Rotation', a shockingly bad track that opened with the English lyrics, 'I want you! I need you! I love you!'

When the song came on, no less than twenty teachers clambered on to the wooden stage at the front of the banquet hall and re-enacted the dance from the music video, using hand gestures to make love hearts and gyrating their hips in a way that I'll never unsee. At times like this, I wish music had never been invented.

The second party wasn't much better.

A Japanese work party can go on through up to three or four after-parties, each in a different venue, deep into the night. The second party is called the *nijikai*, the third the *sanjikai*, and staff numbers drop rapidly with each level, almost like a drunken version of *Inception*.

The *nijikai* took place at an *izakaya* just three minutes' walk from the hotel, yet we lost three quarters of the staff along the way and were now whittled down to just twenty-five.

From here on, the composed teachers I'd been accustomed to became a distant memory. Most notably, a strict Japanese literature teacher in her late thirties called Nakamura sensei, who I'd actively feared as she always looked so serious in the staffroom and I'd never seen her smile, spent the whole time at the *izakaya* rolling on the floor laughing like a maniac.

When it came to the *sanjikai*, the third and it turned out final party, two hours later, Nakamura was deafening the remaining dozen teachers with her abrasive singing at a karaoke bar.

To this day, I despise group karaoke and I suspect it's due to what my eardrums endured that night. Until then, I'd always been confused as to why karaoke had never taken off in the West to the same degree it had in Japan. But as Nakamura screeched the night away, I realized that British people just wouldn't have the patience for it. We'd have to leave the room or smash the karaoke machine. It was testament to the sheer strength of Japanese politeness that, no matter how drunk everyone was or how many ears were bleeding, nobody called an end to the madness.

After Nakamura's nightmare sonata, inevitably, I was in the running for a song myself.

Though I initially refused, the room of inebriated teachers began to clap and chant, 'Chris sensei, Chris sensei, Chris sensei!' over and over, until I had to relent.

Luckily for me, I had an ace up my sleeve. I'd successfully committed to memory the one Japanese song worth knowing as a foreigner in Japan, '*Ue wo muite arukou*', better known in English as the 'Sukiyaki song', by Sakamoto Kyu.

In 1961, the Sukiyaki song took the world by storm topping the Billboard Hot 100 in the US, despite being in Japanese. Incredibly, it was the only single by an Asian artist to top the Hot 100 until 2020, when the South Korean group BTS stormed the charts.

Bizarrely, though the song's Japanese title translates as 'I look up while I walk', in reference to the singer looking up at the sky to prevent his tears from rolling down his face, the English version was robbed of such poetic imagery. Instead, to give the song a snappy, memorable name, it was called 'Sukiyaki', a Japanese beef hotpot, which, while delicious, has absolutely nothing to do with the song.

It'd be like re-titling the Beatles song 'A Hard Day's Night' for Jinternational audiences by calling it 'Fish and Chips'. Even so, their marketing plan worked, and today it's considered a rite of passage for foreign English teachers to learn the song and sing it in front of a crowd of impressed colleagues. I rather liked '*Ue wo muite arukou*'. Even though I must have heard the damn song fifty times in a row while memorizing the lyrics in my apartment for this very moment, I somehow never got tired of listening to Sakamoto Kyu's powerful voice.

Tragically, his career ended abruptly in 1985 when he boarded the ill-fated Japan Airlines flight 123. On a routine flight from Tokyo to Osaka, the 747 suffered a catastrophic mechanical failure, causing the jet to plummet into the mountains of Gunma. Five hundred and twenty passengers lost their lives, among them Kyu. It was the deadliest single-aircraft accident in aviation history.

As I punched the song into the karaoke machine touchscreen,

the room of teachers gave out cheers of joy when they realized what I was planning to sing. There was no going back now. I took a big gulp of beer and went on to butcher Sakamoto Kyu's legacy to ecstatic, drunken applause.

The following Monday when I pulled up to school, I wondered if the shared camaraderie born against the backdrop of alcohol and karaoke would have any lasting effects on my relationships with my colleagues. Perhaps Nakamura sensei would finally smile or say hello to me in the staffroom.

The answer was no.

The cheeky PE teachers gave me an emotionless, silent nod in the corridor.

Nakamura sensei looked straight past me.

And good old Suzuki sensei ignored me, as usual, on his way to class.

The balance was restored.

It was as if nothing had ever happened.

II.

Land of the Rising Waistline

JANUARY 2013

'Chris sensei, you have the cholesterol of a forty-year-old.'

Nishiyama was laughing his way through my abysmal health report.

'Oh Jesus. That's not good. Anything else?'

'Your body mass index says you are obese.'

It wasn't supposed to be this way.

Before arriving in Japan, I'd assumed that after just six months my body fat would magically disappear after I embraced a diet of sushi, rice and pickles. After adopting the Japanese way of life and uncovering the secret to the nation's enviously low obesity rates, I anticipated a spectacular physical transformation the likes of which the world had never seen.

Yeah, not quite.

Things had got far, far worse.

A winter spent hibernating indoors either studying Japanese at my desk with a mouthful of juicy Family Mart fried chicken or drinking and smoking my evenings away with Roy at an *iza-kaya* had taken an appalling toll on my health. My daily diet of raw fish and pickles had remained firmly in the realm of fantasy, though it's true I ate sushi at least once a week. A popular conveyor-belt sushi chain called Kappa Sushi was on my way home from work, and I'd regularly stop by after a long day and order a dozen plates of salmon, tuna and mackerel. I'm not sure it's as healthy when you eat it in bulk.

Far more precariously placed near my apartment was a mouth-watering ramen shop called Shinzan. Ramen. The broth comes in two styles: *kotteri* (thick) and *assari* (light).

Kotteri is a rich broth, typically opaque and filled with emulsified fats and long-boiled bones. *Assari* is usually clear and more delicately flavoured with vegetables and fish. In a nutshell, *kotteri* inflicts a greater sense of guilt, but in my opinion is a far superior broth base.

Shinzan's thick broth was extremely flavourful, with notes of pork and a hint of fish stock, Each region across Japan has a different speciality ramen, from Hakata's tonkotsu ramen, to Sapporo's miso, to Toyama prefecture's tastebud-destroying salty black ramen. The ramen commonly served in Sakata's local shops were soy sauce-based, with thick, juicy cuts of braised pork liberally layered on top and a gooey tea-stained egg on the side.

Ramen is often regarded as one of Japan's most photogenic dishes, due to its mixture of brightly coloured ingredients, from the orange sliced egg and green *nori* to the yellow noodles and glistening fat on the braised pork. Shinzan's ramen, however, looked more like an oil spill.

The soup was so thick and dark it absorbed light like a black hole. The noodles weren't even visible and the pork was always slightly submerged beneath the surface. When they first slapped the bowl down in front of me, broth sloshing on to the table, I was slightly underwhelmed.

But my god was it phenomenal.

After battling the blizzards, there was no greater reward than this greasy, steaming bowl of noodles and, at a ludicrously cheap 830 yen ($6), it soon became a weekly indulgence.

And it wasn't just ramen I was indulging in.

Five minutes from Shinzan was a restaurant called Alba that served up katsu curry with the thickest, creamiest sauce in town, poured over generous helpings of pork cutlets caked in crispy golden breadcrumbs. I would pop in once a week and leave feeling immensely fulfilled and incredibly bloated.

Just about the only healthy meal I was eating were the daily *bento* boxes at school, which we collected every morning from the far side of the staffroom. Each day a well-balanced meal containing either meat or fish, served alongside pickled radishes, was presented in a red plastic box, with the rice in a separate green container.

Monday was hamburger day, and I'd throw off the lid with delight to find a juicy burger drenched in a thick gravy.

Tuesday was boiled whitefish day. Meh.

Wednesday was battered-chicken *karaage* day. Rejoice!

Thursday was boiled mackerel. Not great, not terrible.

Friday was the wild card. On a bad week it'd be more bland, boiled fish. On a good week I'd remove the lid to uncover sautéd pork. Hallelujah!

The *bento* was the perfect size. I'd finish lunch each day feeling satisfied without being stuffed. At the start of the year, I'd often leave half my rice in the container when dropping it off in the disposal pile, to the dismay of one of the staffroom managers.

'Chris sensei, are you leaving rice in your box?' asked the usually cheerful Yuko, a petite, bubbly woman who was one of the friendliest people in the staffroom. The fact that for once she wasn't smiling emphasized the seriousness of the issue.

'Uh, yes, I usually get full when eating rice.' I stumbled over the words, despite my ever-improving Japanese skills.

'*Mottainai*, Chris sensei! Please don't leave it behind. Either eat it or don't order it.'

Ah, *mottainai*.

The most hypocritical word in the Japanese vocabulary.

Mottainai (もったいない) means 'What a waste!' and is usually uttered in regret when some food hasn't been eaten or an item hasn't been recycled or reused. Rooted in Buddhism, waste became a pressing issue in the post-war era amid food rationing and great poverty. I could hardly deny that this hangover from the war was great practice.

But in a country that sells individually wrapped bananas and is second only to the US as the world's biggest generator of plastic packaging waste per capita, it's hard not to see a level of hypocrisy when the term is used.

On more than one occasion I'd been berated for leaving an uneaten piece of salty fish, riddled with bones, in my bento box.

'Chris sensei, won't you think of the fisherman's hard work?' begged Komako sensei, on her usual stroll over to my desk with a handful of KitKats.

'I'm struggling to eat this.' I looked down at the bony piece of fish, knowing that to put it in my mouth would lead to someone having to perform the Heimlich manoeuvre on me.

Meanwhile, Komako sensei's desk was essentially a landfill site, littered with the plastic wrappers of a thousand individually wrapped KitKats.

'We mustn't waste food, Chris sensei.'

I agreed that I should finish it off, and waited until she'd disappeared before throwing on the lid and fleeing the scene of the crime.

While my health report wasn't great by British standards, by Japan's it was nothing short of an atrocity. In the US, a worrying 33 per cent of the population is obese. The UK follows close behind at 28 per cent.

You might be thinking, Well, I know Japan is lower – perhaps 15 per cent?

Nope.

Surely not lower than 10 per cent?

Keep going.

Japan's obesity rate is an astonishing 3.3 per cent.

In an era of ultra-processed and fast food, it's an astonishing feat and one the West would do well to take note of. When I arrived in Japan I was struck by how slim everyone appeared to be, across all age groups. Of the 120 staff at Sakata Senior High, I could count on one hand the number of overweight or obese staff – and I was now one of them.

Where had I gone so wrong?

A study in 2008 found that people in Japan walk on average two thousand steps a day more than Americans do, and portion sizes are significantly smaller, with Japanese people consuming two hundred calories less a day. Not only that, but the food is far less processed than in the West and rich in superfoods, from *natto*, fermented soybeans that I beg you never to make me eat, to pickled radishes and the fermented miso used in the soup that accompanies every meal.

It's thought that the carbohydrate-heavy meals (often featuring rice) make people feel full for longer; also, snacking is much less common in Japan. It was certainly the case that compared to my previous office job, where colleagues had a packet of crisps or biscuits next to their keyboard throughout the day, here I noticed few teachers snacking before or after their *bento* lunch.

Combined, these factors added up to a healthy population. And yet as I was soon to learn, one key element is often left out of the story: societal pressure.

I first experienced this when good old Komako sensei and I were walking to class one morning. Out of nowhere, she blurted out, 'Ooh, Chris sensei, you appear to like food recently.' While eyeing up my stomach.

It was a beautifully roundabout way of calling me fat.

Next, one of my best English students, a girl in the senior class, prodded me in the stomach when I walked past her desk one morning as if to highlight my increasing weight. 'Too much fried chicken!' I declared, to laughter around the room. All I could do was join in.

It's true that my stomach was bulging slightly more than usual. The winter had come as a nasty shock, with the conditions leading me to hide inside for most of my free time, gorging on awful food. It didn't help that convenience stores had a fast-food counter by the tills dispensing boxes of juicy chicken *karaage* or warm fluffy pizza bread for less than 200 yen each. My boozy evenings with Roy were the final nail in the coffin.

Hell, if I carried on down this greasy slope, there would literally be a coffin.

Pressured by my damaging health report and 'playful' bullying from colleagues and students, as the snows began to melt in early spring I began jogging in the evenings and avoiding the reasonably priced convenience-store food I'd grown to depend on.

While I knew colleagues and students meant well, it certainly blew a hole through my perfect image of Japanese politeness. For the first time, I'd been subjected to Japan's unique brand of collectivist bullying. The comments I'd received would have been unthinkable back home in the UK, where people would likely be fired for making such crass remarks.

In 2008, Japan received misleading international news coverage for allegedly 'making obesity illegal' after announcing the controversial 'Metabo law' (*metabo* being a reference to metabolism). To prevent obesity rates from increasing, the new law required companies and local governments to check the waist measurement of people between forty and seventy-five years old each year. If their waistlines exceeded 33.5 inches for men and 35.4 inches for women, the company would encourage these individuals to take weight-loss classes and put a plan in place to get them into shape, or face financial penalties. To many, it sounded like a nanny state gone too far and a total intrusion on the freedoms of Japan's citizens.

However, the law received widespread support from the public. With the Japanese government's burgeoning healthcare costs because of the country's ageing population, an increase in diabetes and heart disease could deliver a crippling blow to the nation's already struggling finances.

The 3.3 per cent obesity rate suggests it's working.

As for me, while I managed to swap my fried-chicken dinners for an omelette and salad, my late-night outings in downtown Sakata weren't going anywhere.

12.

Hostess Clubs and the Art of Expensive Companionship

FEBRUARY 2013

It was 1 a.m. and I was sitting back on a purple leather sofa, sandwiched between two attractive Japanese women, sipping whisky and laughing with the girls about how brilliant I am.

As I leaned over to grab a cigarette, both girls rushed forward with lighters.

'*Kakkoii ne?*' One of the women remarked how cool foreigners are, lighting my cigarette. The other nodded in agreement, depositing some fresh ice cubes and reasonably priced whisky into my glass. I smiled along approvingly, feeling like the gangster I was born to be.

'Are you American?' one of them asked.

'British.'

'*Sugoi!* Amazing!' they exclaimed, before giving me a brief round of applause at this remarkable achievement.

Unfortunately, the inevitable comparison arose.

'Harry Potter! You look like Harry Potter!'

I was in a good mood so I decided to go along with it.

'Oh, really! You think I look like Daniel Radcliffe?'

There are a few confused looks.

'*Nani Radcliffe?* What's that?'

The atmosphere that night would have been relaxing if it weren't for the unpleasant sound of a farmyard animal being electrocuted coming from the other side of the room. As the clouds of smoke in the dimly lit room began to clear, it was revealed that this animal was in fact a middle-aged Japanese salaryman doing karaoke.

Given the group of women crowding around him and the free-flowing champagne, it's safe to assume he was one of the town's wealthier businessmen. It wasn't exactly a flattering display, his seemingly reanimated corpse blaring into the microphone to a comically enthusiastic crowd of cheerleaders.

The attentive female staff cheered him on through the never-ending musical atrocity.

'You must sing! I bet you're amazing!' cried the woman on my right, somehow mistaking the look of horror on my face for some sort of desire to take part.

'Sing! You're British! You have to sing The Beatles!' The woman on the left grabbed the touchscreen karaoke menu and punched in 'Hey Jude'.

Oh god, not again.

I'm suddenly brought back to reality: I'm not a gangster. I'm not cool. Hell, I'm not even Daniel Radcliffe.

The compliments, the flirting, the intoxicating atmosphere of a room where smoke is a substitute for breathable air, the hollers of nearby groups of male customers laughing with delight as their egos and masculinity are massaged . . . Welcome to the *kyabakura*. A hostess bar.

Here you can sit down, flirt with vivacious, sexy women,

become shockingly drunk and fritter away a month's salary in less than six hours.

It almost sounds like a challenge. But trust me, it's worryingly easy to do on a night out in a hostess club. For the all-female staff working in the club, their one job is to keep you there for as long as possible by almost any means necessary.

Your drinks are poured for you, cigarettes lit relentlessly, and every sentence you utter will be greeted with laughter, whether you're funny or not.

It's not difficult to see why the concept of hostess bars has great appeal to fatigued salarymen. Perhaps they're lonely, or don't have much luck with the opposite sex. Maybe they feel they aren't respected at work or are just tired of the day-to-day drudgery. To be able to come to a bar where you're made to feel attractive and charismatic, where you don't have to lift a finger, seems like a pretty sweet deal. And credit where it's due, the staff work exceptionally hard, showing ruthless discipline and attention to detail.

Kyabakura typically reside in large multi-storey buildings, sandwiched between dozens of other hostess bars. While it's undeniably intimidating as a foreigner to explore the labyrinth of corridors and closed doors within – especially as they're often managed by criminal organizations – your anxieties will soon be allayed by the comical English names adorning the doors of each bar. Who wouldn't want to go to Club Sexy Spice or Bar Wonder Dove?

My first time visiting a hostess club was with Kengo sensei, who wanted to treat me to the experience after a particularly stressful week at work. As a complete novice, it all sounded rather seedy.

'No, no, Chris sensei! I think it's a kind of good place to just relax. That's all.'

The moment Kengo sensei heaved open the door to Club Calm House a beautiful woman appeared, like a genie from a bottle.

'*Konbanwa!*' Before Kengo and I had even removed our jackets we were escorted to a lipstick-red sofa. It was as if she feared we were about to back out of the door and disappear into the night.

The room was decorated in striking shades of red ranging from ruby to bloodbath.

Hostess bars are usually on the small side, able to seat around twenty customers on average.

As there are no windows and the haze of smoke is ever present, it can feel a bit claustrophobic at first.

I won't lie, my heart was racing. I had no idea what to expect, and the idea of stammering in poor Japanese to an energetic hostess girl wasn't my idea of relaxation.

From across the room, a raspy voice howled over at us.

'Kengo sensei! *Hisashiburi!* Long time no see!'

Dressed in a sleek black kimono tied together with a black-and-red *obi* belt, a beaming middle-aged lady bolted over and gave Kengo a friendly pat on the shoulder.

While all the staff in the room appeared to be in their twenties or thirties, this lady was a generation or two older, though no less beautiful.

She fixed her gaze on me.

'Hello. My name is Keiko. So nice to meet you!' She introduced herself in impressive English while depositing an *oshibori* towel before each of us. I grabbed mine and held it to my face for a few moments.

These moist towels, often handed out in Japanese establishments so a customer can clean their hands, are served hot in the winter and cold in the summer. Some say *oshibori* should be kept away from the face, but in winter there's nothing better than defrosting your face with a steaming-hot cloth.

Keiko was the mama san, the owner and manager of the club, and I got the impression she and Kengo sensei went way back.

'We've kept your bottle, Kengo sensei. Would you like to drink from it tonight?'

Amid the sheer quantities of alcohol you're expected to drink at a hostess club, standard procedure is to buy a bottle of *shochu* (a distilled rice spirit) and leave it behind if you're unable to finish it. A shelf behind the bar was overflowing with dark brown *shochu* bottles, each with a golden tag adorned with the name of the customer who'd left it behind.

Keiko was busy managing the club, and so the young woman who'd greeted us sat down on the sofa opposite us, having brought Kengo's bottle with a tray of ice and three glasses.

'Customer, may I drink too?' she asked, with a smile so large it'd be impossible to say no.

'*Kanpai!*' she screamed as we clinked the glasses together. I wondered how she could possibly handle drinking all night long, several days a week.

For the next two hours Yukiko helped put me at ease, occasionally rolling out her broken English to meet me halfway through the language barrier as Kengo looked on in bemusement.

There wasn't a single moment when Yukiko lost her smile throughout our conversation, and she moved in closer and closer, laughing at my every word and interrogating me about life in the UK. She was especially delighted to hear that I worked at Sakata Senior High, as she had graduated from there, almost a decade earlier.

There's no doubt that the life of a hostess is a tough one. They are expected to discharge endless amounts of energy while drinking, chatting and charming all night long, with the aim of encouraging customers to buy more drinks.

I'd heard that the highest-earning hostess at a top club in Roppongi in Tokyo had managed to pull in $46,000 a month by enticing customers to splash out on high-end champagne. Out here in Sakata, opportunities to pull in such figures were somewhat remote. Still, Yukiko had already dangled the chance to meet outside of the club – something the girls were encouraged to do. Joining customers on dates as an escort meant the customer would be more likely to return to the club. Better still, the girls might receive expensive gifts from doting customers. Yukiko showed off a glamorous diamond ring that one loyal customer had allegedly purchased for her as a birthday present.

Trying to get my head around this odd form of entertainment, I asked Yukiko what it was like to work as a hostess. However, under the banner of professionalism, she simply told me she enjoyed socializing, singing and drinking.

'Every day, party time!' she cheered, raising her glass to polish off her *shochu*. 'Customer, may I drink more?'

By the end of the night, I could understand the appeal *kyabakura* might have for lonely salarymen looking for company. But when the eyewatering 30,000-yen tab appeared two hours later – about $240 – I realized I certainly wouldn't be coming back in a hurry.

Where possible, I would avoid hostess clubs in the future. Despite the warm, friendly atmosphere, I couldn't shake the expensive elephant in the room. The whole thing had felt very superficial. Nobody smiles for two hours straight without stopping. It felt eerily unnatural and it was difficult not to wonder how happy these girls really were.

More worryingly, as Sakata was a small town, on more than one occasion I'd found myself being awkwardly served drinks by the mother of one of my students. When this happened, when the hostess sat next to me in a revealing outfit, pouring my drinks all evening and flirtatiously touching my leg, I was mortified at the idea of my student witnessing it all. It felt like a plot from an awful romcom, and to avoid finding out how such a movie would end I abstained from hostess clubs for the rest of the year.

13.

Get Out. Now.

They say the hottest temperature ever recorded by humans is a mind-boggling 10 trillion degrees Fahrenheit, at the Large Hadron Collider in Geneva.

That was a lie.

The hottest temperature ever recorded was in my mouth.

So eager had I been to devour my *takoyaki*, searing-hot balls of fried batter with a chunk of octopus in the centre, that I'd popped one in my mouth without letting it cool. This was a rookie error. As I bit through the delicious, savoury, molten batter, and the sweet mayonnaise and Worcestershire sauce topping, it turned my mouth into a river of fire.

I hopped around wildly by the side of a bridge in Dōtonbori, downtown Osaka, sending the *katsuoboshi* fish flakes that had topped the *takoyaki* flying into the air. A Japanese guy hurrying past spotted me writhing in pain. As his eyes flickered between my expression and the polystyrene box of *takoyaki* balls, he put two and two together.

'*Takoyaki, atsui ne!* Very hot!' he chuckled as he disappeared into the crowded streets. Clearly I wasn't the first person to let greed overtake general health and safety.

This brief encounter reminded me how different Osaka is to Tohoku, the northern region where I lived, where the people were famously shy. Umetsu sensei, the energetic business teacher who loved to come and chat with me at my desk, had warned me about this. She was an Osaka native and hilariously outspoken. I figured if everyone from Japan's third largest city was like her, I'd enjoy my trip very much.

When she heard about my travel plans for the upcoming long weekend, she filled me in on all things Osaka.

She had me at *kitchen*. Especially as I discovered that many of my favourite dishes had originated there, including *takoyaki*, *okonomyaki*, (savoury pancakes cooked on a *teppan* grill in front of you) and *kushikatsu* skewers of battered deep-fried goodness. They seemed to have a monopoly on Japan's unhealthiest dishes, and that was the key to my heart.

This was my first solo trip in Japan and my only goals were to eat everything in sight and to bring Umetsu sensei back the ultimate souvenir: *takoyaki*-flavoured Pringles. The branding was superb, even if they did taste like salty cardboard.

In Japan, it's considered etiquette to bring back *omiyage* for all your colleagues after you've been on a trip. This is less a thoughtful gesture and more an obligation. Given the army of 120 staff at Sakata Senior High, there was always a box of *senbei* rice crackers from Iwate or *shiroi koibito* cookies from Hokkaido lingering in the communal kitchen.

However, not everyone agreed with the etiquette of *omiyage*. I'd noticed when chatting with certain teachers that they'd suddenly begin to whisper when revealing their holiday plans. They'd hoped to keep their travel plans a secret, saving the hassle and obligation of bringing back a box of biscuits that would be dispersed across a gargantuan staffroom without so much as a thank you. I shared their sentiments and planned on giving Umetsu sensei her gift away from the hungry eyes of the other members of staff.

The journey to Osaka from rural Yamagata had been quite the undertaking. I set off in the early hours of a spring Friday and drove across two mountain ranges just to get to Sendai airport. The treacherous three-metre snow walls that lined the mountain pass had receded but still loomed over the road as blocks of ice. At Sendai I hopped on a flight one hour south to Kansai international airport and then boarded an express train to Namba station, central Osaka. By the time I'd arrived I was almost as battered as the *takoyaki* I'd be having for dinner.

After ten months in Japan, I'd thought I'd finally got the hang of things, but in this heaving new city I found myself feeling culture shocked all over again. The jarring transition from the windswept rural town of Sakata and the luscious plains of Yamagata to this sprawling metropolis of 19 million people, however, made me eager to explore.

Ebisu Bridge, the site of my *takoyaki* meltdown, lay in the shadow of no less than a hundred illuminated billboards. This assault on the retinas is perhaps matched only by Tokyo's famed Shibuya Crossing in terms of sheer spectacle. But while the draw of Shibuya Scramble Crossing was the sight of 400,000 people pouring across it in a single day, here in downtown Osaka, Dōtonbori's colourful billboards and commercials took centre stage.

Glimmering off the surface of the canal below, the largest billboard was the Glico man, the mascot for a confectionery company who is depicted running with arms outstretched in front of the rising sun. You can barely move in front of this sign for all the tourists mimicking his pose for their Instagram. To the left of the Glico man, the image of a ten-foot-high ice-cold Asahi beer can beams over the crowds, while towering over the bridge the image of Ken Watanabe looks on stoically, promoting some sort of electronic device.

To this day, the view from Ebisu Bridge remains my favourite spot in all of Japan. The intensity of the billboards, the canal boats packed with awestruck tourists, combined with the smell of street food and the sound of young women coaxing passers-by to head to a nearby club, bar or karaoke shop make for an overwhelming and invigorating experience. This is exactly how I'd imagined my new life in Japan – not living in a rice field on the far-flung west coast.

No matter where I pointed my camera, the whole scene looked like a backdrop for *Blade Runner*. In fact, it had been the director of *Blade Runner*, Ridley Scott, who'd helped put Osaka on the map in his 1989 neo-noir action thriller *Black Rain*, featuring Michael Douglas and Andy Garcia. The plot was absurd. The two American cops were hot on the trail of a Yakuza boss and kept running into trouble with their Japanese counterparts.

'You must understand! To them you are *gaijin*! Foreign barbarians!' an American woman working at a hostess club exclaims to the character played by Michael Douglas as he laments the lack of appreciation shown by the Japanese police. With its hilariously over-the-top dialogue and the depiction of Michael Douglas as the rule-breaking white saviour that Japan sorely needed, the film was far from perfect.

But for all its faults, the cinematography captured the grit and grime of Osaka beautifully. For me, a Japanese city at night had never looked so alluring on film.

Osaka was the first Japanese city I'd seen covered in litter. You'll often hear tourists in Japan remark how sparkling Japanese streets are, despite a noticeable lack of bins (a consequence of the sarin gas attacks in 1995). The streets of Osaka had no such sparkle, but this gave them a rough-around-the-edges, lived-in feel that made exploring the streets and back alleys deeply rewarding. While the polished skyscrapers of Tokyo can sometimes feel a little sanitized, here, where power cables snake above, half-empty beer cans sit overlooking the river and steam bellows out of restaurant kitchens, it truly feels like a living, breathing city.

Reluctantly, I pulled myself away from the dazzling sights and headed to my hostel to check in. Given the popularity of Dōtonbori, good accommodation was hard to find and I'd settled for a poorly reviewed place called the Dōtonbori Backpacker Hostel. The guest feedback hadn't been encouraging.

'Five stars out of ten. It was interesting.' – Anonymous

In my experience, the word 'interesting' wasn't usually synonymous with a good night's sleep. My worst fears were confirmed when I came face to face with a black concrete apartment block that on closer inspection was actually white but had been so stained by highway fumes that you could hardly tell.

I took the lift up to the fourth storey and found room 401 in a corridor lined by pink metal doors. It looked like Barbie's prison wing. There was a clunking noise as I struck the metal door.

After waiting thirty seconds for a reply, suddenly, like a jump scare straight out of a horror movie, the door shot open and a man quite literally tumbled out of it on to the floor.

'*Daijoubu?* Are you OK?' I exclaimed, taking a step back.

'*Daijoubu!*' he replied in a gruff voice, standing up and brushing himself off.

The man appeared to be totally unfazed by his eccentric entrance.

'Please, please.' He gestured to the door at the end of the

hallway, and I wondered if this was the part in the horror film where the audiences are screaming at the screen, 'Don't go in there!' Against my better judgement, I followed him into a room that looked like a regular Japanese apartment. It dawned on me that I would be sleeping in this guy's flat.

With his long, ruffled hair and surfer shorts, I got the impression this wasn't your average Japanese guy. He popped a cigarette in his mouth, promptly lit it and opened the refrigerator to reveal the shattered remains of half a watermelon.

'Are you like watermelon?' he asked, switching over to English.

I declined.

It looked like somebody had taken a hammer to it. The damn thing had practically exploded. When I creaked open the door to my room, I caught an unpleasant blast of damp air mixed with sweat and found no less than six bunkbeds arranged in a U-shape in the world's tiniest room. I was shocked this was even legal. In hindsight, it probably wasn't.

It felt like somebody had seriously stretched the definition of a hostel. But it helped to explain the absurdly low price of 2,000 yen per night.

When it comes to accommodation, nowhere has more variety than Japan.

Despite what my 'hostel' experience might demonstrate, you're truly spoilt for choice. At the cheapest end, you have hostels, and I mean real hostels, and capsule hotels, typically costing 1,500 to 4,000 yen a night. These are usually dormitory style, with bunkbeds and communal showers and bathrooms. I normally opt for a capsule hotel, for the extra privacy of sleeping inside what is essentially a jumbo coffin.

A notch above are business hotels, which cost 5,000–15,000 yen. Often smelling of the cigarettes of salarymen gone by, they come with a small single bed and your very own *ofuro*, the classic deep Japanese bathtub, and toilet. Above them come boutique and luxury hotels, which often exceed 25,000 yen a night and boast the very best amenities and gastronomy.

There's also another, slightly more outlandish option. Love hotels clock in at around 4,000 yen for a two-hour stay, or 11,000 yen for the whole night. These short-term rooms, mostly frequented, as the name suggests, for romantic rendezvous, cannot be booked in advance and are often garishly themed. Intimidated by the idea, I had no plans on ever staying in one. Or so I thought.

After being shown to the world's smallest room, I desperately needed a drink. I escaped the building and headed to the nearest 7-Eleven, grabbing a can of Strong Zero. This 9 per cent alcoholic lemon drink came with vodka and was the precursor to many a messy night out.

Drinking in public in Japan is legal, so I ambled my way through Osaka and came across a square full of American iconography.

In the centre, Japanese teenagers were performing tricks on skateboards in the shadow of a tacky model of the Statue of Liberty stuck on the roof of a nearby building.

I'd found myself in *Amerikamura*, literally America town, a celebration of all things American. This was where you could stock up on Western brands or buy clothes branded in very weird English. A red shirt with the phrase 'ARE YOU ENJOY SPRING?' stamped on the front caught my attention, and I made a note to buy one before I left to add to my blossoming collection.

In a world where the English language was pasted across the marketing of every product and service to add a layer of prestige, yet clearly never proofread, Japan had created a hybrid Japanese–English language that often led to more questions than answers.

Just outside my apartment in Sakata, there was an underwhelming steak restaurant that boasted: 'This is the extremity of luxury to bite into chunky meat. How juicy and tasty!! It's beyond the description.'

Restaurant menus read like a horror show. A tofu dish drizzled in cream cheese came with the description: 'Soy sauce reckoning of the cream cheese'. 'Soy sauce reckoning' sounded more like a unique take on waterboarding than an appetizer.

The stores themselves had baffling names. Every day, I walked past a discount clothing store for children called Starvations. In downtown Sendai, another discount store was called Sperm. It was difficult to comprehend the thought process that had led to the choice of these English words, but it made living in Japan all the more rewarding. You never quite knew what you'd find next.

In the humid evening air, groups of friends sat around laughing and drinking in Amerikamura Square, and I felt a sense of calm I'd yet to feel on my visits to Tokyo. The laid-back attitude here felt at odds with Tokyo, where standing around or sitting idle felt like a crime. There was a sense that people in Tokyo were always on the go, always trying to get somewhere.

Having almost polished off my can of Strong Zero, I'd already begun to feel the buzz that comes as a precursor to tipsiness. The drink was living up to its reputation.

As I drank the last drops, I became aware of a girl drinking alone on a bench on the opposite side of the square. In that creepy way humans seem to sense a set of eyes upon them, the moment I caught sight of her, she instantly flicked her eyes up to meet mine.

Maybe it was the Strong Zero taking over, but before I had time to think I raised my can and gave her a friendly 'cheers'. Her formerly expressionless face burst into a smile and she held up her can as if to bump mine.

What followed was a drawn-out game of eye-contact table tennis as we pretended to watch the skateboarders rolling back and forth. Finally, she pointed at the empty seat next to her, beckoning me to come over.

Clutching my empty Strong Zero can, I sheepishly walked over, hoping not to make a fool of myself.

'Are you drinking alone or just getting ready to skate? she asked sarcastically, throwing me with a cheeky smile.

'Very much drinking alone, I'm afraid!' I laughed, tapping the can, the hollow sound indicating it was empty.

'Oh, no, you've already finished!' From within her bag she withdrew a can of sangria-flavoured Strong Zero. 'Fancy another?'

How could I say no?

As we got talking I learned that Mei was from Taiwan and was visiting Osaka for a solo trip of her own.

Osaka was a popular shopping destination for neighbouring countries such as South Korea, China and Taiwan, and it wasn't unusual for tourists to fly in to stock up on a bunch of premium Japanese goods and fly home, almost in the same way British tourists would once pop over to France to buy buckets of cheap alcohol.

In Mei's case, she was hoping to profit from the trip by selling the cosmetics she had bought in her native city of Taichung.

A few cans down, Mei and I had totally hit it off. Not quite ready to return to my prison/hostel and the mushy watermelon, I suggested we continue the night elsewhere.

'I don't suppose you'd like to join me for some *okonomiyaki*?'

We ditched our cans and headed off into the humid, neon-lit streets of Dōtonbori.

Okonomi literally means 'to one's liking'. *Yaki* means 'fried'.

Notice how the ingredients themselves don't appear in the name. The appeal of *okonomiyaki* is the variety of flavours that come from the endless possible combinations of ingredients. No two pancakes need ever be the same. The base ingredients are batter and cabbage, and customers then choose from a number of toppings, ranging from meat to freshly chopped seafood, to all manner of vegetables.

The dish is prepared either in the Hiroshima style or the Osaka style. In Osaka, the ingredients are all mixed together at once, placed upon a smouldering *teppan* and moulded into a circle with a short metal spatula. It's not uncommon to be handed the bowl of ingredients and left to your own devices in front of your very own grill.

Hiroshima style is gradually layered upon the grill, cooking first a portion of noodles, then cabbage, stacking the pancake ever higher and finally layering with batter.

Both styles end up the same way: drenched in Worcestershire sauce, smothered in mayonnaise and doused with shavings of seaweed and smoked bonito fish called *katsuobushi*. These are the same toppings that are used on *takoyaki* and have a similar taste, but *okonomiyaki* are generally a far more filling dish.

Personally, I prefer Hiroshima style, as it's a more complex dish with the bonus texture of the yakisoba noodles. Because it takes more skill to make, restaurants typically prepare Hiroshima *okonomiyaki* in front of you, adding a layer of theatricality to the proceedings. Maybe this is why I prefer it. Or maybe I'm just too bloody lazy to cook it myself.

That's not to say Osaka style is without its charm. It's far less effort to cook and, with no layers, *much* easier to eat. Either way, there was no question: to be in Osaka and eat Hiroshima-style *okonomiyaki* would be considered treason.

Mei and I came across a restaurant overlooking the river which now, at night, was fully bathed in the glow of a hundred illuminated billboards. It was a spectacular backdrop against which to gorge ourselves with pancakes.

Minutes later Mei was prodding and shaping the bubbling

batter of our mixed-seafood *okonomiyaki*. Thankfully, she took me at my word that my attempts at cooking would have us leaving in a body bag.

By the time we finished our meal it was 10 p.m. Despite the deafening sizzling of grills and the whirring of the extractor fan, we'd somehow been able to chat for almost three hours straight. We were both keen to see each other again and made plans to meet the following evening.

The next day, I set out early to explore the nearby town of Nara, famed for its ginormous bronze buddha and its very well-behaved deer. If Osaka was a cacophony of noise, Nara was more like a library. I strolled the peaceful tree-lined streets, the silence broken only by the yelps of a duo energetically pounding rice flour to make soft, squishy *mochi* rice cakes. I then ventured to the main park, where the deer, the heroes of the town, bowed their necks in return for crackers. Ostensibly, they learned this habit from the bowing locals, and it was truly a thrilling sight, until a particularly hungry little bugger bit me on the ass.

Having escaped my tussle with the deer with a hole in my trousers to prove it, I returned to Osaka to meet up with Mei at a British pub chain called Hub.

Hub answers that all-important question: what if somebody who's never set foot in the UK decides to build a British pub?

With walls covered in posters of Spitfires and battleships alongside retro advertisements for British ales, and stools arranged around wooden barrels, evoking the atmosphere of a pirate ship, it was just like home.

My favourite things were the leaflets placed on each table explaining the concept of a British pub.

'Every Sunday, the people of England go to church. After church service they will visit the pub, which is often built into the church itself.'

Ah yes. Pub church. God how I missed those.

Fortunately, they got the one thing right that mattered – the alcohol. Cider was almost impossible to find in Japan, and Hub was one of the few places I could polish off a bottle of my favourite Aspall. I poured our drinks while Mei surveyed the hole in my trousers, almost doubled over with laughter.

'It sounds like you needed me there to protect you, Mr Broad!'

'It was awful. There were hundreds of them.' I exaggerated what had happened, trying not to look completely pathetic. 'But I put up a bloody good fight against the bastards. They won't be messing with me again any time soon.' I took my first swig of the cider and suddenly felt nostalgic for home.

Three bottles later, I'd started to complain about my terrible hostel.

'It's awful, Mei, there's fucking watermelon everywhere.'

Far from being disgusted, she thought it sounded hilarious.

'You need to show me this hostel. It sounds like a movie set.'

'On the contrary, I'm half tempted to avoid going back there tonight.'

Our flirting had reached fever pitch and we were both not so inconspicuously trying to suss out if there was a way we could spend the night together. I wondered if I could steal the plot of one of my favourite nineties movies, *Before Sunrise*, in which two strangers meet on a train and end up wandering around Vienna all night long until one of them has to fly off.

My flight out of Osaka left the next morning at nine o'clock. I proposed that we spend the night wandering the city and then, come 6 a.m., I'd hop on the train to the airport. It was perfect.

Mei was sold. Especially as she'd seen the movie.

I must have missed the scene where there's a mortifying experience in a love hotel.

By midnight, Mei and I had spent several hours hopping from

bar to bar. After all these hours of drinking and flirting we ended up sharing a kiss under the watchful eye of the huge Glico man billboard.

'Have you ever been to a love hotel?' she asked, and looked at me expectantly.

I thought she was joking at first, but she insisted we check one out. I wasn't going to argue. Though the plan of staying up all night sounds exciting, with six hours still to go, the idea of having a few hours' rest seemed appealing.

Lucky for us, one of Osaka's biggest love-hotel districts was on the edge of the Dōtonbori canal, just five minutes away from the bridge, which by now was less busy, inhabited mostly by rowdy nightclub revellers.

Rabu hoteru (ラブホテル) are big business in Japan. With 37,000 across the country, bringing in an estimated $40 billion a year, the service fulfils a vital role in offering Japanese couples a place to escape. Japanese families traditionally live in multigenerational households with grandparents, parents and children all under one roof. Throw paper walls into the equation and it's easy to see the problem.

Beyond married couples, love hotels offer a level of discretion and secrecy to sex workers, singletons hooking up or, inevitably, individuals engaged in an affair. I'd often driven past them in the countryside, where the hotels looked more like tacky theme parks. One in particular, on the outskirts of Sakata, was designed like a castle, while another in Yamagata city had painted the exterior to look like a spaceship.

Despite the quirkiness, they take discretion seriously, with concealed car parks and entrances, and licence-plate covers to mask the identity of the clientele within.

In Osaka, one of our options was Hotel Mickey Cookies, which, confusingly, looked like a daycare centre for children with bright primary-coloured walls and a gigantic teddy bear looming large over the entrance. There was also Hotel Chapel Christmas, which had no less than three Santa Claus figurines mounted around the front door with the festive slogan 'Thank you for coming. Joy to the world!'

The only thing more prominent than gaudy decorations were the signs boasting unbeatable prices. For a mere 2,990 yen, you could enjoy a two-hour stay at Chapel Christmas, where it truly was Christmas every day. A full twelve-hour stint cost a reasonable 6,990 yen.

After walking around in circles unsure of which one to visit, Mei pointed out a more upmarket-looking establishment that thankfully lacked the obnoxious exterior of its competitors.

'This place seems cool?'

Hotel Nest looked almost like a regular business hotel, save for the gushing waterfall by the front entrance. With no idea what to expect, I felt anxious as we entered the lobby. Elevator jazz played softly in the background and a large wall covered in small screens showed images of the accommodation available. Despite the sheer number of rooms, most were already in use, with only four rooms remaining illuminated and available.

It felt very unnatural, especially as there wasn't a single visible member of staff. In love hotels, customers aren't expected to interact with a single human being from start to finish.

At least, that was the expectation.

No sooner had Mei and I agreed on a room than an exasperated man came running out of a side door.

'Excuse me. No foreigner,' he declared, crossing his arms to make an 'X' symbol. The universal sign for fuck off.

I felt like I'd been slapped in the face.

It stopped me dead in my tracks. This felt pretty uncomfortable.

'*Hontou ni dame?* It's really no good?' I scowled back at him.

'No good,' he replied firmly in Japanese, stretching out his arm to collect the key we'd picked up.

'Fuck.' I thrust it into his hand and walked out in embarrassment. It was the first time I'd experienced discrimination as a foreigner in Japan. I'd heard of this happening for renting apartments, but never in a situation as mundane as walking into a love hotel.

I've been to lots of love hotels in the years since to produce YouTube videos, but I was never again rejected for being a foreigner. Since I arrived in Japan in 2012, tourism has boomed, and the market of foreigners looking for a quick, novelty place to lay their head has proved too lucrative to miss out on. Unfortunately, LGBTQ+ couples are not so lucky. I experienced this first hand while shooting videos with my friend Connor. We did find a simple hack for gay male couples, however. Stick on a wig and sunglasses, and the staff monitoring the security cameras are none the wiser. We've never been stopped since, and I've amassed a fantastic wig collection.

As much as it pains me to admit it, on our next attempt to gain entry to a love hotel I was about to live up to the troublesome-foreigner stereotype. The Michael Douglas of our time.

'Don't worry. I'm sure they're not all alike!' Mei reassured me, pointing to another hotel across the road, encouragingly called Hotel Lovers.

This time we were successful.

Armed with a room key and with a growing sense of anticipation, we headed up to the fifth floor and swung open the door to reveal a spacious room drenched in purple with a king-size bed, a fifty-inch TV with karaoke and even a jacuzzi. In a small gift-wrapped bag there was a vibrator and some condoms. Much more exciting than pillow mints. Discretion at a love hotel continues in the room too. The whole experience is masterminded to be completely inconspicuous. Even the soap and shampoo are unscented so that if you're having an extramarital dalliance you don't raise suspicion by returning home smelling of aloe vera and strawberries.

It was both impressive and a little depressing. You certainly got your money's worth in a love hotel.

We slammed the door shut but, just as we were getting down to business, our romantic moment was interrupted by an ear-piercing bleeping.

'What the bloody hell is that? I hope it's not a fire alarm.'

Mei spotted a white screen flashing over by the front door with a few slots built into it for cash and credit cards.

Although she couldn't read the Japanese, her knowledge of Chinese characters, the precursor to kanji, meant she was just about able to make out the words 'Payment' and 'Now'.

'Oh, crap. Maybe we need to pay in advance?'

It seemed the moment the door had shut the clock had started ticking. While most love hotels ask you to pay at the point of departure, we'd picked one that required upfront payment.

'Don't worry, leave it to me!' I gallantly declared, grabbing my wallet while Mei left to start up the jacuzzi.

I selected the three-hour option that would see us through to my early-morning train. The figure of 6,500 yen appeared on screen and I pulled out my British credit card and stuffed it into the machine.

There was a concerning stuttering noise and, moments later, my card popped out. A red exclamation mark appeared on screen.

Uh oh.

I tore my wallet open to see if I had any cash left. Nope. All gone. Of course it was. We'd been drinking the town dry for the last nine hours.

Fuck.

I tried my card again. It was promptly rejected.

Even more fuck.

By now I could hear the sound of water gushing into the jacuzzi. The shower was going too.

I poked my head into the bathroom to see that Mei was fully naked and covered in soap. Any potential arousal I might have felt had been snuffed out by the impending sense of dread.

'Mei. I don't suppose you have any cash, do you?' I yelled, embarrassingly.

'No, I spent it all at Hub. I left the rest in my hotel room,' she shouted back calmly.

I walked back past the jacuzzi we'd never get to enjoy and over to the payment machine.

What happens now?

In a haze of panic, I was just about ready to start stuffing any physical object I could find into the card reader, whether it was my driver's licence or our complementary pack of condoms. Then I spotted the red call button for the intercom. Maybe we could negotiate with the staff? Perhaps they would have a machine that accepted my card?

I pushed the button and a woman responded, sounding unimpressed.

'*Hai. Dozo.* Go ahead.'

I could tell by her tone that somehow I'd already pissed her off. Now I had to explain in my awful Japanese that I had no money.

'I'm sorry, my credit card is no good.'

'Do you have cash?' she snapped.

'Just a credit card. But it's no good,' I reiterated.

There was a pause, followed by the sound of an irritated sigh as the woman abruptly hung up.

At last, the payment machine had stopped beeping. Had they

let me off? Maybe, out of the kindness of her heart, the woman had given us the room for free.

'The bath is ready!' shouted Mei, still blissfully unaware of our predicament.

Just then I heard a knock. I realized that the door, which had bolted shut automatically when we stepped inside, had been unlocked remotely.

I pushed it open to reveal a stony-faced middle-aged woman. She wore the expression of someone who'd trodden this path before.

Without any pleasantries, she held out her hand.

'Show me the card.'

I fumbled in my wallet and pulled out the card, hastily handing it over. Expressionless, she examined the front and back before handing it back.

'*Dame!* No good. Do you have cash?' She was growing increasingly angry.

'No cash. But I can get some now.'

She shook her head and snapped, '*Dete kudasai*. Get out.'

Double fuck.

I looked from the woman to the bathroom door behind me, where the sound of Mei splashing in the water was clearly audible.

'But she's in the bath,' I explained, hoping to arouse some sympathy.

'Get out. Now.' The woman glared at me. I suspected if we didn't make a move sharpish, she'd be calling in the heavy-handed individuals that run Japan's nightlife districts to come and sort us out.

I poked my head into the bathroom to find Mei up to her neck in bubbles. It was like a scene straight out of a movie, but it was less *The Notebook* and more *American Psycho*.

'Mei, I'm really sorry, but we've got a slight problem. We can't pay for the room.'

She thought I was being my usual joking self, until she caught the look of horror etched on my face.

Mei jumped out of the bath and threw a towel over herself. As she hopped around, pulling her clothes on, I stood like an awkward fool in the doorway, trying once again to garner some sympathy from the woman who was about to sling us out.

'This is my first time in a love hotel,' I quipped. Surely she could find the humour in the situation?

Nope. The woman folded her arms and glared at the bathroom door angrily as we waited uncomfortably for Mei to get dressed. I'd never felt so embarrassed in all my life.

Shockingly, considering our two failed attempts, we remained undeterred. After storming into a 7-Eleven and withdrawing half the contents of my bank account, we picked another love hotel. At long last: our third and final attempt proved successful. But we were so tired after our long night of rejection we crashed on the bed almost immediately, waking groggily three hours later, just in time for my train.

'Three love hotels in one night. Gosh, what a night,' Mei giggled. I tried not to die of embarrassment as I headed off to the station.

For me, the trip taught me a valuable life lesson. Though the memory of that night would make me cringe for months to come, ultimately it turned out to be one I'd treasure fondly. The key to turning a good trip into an unforgettable one is the encounters you have along the way. It's easy to walk around a city and keep to yourself, but it's these encounters with strangers, embarrassing or not, that stay with you for ever. This realization left a lasting impact on me and made me more open-minded on my future adventures around Japan.

Mei and I stayed in touch, as friends, and two years later we caught up over drinks in Taipei and reminisced about our not so romantic weekend.

Meanwhile my love affair with Osaka is still alive to this day.

Whenever I'm tasked with acting as a tour guide for friends visiting Japan, the part I look forward to most are the days spent in Osaka. For the food, the people, the nightlife and the grittiness, Osaka will always have a special place in my heart. For the love of god, feature it in your itinerary.

And if you're looking for a great hostel with a complementary watermelon, I've got you covered.

14.

Japan's Most Eccentric Man

Somehow, my first year in Japan was over – a year that had simultaneously felt like the longest and the shortest year of my life.

It had been the most intense, challenging, yet rewarding twelve months, but despite all I'd seen and done, I still felt like a glorified tourist. For so much of my year, I felt like a failure at work, with many teachers forgetting to take me to class or purposely avoiding me as they headed out of the staffroom. A few teachers saw the employment of a foreign teacher as a pointless expense; others weren't quite sure how to put me to good use. Meanwhile, my Japanese language abilities were still practically non-existent and, to top it all off, most of the friends I'd made were foreigners who were about to leave Yamagata, including Roy, whose five-year contract on JET was finally up.

The Japanese colleague who I'd bonded with the most, Kengo sensei, was retiring and heading off to spend more time working on anti-war projects in Tokyo. As my closest Japanese friend and mentor, his departure was a real blow.

To make matters worse, some of the other teachers I'd got to know well were being scattered to the winds. While the school year ends in August for most of the world, in Japan it finishes in March. As the students enjoy spring break, Japanese teachers are re-dispersed around the prefecture – an unusual quirk of Japan's education system.

Teachers are constantly shuffled and moved between schools, cities and sometimes regions. Where they end up can be completely random, and a few English teachers I'd worked with seemed resentful at their imminent departure from Sakata Senior High.

Naoko sensei, my Beatles-loving colleague, had been shifted to a rural school in a hot-spring town called Atsumi, about one hour south of Sakata.

'I'm not sure why they've put me there, but I'll be OK.' She didn't sound too convinced.

I suspected one reason was that she was an easy target. As a single middle-aged woman with no family to prioritize, she could be placed wherever she was needed. Teachers with partners and children were much less likely to be uprooted and moved to a far-flung corner of Japan.

Saitou sensei was another casualty of the re-organization. Though we'd struggled to forge any real relationship, given the language barrier, it was a shame to lose another familiar face.

Watching colleagues and friends depart and the students I'd taught graduate was a strong reminder of the transience that underpins the world of teaching and the revolving doors of education.

On Kengo's final day, he called me over to his desk, tucked away in a side room and shared with several other teachers who'd all headed out for lunch. During our classes together, he loved to sing to the students while playing the guitar, typically songs from the sixties, although, unfortunately, 'I am the Walrus' never seemed to make his hit list.

'Chris sensei, I'd like to play you one last song before I go.'

I perched myself down on a chair as he rested on the edge of his desk clutching his acoustic guitar.

I was treated to Bob Dylan's legendary 'Blowin' in the Wind', a great song and the perfect choice, given Kengo's affiliation with Japan's anti-war community. As he strummed away, staff wandered through the room, acting as though nothing was happening. It was heartbreaking to know that the school was about to lose such a brilliant, irreplaceable teacher. And yet his talents seemed to have gone unnoticed.

We shook hands and he handed me his private *meishi* business card.

'Let's drink again soon, Chris san.'

Soon after, Kengo sensei left. Occasionally, I'd receive an email asking how I was getting on and for updates on Sakata Senior High. Once every six months or so, he'd reappear in Sakata and we'd grab dinner together. But for the most part, he'd moved on to his new life in Tokyo and I wished him well.

As the summer holidays rolled in, I felt deflated by the absence of my two closest mentors and friends. Little did I know, my luck was about to change. In one August, I was about to make more Japanese friends than I'd made in the previous twelve months. On a cool summer's evening, on a night out on the town, I'd bump into an eccentric stranger who would go on to shape my time in Japan more than anyone else I met there.

Sakata's run-down streets always looked best at night. The shuttered shops of the day were hidden in the darkness. The neon haze of illuminated billboards and bar signs eclipsed the faded glory of the shops: a family-run clothing store made redundant by the towering department store by the highway, a yakisoba restaurant whose elderly owner had passed away without an heir, a souvenir store with no tourists left to sell to. Sakata wasn't exactly a booming tourist destination.

It was a Thursday night in early August and I'd joined Roy for one last drink downtown. Given it was a work night for me, I'd snuck off at around 11.30 p.m. and wandered into the humid late-night air, trudging in a drunken haze to my apartment on the far side of town.

The walk took me past shabby buildings packed full of hostess clubs that were open into the early hours of the morning, their doors firmly shut, windows covered, the sound of girls' laughter echoing from within as a salaryman made a mockery of the kara-oke machine.

As I made my way towards the now-familiar *hentai* billboard that had shocked me a year ago I noticed a Japanese man strolling in my direction on the opposite side of the road.

Puffing on a cigarette and gazing down at the ground, he was deep in thought. He was wearing a dark grey T-shirt and jeans and I reckoned he was in his late twenties or early thirties.

As we passed each other, his eyes darted over towards me, and he did a double-take and stopped in his tracks.

Oh crap, here we go.

I still found chatting with strangers in Japanese fairly stressful. Knackered after a long day, I wasn't keen to go for a round of small talk.

'Wow! Hello!' To my surprise, he spoke in English.

'Hello,' I nodded, continuing to hurry down the street.

'Where you from?' He was now beaming in delight. I got the impression he hadn't spoken to many foreigners out here. 'Are you from America?' he followed up, before I had a chance to reply.

By this point, I'd stopped walking, realizing there was no escape.

'No, no, British. Nice to meet you.'

The moment I said the word 'British' the man's eyes lit up.

'No way! Oh my god! I love England culture.' He walked over and shook my hand frantically. This kind of encounter wasn't overly rare in rural Japan. Every now and then, you'd find an Anglophile, but this guy was on a whole other level. I stood, gobsmacked, as he began to reel off a list of nearly every British musician who'd ever lived.

'Oh my god, I love David Bowie, Pink Floyd, Queen, Billy Idol—'

'Very good bands.' I tried to cut him short, but he kept going.

'Led Zeppelin, The Beatles, Sex Pistols. So good!'

'Well, it's so nice to meet you!' I said, taking a step away and trying to bring a swift end to the interaction.

'Can you karaoke?' He gestured as though drinking an imaginary beer, the universal sign for 'Let's go for a drink!'

I was still trying to work out if I'd just met Yamagata's kindest man or the craziest one, but I figured, what the hell, I had nothing to lose. My trip to Osaka had taught me to say yes to hanging out with strangers more often – so long as there were no love hotels involved.

'OK, maybe one drink.'

He clapped his hands together in victory, shouting, 'Yeah, fucking let's go,' and ushered me back up the street from where I'd just come.

Rather worryingly, he escorted me around the corner, to what I'd always assumed was a large, abandoned building. He pointed upwards to the third floor, where I could just about make out a dimly lit window.

He opened a door on the side of the building leading to a dark concrete staircase and I started to wonder if my remains would ever be found. It dawned on me that perhaps this stranger was some kind of street tout for local bars.

We climbed up three flights of stairs and arrived at a door wedged open with a pile of broken computers. Fairy lights flickered underneath a sign with a snake and an indecipherable kanji. I had a feeling this was going to be a very special bar indeed.

It's not uncommon for family-run bars and restaurants in Japan to feel like a converted room in someone's home or apartment. Coming from the UK, where bar licences are essential and the idea of wandering into someone's home for a drink sounds like the start of an episode of *Crimewatch*, I'd had difficulty adjusting to this style of Japanese drinking hole, as delightfully characterful as they were. Tokyo alone is believed to have 29,000 bars, and it's not hard to see how, given the apparently very relaxed requirements to be able to set one up.

Snake bar was nothing more than a filthy counter covered in ashtrays, trinkets and, inexplicably, broken electronics. There were four stools, one of which was occupied by a man cradling a glass of whisky, and a small sofa by a coffee table over in the corner. Above the counter was the only visibly functioning electronic device, a TV playing *Ghost in the Shell*, though it was hard to see through the thick cloud of cigarette smoke emanating from the barkeeper who stood beneath it.

A gruff man in his fifties in a beanie hat called over to my new acquaintance/potential murderer in a raspy voice. 'Natsuki, *hisashiburi*!' Long time no see.

'Master san, *hisashiburi*!' He gestured over to me as I stood trying to take in my absurd new surroundings.

'This is my friend. He's from England!' Despite the glee in Natsuki's voice, the barman wasn't overly impressed, and pointed us over to the couch in the corner.

The couch and coffee table were covered in broken computer motherboards. The place was like a hoarder's den. It felt like I was on the set of a post-apocalyptic movie, but just as I started to get into the dystopian setting, I realized I'd soon have to drink real-life drinks in what might be Japan's filthiest bar.

But at least I had a name for the man responsible for bringing me here. Natsuki. I made a mental note, in case I'd be needing it for a police report later.

I took a sip of my very warm beer, which gave me a solid theory as to why the bar remained so frighteningly empty.

'Why do you come to Sakata?' Natsuki asked me, popping another cigarette in his mouth and offering one to me. I accepted.

I figured that as Natsuki had made quite the effort speaking English when he clearly wasn't fluent, I'd make the effort too, and switch to Japanese. I'd assumed he'd find this a relief, but he was having none of it.

'I wanna learn British English. British English is so cool.'

Having spent the last year with Roy, who was about to be demoted to the world's second-heaviest smoker, I'd picked up some bad habits. Evenings spent in an *izakaya* fuelled by cigarettes and alcohol had become a very regular occurrence.

Fortunately, one puff of Natsuki's Marlboro Red was enough to almost put me off for good. With its 12 milligrams of tobacco, it felt like being smacked in the throat with a hammer. While I struggled to keep my composure, Natsuki was making a mockery of Roy's smoking habit, having already lit up his fourth cigarette in the roughly ten minutes we'd been acquainted.

'I like Queen Elizabeth. So good England grandma,' he said through a cloud of smoke.

I was starting to regret not bringing my camera out with me, as this was turning into one of the most bizarre interactions I'd had in Japan. It felt like the kind of experience foreign tourists expect to have when coming to the country but rarely did, especially here in north Japan, where strangers were more likely to flee from my presence than strike up a conversation.

Natsuki was one of the few people I'd met who seemed like an absolute anomaly. The pressure to blend in was keenly felt in Japan and, despite what travel documentaries might suggest, it was not often that you'd come across such a large and singular personality. In his teenage years, Natsuki told me, he'd constantly been in trouble with the police for skipping school. He took up smoking when he was thirteen – a full seven years before he hit the legal age.

He'd got in with Sakata's burgeoning punk-rock crowd and, exposed to the influence of the Sex Pistols, The Damned and The Clash, became the living embodiment of punk rock. When his career as a guitarist and frontman didn't go to plan, he moved to Tokyo to study fashion and beauty, ultimately returning to Sakata, where he met his girlfriend, Asami. They now ran a beauty salon together.

Our conversation started to head in a more serious direction, and I asked him whether he had been able to walk away from his punk-rock lifestyle. Inspiringly, he believed he'd done quite the opposite. If the essence of the punk-rock spirit is celebrating one's individuality, he said, then the beauty salon is where he helps people become who they want to be.

Hearing Natsuki's passion for his business made me appreciate that there was more to him than the drunken chaos on display when we first met. Here was a guy who loved his life and truly cared about his work.

We'd long since given up speaking 'British English' and had switched to Japanese. It had happened so seamlessly that midway through our conversation I had to pinch myself at the realization that we had been conversing in the language that had so plagued me. The training wheels were finally off.

I'd made more linguistic progress in one evening, speaking with my new, laidback friend, than I had done in the last three months of studies alone in my apartment. I felt at ease chatting with Natsuki, as he had seemed so at ease speaking English with me. For both of us, the ability to switch back to our mother tongue completely took the pressure off.

After an hour of drinking, Natsuki stood up with a jolt, walked over to the bar and pushed aside a pile of broken hard drives to reveal two microphones and a working touch panel. Who knew what else was nestled amid that pile of crap.

'Let's karaoke together! British music! Do you like The Clash?' He handed one of the microphones to me as I stubbed out my horrific cigarette.

'Sure. "Rock the Casbah" is my favourite.'

'Oh, so good choice!' He laughed and punched it into the touchscreen.

Speakers hidden around the bar blared out an appalling karaoke version of the track, drowning out *Ghost in the Shell*, which was still playing on the TV.

I still wasn't a fan of singing karaoke in front of a crowd but, fortunately for me, the guy sitting at the bar looked dead and the barman was just staring at the TV screen, oblivious to our whirlwind duet.

Credit to Natsuki, while the guy's English wasn't great, his knowledge of English lyrics was certainly impressive and he had a fantastic singing voice.

Half a dozen British songs, two more warm beers and a pack of Marlboro Reds later, I realized to my horror that I had to be at work in six hours. The curtains came down on my drunken karaoke session.

Natsuki insisted both on paying the tab and meeting again the following week.

'Please let's meeting again. I wanna learn British English.'

At first I thought the guy was just being polite. Nearly every

Japanese person I'd spoken to had asked me to teach them English. It was a polite comment often used to fill awkward silences and rarely led anywhere. Despite the fun we'd had, I was pretty sure it would be the same with this guy.

But Natsuki pinched my phone, entered his phone number and made me promise to meet him the following Thursday.

'Sorry, Natsuki. Next week I'm climbing Mount Fuji.' It sounded like a lie, but I actually was.

'Ee! Be careful. Don't die, please.'

I took his sage advice, and assured him that, in the event that I survived, I'd meet with him in two weeks' time. As we left the bar, he kindly hailed a cab for me and saw me on my way.

We shook hands and I flopped into the back seat of the taxi, wondering if I'd see Natsuki again.

At the very least, I thought, it was a fun night out, and I had at last put my Japanese speaking skills to the test. Like riding a bike without training wheels, I was finally off and away. The fact I'd made a new friend out of it was the icing on the cake. Thank god I hadn't continued walking home when I collided with Japan's most eccentric man.

15.

The Wise Men of Fuji

'THE CLEAN AIR AT THE SUMMIT OF MOUNT FUJI: Packed in this can is the clean natural air you can breathe only when you are at the top of Japan's number-one mountain, Mount Fuji.'

– 850 yen ($7)

Wow! Why bother climbing 3,776 metres to the summit of Mount Fuji when I can simply buy a can of air from the summit instead?

As I held the blue tin can, the image of Fuji emblazoned on the front, I was awfully tempted. In mere seconds, I could crack it open, inhale the enchanting air within and then hop back on the bus to Tokyo.

But then again, how could one be sure it was filled with authentic air from the summit?

It seemed preposterous that a team of people would climb almost 4 kilometres to the summit of Japan's tallest mountain with rucksacks bundled with empty cans simply to 'capture' the air.

And yet if it were any other mountain, I wouldn't have believed it. Mount Fuji is no normal mountain. So sacred are its slopes that until 1868 women were banned from climbing it, for fear they would distract men from their religious duties. A symbol of Japan, the stratovolcano, with its almost perfect conical shape, had inspired countless artists, writers and poets and had been declared a cultural site by UNESCO that year.

Nothing said cultural appreciation better than devouring a mouthwatering plate of katsu curry with rice moulded into the shape of the mountain at the rest stop at the base of Fuji one hour before setting off on my climb.

I placed the can back on the shelf and walked out of the souvenir store at Mount Fuji's fifth station, the main starting point. I gazed up along a gentle slope that grew steeper, practically vertical, to the distant summit. The dark black volcanic peak didn't exactly look inviting. Somehow that hadn't dissuaded the 300,000 people that did the climb each year.

I was about to embark on the toughest physical challenge of my life and I didn't feel at all ready. Nishiyama sensei's voice replayed in my head:

'Remember, Chris san. A wise man climbs Mount Fuji once. Only a fool climbs it twice.'

I was starting to think a wise man would avoid climbing bloody Mount Fuji at all.

It was 5 p.m. Fuelled by my mound of Fuji-shaped katsu curry, I fastened my backpack and began the hellish fourteen-hour round trip into the sky. A journey that would take us through the night and hopefully reward us with a life-changing sunrise.

I just wish I'd slept the night before.

The cheapest way to travel in Japan is by night bus. It cost just 3,500 yen to make the eight-hour journey from Sakata on the far-flung west coast to Shinjuku bus station, arriving in the heart of Tokyo at 6 a.m.

But it came at a price. Sleep was no guarantee.

Japan has some truly fabulous night buses with seats that fully recline and are walled off like cocoons for privacy. Mine had none of that.

I'd boarded the bus and clambered into my narrow seat to find a small leg rest that sprang out from underneath and a curtain that gave me some degree of privacy. Not great, not terrible.

What I hadn't anticipated was the noise emanating from my fellow passengers.

Japanese people have a superpower that I greatly envy. At the click of a finger they're able to fall asleep and stay asleep until exactly forty-five seconds before they reach their destination. I promise you. Watch a Japanese commuter on a plane, train, bus or horse-drawn carriage. They'll sit down, sleep, then, as if there's an alarm clock built into their brain, they'll snap awake and stumble off at the right stop. Perhaps it's less a gift and more a symptom of overwork and constantly being switched on. Or perhaps it's all the rice and the heavy carbs. It's one of life's great mysteries.

All I know is, the moment we were seated on the bus, as if a hypnotist had snapped their fingers, everyone promptly fell asleep and burst into a chorus of snores. I soon hated myself for not bringing headphones, but it wouldn't have made a difference. Packed into the narrow chair, unable to recline or use the footrest, I arrived in Shinjuku having had a solid three hours' sleep.

I tried to trick my subconscious into believing it was longer.

Gosh, brain, what a fine six hours of sleep that was!

To which my brain replied, *Uh, you can fuck right off.*

Joining me on my ascent was my good friend from university, George. A cheeky Londoner, two years younger and two times fitter than I was, he'd completed an Ironman triathlon a few weeks earlier and was ready to dive into his next physical challenge.

I'd picked him up from Narita airport and, riding back to Tokyo on the train, he was blown away by Japan from the get-go. 'Mate, we've got to stay at a capsule hotel. I want the real Japanese experience,' he insisted.

'I mean, we should probably get a decent night's sleep at a business hotel, mate. We've got a big climb coming up.'

'I can get a decent sleep any time. Let's stay at a capsule hotel.'

As he was my guest, I gave in, booking a frighteningly cheap capsule hotel just south of Shinjuku station.

Capsule hotels are synonymous with Japan today, but they've only been around since 1979, when architect Kisho Kurokawa designed the Capsule Inn Osaka.

In the booming post-war years, Japan's growth was unstoppable and land prices became eye-wateringly high, so designers were led to think ever smaller.

For around 2,000 yen ($18) a night, guests have access to their very own capsule pod, typically two metres in length, one and a half wide and one high, allowing some limited movement, and often featuring a TV. With a single dorm holding up to fifty capsules, a communal shower and a locker room, guests can enjoy the amenities of a real hotel at a third of the price.

What started out as cheap accommodation, however, soon became the saviour of drunken salarymen who would check in spontaneously after a long evening spent drinking, rather than heading home and suffering the consequences.

To appease George, I'd hastily booked the first capsule hotel I could find online, but it soon transpired I'd booked what might be Tokyo's most decrepit accommodation in the heart of Kabuki-cho's red-light district. A male-only capsule hotel. I knew we were stuffed when we arrived at a dirty building sandwiched between air-conditioning units and pipes. A stained green sign read 'Hotel Star Capsule' and the doorway led into a lobby with a tattered carpet that hadn't been replaced since the eighties.

We removed our shoes and put them in the lockers, and a man at the front desk gave us each a bag containing a shower towel, a modesty towel for the communal baths and a toothbrush. We rode a crowded elevator up to the third floor, where the doors scraped open to reveal twenty-four capsules, stacked two rows high, stretching out down the hallway like a futuristic morgue.

A couple of people were climbing the ladders to hop into their bunk, or changing clothes, and the hall felt eerily silent, save for the rustling of bags and clothes.

I realized why. Several of the capsules were already shuttered. Presumably some people were already asleep.

'What is this?' George blurted out.

'Shh. People are sleeping.' I pointed to the closed capsules.

My capsule was on the top row and I scrambled into it using the metal ladder. Inside, everything was round and cream-coloured, save for a panel with a wall socket and light controls. The white sheets helped illuminate the interior, but I still felt that I was about to sleep inside what was basically a coffin.

But it was surprisingly comfortable. In the same way I'd learned to enjoy sleeping on my futon every night, turning the floor of my apartment into one big bed, I found a similar satisfaction in knowing that I couldn't fall out of this bed.

Is this what it feels like to be dead? I gazed at the ceiling, barely a foot from my face.

Unfortunately, as night rolled in and I attempted to get some much-needed sleep, two problems became apparent. Number one was the snoring.

By 11 p.m., the room had erupted into a chorus of snores,

courtesy of the many drunkards who'd stumbled into their pods after a night out and crashed.

Number two was the lack of ventilation. The dorm itself had air conditioning, but the moment I slid the door down to seal myself in, the lack of airflow felt suffocating.

As I tossed and turned through the night, finding innovative ways to turn my pillow into sound insulation, I vowed never to set foot in a capsule hotel again.

It was eighteen hours later, sleep-deprived and fuelled on katsu and adrenaline, that we began our ascent of Mount Fuji, from Fujinomiya, the fifth station, already 2,400 metres up the mountain.

Odds are, if anyone claims they've climbed Mount Fuji, what they're referring to is the final 1,600-metre climb to the summit, though hardier climbers can begin their trek way down at sea level.

I wasn't brave.

And I wasn't prepared at all.

I'd come along to the climb wearing extendable shorts and a T-shirt, although I did have a jacket.

George had come in shorts and a hoodie. I'd warned him he might need something more, but fresh from his Ironman success, he felt emboldened that he could survive whatever Mother Nature threw at him.

'I'll be fine. Let's just get up this mountain.'

'Eeh! You must be so very cold?' a veteran Japanese hiker declared as he shuffled past buried in a ski jacket and clutching a hiking stick.

'Don't worry! We'll be fine!' I joked, acutely aware that the temperature had already dropped from 34 degrees at sea level to a chilly 14°C. We might be in for a nasty shock at the summit.

'*Ganbatte ne!* Do your best!' he cheered me on, leading off a group of hikers holding gigaton rucksacks.

At the start of the trail a warning sign had cautioned against 'bullet-climbing' to the top – racing to the summit then rapidly down in a matter of hours. At 3,776 metres, it wasn't uncommon for climbers to experience altitude sickness and fatigue, as the levels of oxygen there were lower than at sea level.

Most climbers start in the early evening, climb to one of the mountain lodges at the eighth station, at around 3,400 metres, and catch a few hours' rest, continuing at 3 a.m. to reach the summit in time for the glorious sunrise.

George and I hadn't booked the lodge.

We tried. But it was fully booked.

We weren't entirely sure what our plan was as we snaked our way up the mountain through the crowds of fellow hikers. The vending machines got increasingly expensive the higher we climbed. A can of coffee you'd usually buy for 120 yen soon cost you 400 yen. But we didn't have much choice.

My main impression was that the climb felt like a theme-park attraction. It wasn't an easy climb, but with toilets, noodle restaurants and vending machines peppered at pit stops throughout, and with the sheer crowds of hikers, the experience felt far from being at one with nature.

'I hope this bloody thing doesn't erupt today,' George remarked as we tucked into a bowl of udon in a soy-sauce broth. Given all the sweat I'd lost, the salty soup was welcome.

'I mean, technically, it is an active volcano, mate. It last erupted in 1707.'

'You what!' He nearly spat his noodles out. 'I hope you're winding me up.'

God forbid Fuji should erupt. It's estimated to have the

capacity to unleash a level of destruction not seen in Japan since the 2011 earthquake and tsunami. If it did erupt, raining ash down upon Tokyo, the world's biggest metropolis, just 100 kilometres east, it's projected to cost the economy $25 billion in damage.

Still, at the moment, I was more concerned about dying of hypothermia.

The sun disappeared and Fuji turned to darkness. George, being the marathon-running madman he was, had gone ahead, and I'd given him our only torch. I was left with my phone light for guidance. My legs were beginning to throb and my chest to burn as I pushed on higher and higher.

On the final stretch of Mount Fuji the ground turns to thick, black volcanic soil that absorbs all the light around you. I turned around and looked back down the mountain and saw hundreds of tiny lights far below, hikers snaking their way to the summit through the darkness, as Tokyo's lights illuminated the horizon. I stopped for a moment to appreciate the view and take it all in.

'Come on. We're almost there!' George cried out ahead.

Godammit!

It was midnight when we reached the wooden lodges of the ninth station. We peeked in through the window with envious eyes: dozens of people asleep on the floor, or laughing and talking around pots of hot tea. I gazed at the paraffin heater blasting away, keeping the occupants toasty warm, as we stood outside, exhausted from the climb, in the freezing winds.

There wasn't even a free bench outside. Every one was occupied by hikers buried beneath blankets and coats trying to get some shut-eye.

In the end I propped myself up against a large boulder and, by some miracle, was able to get an hour's sleep. Until a Japanese couple wielding a flashlight so powerful it could bore a hole into the ground shone it straight into my eyes. Perhaps they thought I was dead.

The next morning we set off for the summit and arrived one hour before sunrise, to find ourselves in a queue of people. A bottleneck had formed on the ever-narrowing pathway. It felt more like waiting to get into an overhyped ramen shop than arriving at the summit of Japan's tallest mountain.

'Beer! Sake! Sake time!' A jubilant salesman clutching jars of one-cup sake attempted to thrust a drink into my hand. On paper, in celebration of reaching the summit, I should have snatched it from his hand and drunk to our achievement. But, obliterated after having carried myself 1,300 metres into the sky powered by katsu, udon and Pocari Sweat, the idea of drinking alcohol seemed like it could be a fatal error.

The summit was even busier. There was only one public toilet in a smelly stone building with a lengthy queue outside. I eventually reached the front and ventured inside, to discover half a dozen foreign climbers sleeping shoulder to shoulder, squeezed between the warm pipes beneath the sink. So exhausted were the sleeping climbers, the splashes of water from the sink above failed to stir them from their slumber and, despite the horrendous conditions, the toilet provided the only shelter from the cold. I couldn't blame them for making use of it.

We were sitting on the summit among hundreds of hikers, and I was starting to worry about George. His legs had been exposed throughout the climb. The icy wind had now brought the temperature to below zero, and he was shaking uncontrollably. The guy was tough as nails, but frostbite was a real concern. George wrapped his arms around his legs to warm them. I thought we should get moving.

'We're staying for the sunrise. We've made it this far,' he insisted.

At long last, around 5 a.m., the sky turned from black to blue to orange as the sun rose slowly from beyond the horizon of the Pacific Ocean. The stoic hikers screamed in excitement.

'*Dekita!* We did it!' a woman cried out.

The spectacle of the stoic, reserved hikers breaking into cheers and cries almost outweighed the sunrise.

We'd done it.

Before beginning the long climb down we peered into the sinister, dark crater on the summit of Mount Fuji, silent for over three hundred years.

As we were leaving, the enthusiastic hiker from the fifth station caught sight of us.

'*Sugoi!* You are alive!' he cheered. 'Next time, please bring more clothes.'

'There won't be a next time,' George said with a grin, darting his way over to the pathway down the mountain and into the warmth.

We were now officially wise men.

And we need never climb Mount Fuji ever again.

16.

Doctor Who

My legs in ruins and both of us triumphant, George and I parted ways and I returned to Yamagata with the ultimate souvenir.

The worst throat infection in human history.

What started as a tickle evolved into pain so intense I was struggling to swallow food. My tonsils had swollen to the size of beach balls and saliva drooled from my mouth. If I did manage to sleep through the throbbing pain, I'd wake up with my head in a puddle of spit.

The first thing I did when I got to work was ask Nishiyama sensei to point me to a local doctor. He recommended one a few blocks from my apartment, but none of my colleagues were available to accompany me. I was on my own, and feeling daunted by having to explain my symptoms using my very limited vocabulary.

The Yoshiharu Ear, Nose and Throat Clinic was in a drab single-storey pink building. It was almost windowless, and a cartoon elephant had been painted on the wall in a weak attempt to cheer the place up.

As I wandered into the clinic, anxious and praying that I'd be able to communicate with the staff, I felt the inevitable barrage of stares. By this point I'd got used to it, but I'd rather it didn't happen when I was dribbling.

I marched over to the desk to make a walk-in appointment and, without a word, the receptionist handed me a clipboard. On it was a piece of paper with a drawing of a stick figure on it.

Relief washed over me. All I had to do was to circle the afflicted region on the picture – no explanations needed. I furiously scribbled circles around the stick figure's neck and, feeling emboldened by my drawing skills, followed it up with a simple Japanese sentence: *Nodo ga itai* ('My throat hurts'). At last, after almost a year of study, I could write three whole words.

A small TV on the wall was blaring out a cookery show. An irritating, over-enthusiastic young man was fawning over a bowl of ramen.

'Amazing! Oh my god! It's so delicious!' he wailed. The sound of his slurps filled the room.

Half a dozen patients sat slumped in the waiting room. Most of them looked at least two hundred years old. I was the only person in the building not wearing a face mask; in Japan it's considered good manners to wear a face mask in public when you're ill, so as not to pass it on.

This habit was common long before the pandemic. In Tokyo, where 3.6 million commuters pass through Shinjuku train station, the world's busiest, in a single day, it's not uncommon to find half the passengers wearing masks in winter as a preventative measure. Bizarrely, the younger generation view masks almost as accessories, often communicating the same message as earphones: *Stay the hell away from me*. I'd get frustrated with certain pupils who kept one on at all times, including one of my top English students who hid behind the mask purely out of shyness. In the space of an entire year, I only caught sight of her face three times.

'BOOROORDO SAN . . . BOOOROOOORDO SAN.'

It took me a few moments to realize that Broad san was me.

A young nurse had come to escort me to the GP. Dressed in a dazzlingly white collared shirt, her face hidden behind an equally dazzling white hat and mask, she seemed to illuminate the dimly lit waiting room.

In the UK, when you go to see a GP you go into a small office and discuss the problem behind closed doors. Typically, a large desk separates you and the doctor has often made some attempt to make the room a little homier with pictures of their kids or pot plants. A discussion of the problem is followed by a quick examination, the tapping of a computer keyboard and the collection of a prescription a few minutes later. I expected a similar experience in Japan. Boy was I wrong.

The nurse ushered me into what looked like an operating theatre, where no less than three female nurses, each dressed in the same blinding white, bowed in welcome.

With the glowing nurses and the bright lighting, it was almost like an image of heaven – but for the slightly chubby elderly doctor on a small chair in the centre of the room examining the stick figure I had drawn on. He looked like a disapproving father gazing on his child's messy crayon drawing.

He waved me over to the chair opposite him without looking up.

I wasn't sure about being looked at by four members of staff – for a sore throat. It looked like the set-up for a patient going into surgery, and I half expected the nurses to leap in and hold me down.

No desk between us, I sat facing the doctor, trying not to bump my knees against his. Given the room itself was massive, the uncomfortably small space separating us felt almost comical.

From what I could see, the doctor was somewhere in his sixties. He wore white surgical clothing and a facemask and, on his head, held by a leather strap, a torch so large it would light up a coal mine.

He sat looking at my form, not saying a word. After what felt like a lifetime he finally broke the uneasy silence.

'My English, no good!' he barked, slapping the documents down on the table beside him and switching on the powerful torch, dazzling me. I felt like the proverbial deer in the headlights.

'Let's open mouth!' he demanded, leaning in to get a closer look.

I opened my mouth as wide as I could, which was barely at all given the painful swelling.

The doctor peered in for five seconds then recoiled. This didn't fill me with confidence.

'Eh? Eh!? Eeee! *Sugoi!*' he exclaimed.

In the UK, a doctor might say something like 'That looks painful,' so to see a doctor backflip from me so suddenly had me worried.

'Incredible! Very big throat!' He grabbed a piece of paper and muttered something to one of the waiting nurses. She left the room and returned a few moments later with a box of crayons and a pencil.

He sketched with the pencil then picked up a crayon and smothered the drawing in red.

He mumbled to himself as he worked on his masterpiece, sketching here and there, throwing in a bit more red.

I was really starting to worry now – perhaps it was something more serious than a throat infection. It had to be something out of the ordinary to elicit this level of frenetic activity.

The doctor dusted off a few loose crumbs of crayon and showed me his magnum opus.

'THIS YOUR THROAT!' he yelled. 'SO BIG THROAT!'

Judging from the drawing, I couldn't deny it was a big throat.

I surveyed the terrifying red squiggly thing on the paper and nodded in agreement, wondering if this random art session was completely necessary.

He turned to his fleet of nurses and barked something I couldn't understand. They nodded in unison.

Without explaining his diagnosis, he motioned for me to follow the closest nurse. I was escorted along a corridor and into a narrow room with a bed and curtains.

The nurse indicated that I should pull up my sleeve, and I obliged. She left for a moment, and when she returned she was wheeling in an IV drip attached to a pole. I hit peak anxiety.

What the bloody hell was going on? Minutes ago, I had been watching a doctor drawing like he was in a primary school art class, and now I was having an intravenous drip fed into the back of my hand.

The nurse checked the drip, threw a thick woollen blanket over me, switched off the lights and walked out of the room, closing the door behind her. It had all happened so fast I'd had no chance to question what was going on. I just let a woman hook me up to a bag of god-knows-what.

Alone in that dark room, far from home, I was growing more and more worried that something was seriously wrong with me. Perhaps they were talking about my chances right now.

After twenty minutes I drifted off to sleep under the warm blanket, but woke when the door was opened and the nurse returned. Out popped the drip and off we went, back down the corridor for another audience with Japan's greatest living artist.

As soon as I sat down the doctor showed me his drawing.

'YOUR THROAT SO VERY BIG.'

I agreed again that it was indeed a very large throat.

He launched into an explanation in Japanese, with a few anxiety-inducing English words thrown in.

'*Something something* infection! *Something something* dangerous! *Something something* very pain.'

I was furious that my Japanese studies had failed me so spectacularly. For all the progress I thought I'd made, I'd been stumped. All that remained were the words 'very pain' ringing in my ears.

He scribbled out a prescription and handed it to me, then clapped his hands to signal the end of proceedings.

'GET BETTER, BURODO SAN!' he bellowed, as if it were my ears that were the problem.

In Japan, National Health Insurance is taken from your monthly salary and covers 70 per cent of the costs. It's up to you to pay the last 30 per cent. In total, it had cost about 1,000 yen. What a bargain.

The nurses called out '*Odaijini*', the Japanese word for 'Get well soon', and I wandered out of the clinic confused, disoriented but weirdly energetic. What *had* they given me?

The IV drip seemed to have worked its magic. For the first time in a week, I didn't feel like death. Drips are a very popular treatment in Japan. Nearly every trip to the doctor has a complementary drip thrown in, like getting a free air-freshener at the carwash.

While I preferred the GP consultations I'd been used to in the UK, Japan's health service was certainly efficient. And I'd never had anyone in the NHS do me a crayon drawing.

17.

The Fried-chicken-addicted Bear

AUGUST–OCTOBER 2013

While Sakata's shuttered streets were practically empty during the day, it wasn't hard to find where the locals were spending all of their free time.

Family restaurants such as Gasuto, Saizeriya and Cocosu were often the life and soul of the town, full of students doing their homework after school, pensioners reading a newspaper over a coffee or couples on awkward-looking dates in the corner.

The following weekend I was in Gasuto, finding myself in the last category. Without realizing it, I was on my first date with a Japanese girl.

With bottomless drinks and reasonably priced Western food, it was easy to see the appeal of family restaurants such as Gasuto. You could sit for hours on end devouring French fries and gravy-drenched hamburgers. The 'Cheese Hamburg' costs less than a thousand yen (about $10), and it's totally delicious. I prodded the lump of beef and watched the melted cheese ooze out from within. My cholesterol was about to take a beating.

It has to be said that Gasuto wasn't exactly a romantic location. In my defence, I thought I was teaching a private English lesson.

At the start of August, I went to a house party in the neighbouring town of Tsuruoka to welcome the new JET intake. There I'd met a girl called Aika.

While most of the Japanese girls I'd met in the countryside were self-composed, shy and often hard to read, Aika was extremely animated, with a wide smile and a warm, bubbly personality. She was fun to talk to, despite my appalling Japanese and her rudimentary English.

She fired questions at me, delighted to discovered that I, like her, lived in the town of Sakata.

'Amazing! Won't you teach me English?' she joked.

'Of course. Let's hang out in Sakata!' I said. It was an empty promise, but we exchanged details and at the end of the party I gave her a goodbye hug, thinking that we were unlikely to see each other again.

Now here we were, watching the gooey cheese burst out from my greasy Cheese Hamburg. Time to unravel months of jogging with one mouthful.

'When I was student, I like English. But I'm very bad.' Aika spoke slowly, but her pronunciation was very impressive.

'I like studying Japanese. But it's very difficult!' I replied.

By the end of the meal, I'd barely spoken any English, let alone taught it, and as her questions were focusing increasingly on my private life, my impressive detective skills had deduced we were in fact on a date.

We'd followed our not so romantic Gasuto date up with dinner a few days later, ending our evening with a kiss outside my apartment.

'Today was a lot of fun! Thank you,' Aika said as she hopped into her pink Nissan and drove off into the night.

It was only our second date, so I felt we were still making up our minds about each other. Aika seemed laid back and fun, with an openness I'd not seen in many Japanese girls. We'd spent almost six hours at two *izakaya*, eating our way through the menus, chatting about languages and life in a Japanese school, and British food.

'Japanese television always say English food is so bad!' Aika insisted.

I feigned irritation.

'Lies!' I retorted. 'British food is way better. We have pies.'

Who knew where things would lead? But I was in no rush to figure out whether this could be something serious.

But less than an hour later, Aika gave me an ultimatum. As I was settling down in bed my phone buzzed with a message written in blunt English.

'Today was so fun! Thank you! Do we become lovers? X'
Well, that was fast.

I wasn't quite sure how to respond. In the UK, if somebody sent you that after a second date, you'd likely run for the hills. I wasn't sure if it was cute or desperate.

It turned out it was neither. Roy had mentioned that couples in Japan tend to formally agree they're an item early on and get it out of the way. There was no setting your status to 'it's complicated'.

I didn't want to throw away this connection, the first I'd made with a member of the opposite sex. 'Sure! Let's meet up again this week!'

I received a flurry of bizarre Japanese love-heart stickers in return. We were away.

Having made a new Japanese friend and found a girlfriend in the space of a fortnight, the only thing I needed now to complete the set was a Japanese teacher and mentor. Luckily for me, the last piece of the puzzle fell into place a week before the summer holidays were due to end.

Sakata held an annual 'Culture Day' at the International

Centre downtown. Foreign residents run stands showcasing and celebrating the food and culture of their home country.

While the town had a sizeable population of Chinese, Korean and Filipino residents, I was more or less the only Brit in town and I had been asked to attend. I was initially reluctant, until I learned there'd be free food. Sure enough, upon my arrival, I'd worked my way around the many food stalls, stealing dishes of kimchi and gyoza. It was an excellent display of British greed. A fine cultural contribution.

While I was devouring a mound of yakisoba a familiar face appeared through the crowd. Naoko sensei came darting over in a bright purple top.

'Chris sensei, *hisashiburu!* How have you been?'

There was an awkward pause as I tried to swallow a wodge of greasy noodles.

'You seem to be enjoying the food, as usual, Chris sensei!'

Cheeky. But fair point.

We hadn't seen each other since April, given the annual teacher reshuffle had cast her out to the formidably remote hot spring town of Atsumi. The educational equivalent of the Bermuda Triangle, teachers sent to the town were typically never seen again, so her appearance was a pleasant surprise.

I missed teaching with Naoko sensei. She had a positive attitude and a genuine passion for teaching languages – a rare thing in the English department.

'Actually, Chris sensei, I was hoping to run into you. How are your Japanese studies?' she enquired.

'*Ma-ma,*' I joked. It's a common Japanese expression meaning neither bad nor good.

She smiled, but then her tone stiffened.

'I was wondering, would you like to take part in the local Japanese speech contest?'

'Haha, sorry, Naoko sensei. I don't think that's a good idea. I'm not ready.' I chuckled, dismissing the notion and stuffing in another mouthful of noodles.

'No, no, no, Chris sensei! You can do it.' It sounded less like an encouraging compliment and more like begging. It transpired that she was headhunting me for the competition.

'I'm helping to run the speech contest this year and we'd love you to take part.'

'When is the contest, Naoko sensei? Maybe if it's next year I can do it.'

'Well, actually, it's in November.'

I laughed aloud and dismissed it. Three months was no time to get my skills up to scratch. I could scarcely hold a basic conversation for a few minutes, let alone stand in front of a crowd of people delivering a fifteen-minute speech in Japanese from memory.

But Naoko insisted and pointed to an ad on the wall of the International Centre promoting free Japanese lessons.

'I know the teachers. We can find someone to help you with your studies!'

I thought about my poor progress. I could read a few hundred kanji and knew over 2,000 words, but my listening and speaking skills were still shocking. It dawned on me that this was a golden opportunity to ramp up my efforts at the start of my second year in Japan.

'If we can find a teacher, Naoko sensei, then I'll do it.'

She'd shanghaied me.

'Don't worry, Chris sensei, I can find you a teacher.'

A week later I was back at the International Centre, sitting at a table of students quietly doing their homework. An elderly man strolled in carrying a handful of textbooks.

I recognized him straight away, and not just because he shared an eerie resemblance to the actor David Carradine, best known for playing the eponymous character in *Kill Bill*. I'd seen this man in my Monday-night *eikaiwa* class a couple of times, sitting at the back and not returning again after those two sessions. Most likely as he'd not been able to get a word in, while Noriko and her gang took centre stage.

'Hello, Chris san. I'm Fumio Itou,' he said, extending a hand.

'Evening, Itou sensei.' I stood up and shook it. 'I think we've met before! You came to my English class once.'

'Oh yes! Good to see you again.' He definitely didn't remember.

He was in his late seventies, but Itou sensei was sharp and had an impressive knowledge of English, despite never having lived overseas and having no specific reason to learn it.

'Did you use to teach English?' I asked, assuming his excellent pronunciation, better than many of the teachers I worked with at school, must be the result of years of experience in the field.

'Actually, I was a train conductor!' He laughed, acknowledging my surprise. 'I just always loved English since I took a trip to Europe in my twenties.'

As a young man, Itou had saved up his earnings to marry the girl of his dreams. At twenty-seven he'd proposed to her, but her parents thought he wasn't good enough for her. Heartbroken and rejected, he took the wedding money he'd saved and spent it on a six-month trip around Europe, and this had inspired him to learn English.

'Travelling around Europe was fun. But very difficult with just Japanese. So when I came back I started studying English from a dictionary.' He chuckled.

'Good god. You literally read a dictionary?' The idea sounded like absolute hell.

'Yes, it was very difficult.' He looked solemn for a moment. 'I think I made it all the way to the letter G.'

From then on, every Wednesday, whatever the weather, Itou sensei and I would rendezvous downtown at the International Centre so I could practise Japanese, thankfully without once using a dictionary.

The aim was for me to make my way through the Genki textbook series and to speak only in Japanese for the full ninety minutes. Inevitably, more often than not, our tutoring sessions would descend into the two of us speaking in English, and we'd chat about Itou's adventures through Europe or life working as a train conductor on Japan's west coast line.

My weekly schedule was starting to fill up, what with the *eikaiwa* and my new Japanese class. But it was Thursday night that quickly became my favourite night of the week.

The eccentric punk rocker I'd bumped into on the street had fast become my best friend in Sakata.

Around 6.30 p.m. Natsuki and I would meet downtown at a yakitori restaurant called *Kichi Kichi* (literally, Lucky Lucky).

A mom-and-pop shop overlooking the town hall, when you stumble through the doors you're welcomed by the heavenly smell of a dozen juicy chicken skewers sizzling slowly over the charcoal grill.

Yaki means 'grilled' and *tori* means 'chicken'. From chicken breast and thigh, to less appealing cuts such as gizzards and tail, yakitori makes use of every part of the bird. Nothing goes to waste. Even the cartilage was battered and turned into popcorn-sized nuggets called *nankotsu*.

While the husband ran the kitchen and prepared the skewers, the wife dashed tirelessly around the store taking orders and serving food and drinks. After a long day teaching, few things excited me more than the first tray of skewers, usually no less than six, a mix of chicken breast and tail. The beauty of the charcoal grill was that it cooked the meat slowly, leaving it tender and juicy. The only decision you need to make is the flavour: either dipped in sweet *tare* sauce or seasoned with *shio* (salt). Natsuki and I always chose salted so we could savour the flavour of each cut. We kicked it all off with a gleeful 'Kanpai!', clinking our ice-cold glasses filled to the brim with the golden nectar of Suntory Premium Malts.

'Oh my god. Fifteen-minute Japanese speech. Very crazy idea!' Natsuki blurted when I revealed that I'd signed myself up for the speech contest.

'I have one month, mate. Please help me,' I pleaded, gnawing the last morsel of chicken thigh off the end of a skewer.

The sudden absence of Natsuki's 'screw it, just do it' mentality concerned me. There wasn't much he cowered from. He lit up a cigarette and shook his head.

'Hmm, I think maybe very difficult!'

The scale of the task before me was laughable, and it felt even more so now.

I had a month to write a speech in English, translate it into Japanese and learn the script off by heart. Oh, and then deliver it in under fifteen minutes, before three judges and a crowd of 150 people.

Why the fuck did I say yes?

Step one was to pick a topic about which I could speak from the heart.

My runaway addiction to Family Mart fried chicken seemed like a good starting point.

Over the course of the weekend, I bashed out a speech about my struggles to learn Japanese against the backdrop of culture shock and my disappointing weight gain. I painted an image of myself hibernating indoors throughout the winter, studying remorselessly and munching on cheap convenience-store chicken.

By the end I'd written a 1,500-word speech and given it the ludicrous title 'The Family Mart Chicken-addicted Bear'.

It took me a week to translate it into rudimentary Japanese, which I had looked over and improved by a crack team including Roy, Nishiyama and Itou sensei.

Annoyingly, each of them took the speech in a different direction.

As if the Japanese language isn't already a nightmare, to make matters worse, there's *keigo* – a system of honorific speech.

In Japan, *who* you're talking determines *how* you talk, and this explains why, in most ice-breaking interactions, the conversation seldom deviates from a formal fixed pattern. It's rare to chat with a Japanese person and not have the same three questions pop up.

'Where are you from?'

'How old are you?'

'What do you do?'

In Japan, understanding your position within a hierarchy relative to the person you're talking to is of the utmost importance. This is why these questions are asked upfront – to establish how to continue the conversation.

In the West, we seem to place importance on all the wrong things. Power. Wealth. Celebrity status. In Japan, age is often the determining factor.

Senpai means 'elder', or senior of the group. A *senpai* demands respect simply by virtue of being older, in the time-honoured manner set out by the Chinese philosopher Confucius two thousand years ago. A *kouhai*, or junior, is supposed to speak to their *senpai* using *keigo*.

I remember hanging out with a Japanese guy in his twenties, chatting casually at a party, and the moment he discovered he was older than me, he started to act and speak differently. His tone changed and he began to sound like he was mentoring or guiding me. He'd switched from being a joker to trying to give me useful advice.

It felt bizarre at first, but I soon grew to respect this way of doing things. It was endearing to see people in positions of power act humbly in the presence of their elders. It felt like society as a whole was far more respectful as a result.

As for *keigo* – there's a simple golden rule: the longer the sentence, the more polite it is. For example:

When speaking to a friend, you might say:

'It's hot today, right.'

Kyou wa atsui **desu** *ne*.

The *keigo* variant you'd likely hear from a shopworker speaking politely to a customer would be:

Kyou wa atsui **de gozaimasu** *ne*.

It's the same sentence. But the *desu*, meaning 'it is', has been elongated into its polite form.

Even Japanese people admit to having trouble keeping up with it all or always knowing which speech form to use and where. This was evident when Roy, Nishiyama and Itou went through my speech: each of them set on it and tore it apart, one changing it to everyday Japanese speech and another converting it into *keigo*. Were we aiming it at the audience or the judges? Or should it be like I was chatting to a friend?

Eventually, we chose the last option. Given the informal, jokey tone of the speech, it made sense for me to speak casually. I mean, it was essentially a fifteen-minute speech about fried chicken.

I spent another week learning how to read the speech, including some new vocabulary and some grammar I'd never grasped, and then I found myself just one week away from the big day. It dawned on me how screwed I was.

That Thursday evening, Itou sensei and I were tucked in the corner of a classroom against the backdrop of howling winter winds. I stood up to deliver my speech to him for the first time but, far from having it memorized, I was practically reading it off the page.

'Your pronunciation is actually pretty good, Chris san,' remarked Itou sensei encouragingly. 'You just need to focus on memorizing the script. Have you heard of the Roman Room method?'

'I don't believe I have,' I replied, dropping the speech on the table and slumping into my chair, dejected.

'When I was learning English, I tried many memorization methods once I realized that reading from a dictionary was a waste of time. I found the Roman Room method worked well. You imagine you're inside a room or building you know well and, in each room, you place an object. Using your visual memory can be quite effective.'

It sounded intriguing, albeit more of a party trick to memorize a list of objects and repeat them back. But a year earlier I'd initially laughed at the idea of using word association and yet, as if by magic, I'd successfully committed 120 names to memory in just two days.

'It'll take a miracle for me to memorize this,' I replied, waving the paper the speech was written on. 'But I'll certainly give it a try. Thank you, Itou sensei.'

Astonishingly, I soon found the Roman Room a frighteningly effective method. Far more powerful than anything I'd tried before.

Using the visual, spatial-awareness part of my brain, I imagined walking through the school corridor, looking into the rooms, a trigger item inside each one. It could be a person, a place or an object. I'd associate each room with the first sentence of each paragraph of the speech, which I'd broken down into fifteen chunks.

One paragraph contained a joke about how I'd dreamed of owning a chocolate factory and referred to myself as a bear in hibernation. For this paragraph, I pictured Paddington Bear in his red hat throwing greasy portions of Family Mart chicken at the classroom chalkboard. The more vivid and ridiculous the image, the easier it was to recall.

I found that after picturing the corridor in my mind and going through each room once or twice, in a matter of minutes I could recall what was in each and every one. I could walk up and down the corridor in my memory, peer into the classroom and be reminded of each paragraph.

It was a genuine light-bulb moment. Once again, thanks to a simple memorization technique, what had previously seemed impossible felt achievable.

The only question was, with one week to go, had I left it too late?

The day of the speech arrived and 150 locals, among them several of my students and colleagues from Sakata Senior High, showed up to the contest, which was being held in a large, modern lecture theatre at the local university.

As I sat near the front of the room anxiously fidgeting and with my heart racing, I felt beyond terrified. I was about to completely butcher the Japanese language before 150 Japanese people, some of them colleagues and friends I respected.

Itou sensei, Nishiyama and Aika were dotted around the room. Natsuki couldn't escape his salon but had sent an encouraging text that morning: 'So fucking good luck, mate!'

Aika was holding my camcorder, capturing the spectacle, and Itou sensei was sitting next to me at the front of the crowd.

It would take a miracle to pull this off.

So far, the Roman Room technique had succeeded, but I'd only successfully recollected the whole speech once, when practising with Itou sensei the day before.

There were eight foreign speakers, all residents of Sakata and from a diverse range of countries including the UK, the US, South Korea and China. As the penultimate speaker, I sat for over an hour wriggling in my seat. My heart felt like it was going to explode.

Itou sensei must have noticed I was nervous and patted me on the shoulder in encouragement. 'You'll be fine,' he said. 'Trust me.'

It wasn't just the fear of forgetting my speech and massacring the Japanese language that had me on edge. I'd started to wonder if the content of my speech was at all appropriate.

The previous speaker, a middle-aged South Korean woman who'd raised a family here in rural Japan, gave a powerful and rousing speech about her conflicted sense of identity as a Korean living in Japan.

My speech was literally about my favourite snack.

How could I follow her?

'Broad san! *Douzo.*' One of the three judges – a group of three elderly men, two school principals and one governor – called me to the podium. I found them intimidating, which added to the horror of it all.

I stood before the lectern and placed my speech down before me in case I totally blanked, then looked up to see 150 faces gazing at me intently, a mixture of smiles and intrigue. Aika trained the camcorder on me, Nishiyama gave a thumbs-up and Itou sensei nodded.

My name was read out, and the title of my speech, which elicited a wave of muffled laughter around the room. It was an encouraging start.

I'd always found public speaking crippling; the thought of dozens of eyes all on me sent chills down my spine. It sounds ridiculous, given my job as a YouTuber, but there's a key difference between standing in a room and engaging a live audience and producing a video alone in your apartment.

Becoming a teacher and giving lessons to classes of forty students over the course of the year had helped, but this was on another level.

I gave a bow, uttered, '*Yoroshiku onegaishimasu*,' and dived in.

For the past fifteen months, I feel like I've been on a long journey. It's a strange feeling because I've been living and working here in Yamagata the whole time.

I took a brief pause to look around the room.

However, it wasn't a physical journey. It was a mental journey. When I moved to Japan in August 2012, I knew it would be a challenge. It was my first time living and working abroad. More importantly, it was my first time living in an environment where I couldn't understand the language.

The experience has led me to feel many emotions. Excitement, surprise, fear and frustration, often daily. My personality has changed. But yet, without a doubt, it's been the best year of my life.

My eyes swept the room, and I was relieved to see reassuring nods from the audience.

The first time I thought things were going to be tough was at work. I work in a large school. There are over a thousand students and a hundred teachers. We had a school assembly and everyone went into the gym hall. As I sat there trying to listen during the assembly, I realized that of the thousand people in the room, I was the only one that couldn't understand what was going on. It was a scary thought.

I took another brief pause, pretending that I was speaking the whole thing spontaneously from the heart.

And then, as I went to continue, my mind skipped a step.

Oh shit, what was the next paragraph?

I panicked. And the memory went further from my mind.

Uh oh.

By that point it was too late. I was screwed.

The room seemed to go very quiet. My eyes darted up to the ceiling as I desperately tried to remember. My mind attempting to latch on to anything.

But it was too late. My memory had failed me. I was done.

I looked down at the speech on the lectern and uncomfortably read out the remainder of the speech, instantly disqualifying myself and sapping my presentation of any real emotion.

I got a few laughs and a round of applause at the end but, ultimately, I'd failed.

'That was good!' Itou sensei reassured me. 'Everybody seemed to enjoy it.'

But I couldn't shake the feeling of failure. I felt I'd let everybody down.

'You did well, Chris sensei,' commented Nishiyama, after the event was over. 'For one year of studying Japanese it's great progress. I particularly like the story about you being a bear.'

Looking back on it, I was foolish to attempt the speech

contest so early on. I was still cramming basic Japanese vocabulary into my head in the run-up to it.

But from that failure came resolve. Resolve to take part again the following year, with a better speech and greater confidence in my Japanese speaking abilities. I would memorize the whole thing way earlier, using the Roman Room method.

Twelve months later I went up against ten contestants armed with a new speech, 'Japan's countryside changed me'.

The speech focused on how living in the countryside had helped me to appreciate being in the moment and the slow pace of life that came from living in rural Japan.

To my relief, I was able to not only recall the whole fifteen-minute speech – I won the contest, something that had seemed unthinkable one year earlier. In hindsight, had I not tried and failed so spectacularly in my first attempt, my successful win a year later would not have been possible. It taught me to value failure every step of the way.

Best of all, I shared the victory with Itou sensei, who had continued to tutor me all through the year. At the end of the competition, we shared an emotional hug and I knew that I'd made him proud. That meant more than anything.

18.

The Worst Possible Start

It was the first day of my second year at Sakata Senior High. As a JET, my school year started in September – to fit in with the rest of the world – while for students in Japan, their academic year started in April. With their summer holidays over, I'd been looking forward to returning to the classroom and showing off my rapidly advancing Japanese language skills. I was still riding high from my successful ascent of Mount Fuji, and the all-powerful *Kouchou sensei* (school principal) had added to my euphoria when he had awarded me my contract for the next year of employment the week before.

'We need your help again,' he'd declared dramatically as he held the contract out to me with two outstretched arms.

He did so with such ceremony it felt like he was handing me a legendary sword and tasking me with vanquishing a mythical beast in his name. In reality, it meant one more year of standing in a classroom five days a week, teaching students how to properly pronounce 'penguin'.

I received it with a deep bow of appreciation. *Kouchou sensei's* cheerful demeanour would soon be a distant memory, as this was his final year before retirement. I couldn't quite imagine the school without his booming voice.

Parking up in my brand-new twenty-year-old Toyota Starlet, which Roy had so generously gifted me before his departure, I wound up the windows and stepped out into another blazing September morning. It would be a while until the weather cooled down and I looked forward to it like a child would Christmas.

I'd got in earlier than usual, at 7.30 a.m., hoping to set a good example for the first day of the autumn term. I'd noticed that Japanese staff would compliment me without fail every time I arrived early or stayed at my desk late into the evening. Overtime was the key to claiming brownie points, even if you were doing nothing of conceivable value. Being present was prized far more than being productive.

As I changed into my work shoes and began climbing the stairs to the sprawling staffroom, a teacher sprinted past me.

'*Ohayo gozaimasu!*' I cried out a morning greeting.

He kept running, blatantly ignoring me as he disappeared down the stairs and out into the school courtyard.

Great. The first day back and I'm already being ignored.

I continued down the freshly waxed wooden corridor to the staffroom, wondering if this year would be any different to the last. This wasn't the best start.

As I turned the corner to the staffroom, the wooden sliding doors rolled open to reveal an exasperated Kouchou sensei, who came sprinting out with his assistant. He was sweating profusely, even for a day as hot as this, and he darted straight past me, scarcely acknowledging me before disappearing off towards the stairs.

The mood felt fraught the moment I walked into the room. Half a dozen teachers were huddling in a corner murmuring things I struggled to catch in Japanese. One of the female teachers had her hand over her mouth. I sensed that something was unfolding.

Reaching my desk, I was relieved to bump into Nishiyama sensei, who gave me a solemn wave as he approached.

'Is everything OK, Nishiyama sensei? Something seems off today.'

'Good morning, Chris sensei. I'm afraid it is not OK,' he replied in slow, meticulous English, his tone sounding ominous.

'A few minutes ago, a first-year student jumped out of a fourth-storey window.'

I was in utter shock. I'm not sure what I'd thought was going on, but it certainly wasn't that.

'Oh my god. How are they?' I said, expecting the worst.

'Right now I'm not sure, but he seems to be conscious.' With that Nishiyama excused himself and ran off to inform an arriving colleague.

Amid the morning chaos, I felt helpless. I watched over the course of the ensuing hour as fresh-faced teachers strolled into the room, their expressions turning to shock when they learned that a student had attempted suicide on the first day of term.

During the morning staff meeting, a breathless Kouchou sensei stood before the 120 teachers and staff and declared that the student was thankfully stable, though he'd broken nearly every bone in his body, including both arms and legs. Given the student had fallen around 12 metres, that he'd survived was nothing short of a miracle.

The incident had a wide-reaching impact. All major school events were cancelled with immediate effect, including the much-loved annual school fair. While many of the students seemed unaware of the incident, the shockwaves that coursed through the staffroom were palpable even weeks later. Many staff looked perpetually distressed as we all started to ask ourselves why a sixteen-year-old student had attempted to take their own life and whether we could have done anything to prevent it. Rumours began to swirl that the boy had been the victim of bullying.

Ijime is an issue that is, unfortunately, entrenched in Japanese schools.

A study in 2013 by the Tokyo Metropolitan School of Personnel in Service Training Centre had found that 66.2 per cent of the 9,000 children surveyed had been victims of bullying. Almost half of the respondents – 46.9 per cent – claimed they'd experienced both suffering it and inflicting it. These statistics are hugely worrying, but sadly not difficult to believe.

I'd witnessed first hand the level of fear students had when raising their hand to answer a question. Every action taken in the classroom ran the risk of being mocked by classmates for being incorrect or, worse, resulting in being seen as a know-it-all nerd. While this sounds no different to any school world-wide, the pressure to avoid standing out and being rejected is far greater in Japanese society.

The Japanese proverb you'll hear most is *Deru kui wa utareru* – the stake that sticks out gets hammered down. No proverb sums up better Japan's adherence to group conformity and collectivism. To be cast out and avoided is unthinkable in a culture that prioritizes the needs of the group over those of the individual. With tradition so ingrained in daily life, divergence from what is considered the norm is almost always looked down upon. It can be hard to comprehend, especially in a country so often lauded as futuristic and eccentric, but the reality is that the status quo is king. Worst of all, classmates are often more likely to join in with the bullying so as not to go against the grain. Whichever way the group goes, everyone must follow or suffer the consequences.

In Japanese the word *haafu* (literally 'half') is used to describe individuals with one Japanese parent and one foreign parent and, though not intentionally derogatory, being branded as *haafu* is another potential way to feel excluded from the group. To my frustration, I'd watched as two of my top English students, a half-Chinese girl and a half-Filipino girl, were actively suppressing their abilities so as not to become targeted.

In our interactions outside class or in private tutoring sessions, I marvelled at their fluency. But in the classroom they hid their prowess and kept their heads down. It was heartbreaking to see them hold back their potential in order to remain a part of the group dynamic, and it was something I saw time and time again. From what I'd seen, it wasn't their ethnicity but their abilities that were the cause for potential bullying.

Bullying manifested itself in different ways. At the most extreme end were acts of violence, but often the cruellest and most affecting tactics were those that left students feeling completely isolated. A report by MEXT (the Ministry of Education) in 2014 found that 19.1 per cent of victims reported bullying through being ignored or excluded by their peer group. It's hard to imagine the damaging effects, going through this five days a week for years on end.

Japanese schools faced greater pressure to handle bullying after one incident received national attention in 2011. A thirteen-year-old student in Shiga prefecture jumped to his death after being the victim of intense bullying. Interviews with his fellow students found that the boy's homeroom teacher had been aware of the ongoing bullying, and had witnessed and laughed along with it. The incident shone a spotlight on the disconcertingly blasé attitude Japanese teachers had towards the subject.

I'd witnessed on numerous occasions a student being beaten up by classmates while teachers stood there and failed to intervene. I wondered, with a sense of guilt, if the student had been from one of my classes.

A few weeks later I learned from Nishiyama sensei that the newly enrolled first-year student had indeed become the target of bullying, with classmates regularly harassing and stealing from him. When no one intervened, he'd given up hope and taken what he believed to be the only way out. The bullies responsible were suspended for several weeks and, after a leave of absence, the victim returned to school several months later, fully healed. Fortunately, he seemed to thrive in the following months.

There's no doubt that the teachers at Sakata Senior High took the issue of *ijime* more seriously after the incident, but it was a tragedy how far things had to go before they reached that point.

That year, because of the public outcry at the suicide student in Shiga, the Japanese government implemented the *Ijime* Prevention Law, requiring schools to take action to prevent bullying.

Unfortunately, it doesn't seem to have worked. In 2022, 612,000 cases of bullying were recorded in Japan. A record high.

19.

A Letter from the Colonel

DECEMBER 2014

'Do me a favour and just shut the fuck up, for fuck's saké.'

'Sorry, Itou sensei . . .'

It was rare to hear a Japanese person swear in Japanese, let alone English. It felt wrong.

'Sorry, Itou sensei. It's sake. Not saké.'

'Oh sake! I see!'

Itou sensei was clutching a Japanese–English book called *How to Use Fuck*. Quite possibly the most ridiculous book I'd ever bought.

No one was more eager to learn than Natsuki, who used swear-words in practically every sentence.

'Wow! I like fuck. Fuck is important!' he observed as he skimmed through the book, reaching a page containing a hand-drawn image of Hitler with the phrase 'Fucking bastard.'

'What is shit a brick?' asked Aika, confused at the inclusion of a building material.

'I'm trusting you with the drugs. Don't fuck me over,' declared Chounan sensei, then gave his usual booming laugh.

It was so funny to hear my polite Japanese friends using

vocabulary more suited to a gangster, a thug – anyone British, really – I filmed the four of them as they read through, popped the video on to YouTube and had my biggest viral video to date, with half a million hits in a day.

The *Metro* newspaper had run an article about it called 'English "swearing missionary" shows Japanese how to say f★★★ correctly', almost with a sense of pride, as though I was doing the Lord's work.

The truth is the book was genuinely useful. It was the first time I'd seen Japanese people excited by an English textbook. It helped them understand half the dialogue in Western films and on TV in one hit.

Yet for all the praise I'd received in my role as a swear-word missionary, the video had also inspired more hateful comments than ever before.

'Don't spoil the mouths of foreign people with your
    dishonourable, disrespectful Caucasian profanity.'
'Despicable garbage!'
'Disliked the video for swearing. It's not NOT funny. It's
    NOT clever and it's downright disrespectful to the
    Japanese.'

Disrespectful to the Japanese? The gift of knowledge.

I'd started to encounter a creepy community of Japanese-obsessed foreigners online who felt a great sense of importance as the self-appointed gatekeepers of Japan.

In one video I'd attempted to consume some horrific food I'd bought in a jar from the mountain region of Nagano.

Hachinkoko. A pot of fermented bee larvae.

That's right. Served in a brown glass container, the bee larvae were painfully visible, contained in their sticky, muddy paste.

On camera, I'd tried it, and was almost physically sick.

I'd given some to Natsuki, and he *had* been physically sick.

Hell, the woman at the souvenir store had ominously pointed out, 'It's not particularly delicious,' as she sold it to us. 'I'm not sure who eats this stuff.'

No sooner had the video come out, the foreign gatekeepers went to war.

'Disrespectful to Japan. And people wonder why most
    Japanese don't like foreigners.'
'Why live in Japan if you hate it. Go home.'

Somehow the viewers had glazed over the fact that a Japanese person had tried and failed to stomach this uniquely Japanese product. For the longest time, I found this attitude baffling and borderline condescending. People around the world feel a sense of entitlement when it comes to protecting Japan's culture, even if they've never set foot in the country. There's a bizarre perception that only the outside world can defend the Land of the Rising Sun, a phenomenon I've come to call 'Last Samurai Syndrome', This refers to the movie where Tom Cruise plays the heroic white saviour, who comes to appreciate the way of the samurai better than the Japanese characters ever could, even the emperor himself.

Over the years, I've begun to comprehend why my presence in Japan has sometimes elicited such ire from overseas viewers. I've constantly been amazed by the myriad of ways foreigners have found themselves drawn to the country. Naturally there is the lure of manga, anime and martial arts but I've met fellow Brits who came here to master sword-making, build a craft gin distillery or become an acclaimed top sake sommelier. It's a testament to the breadth and depth of Japan's culture, arts, history and unique sense of identity that the country has become the obsession of so many around the world. So, it's perhaps unsurprising that those romanticized notions of life in Japan are rather ruined by You-Tube videos of a sarcastic British guy bumbling around the country, revolted at bee larvae. It was never meant to be this way.

Besides, defending Japan against Western culture sometimes seems a pointless endeavour, given the country is so willing to embrace it. Case in point, enter Colonel Sanders.

Christmas has always been my favourite time of year, all the family together for once, against the backdrop of good food, music and games.

My first Christmas in Japan a year before had none of that.

For a country that had worked so hard to fight off Western ideals and hold on to its sense of cultural identity, there was one glaring area in which they'd failed.

Not only had the nation of Buddhists and Shintoists embraced Christmas, they'd completely bastardized it, with a little help from good old Colonel Sanders.

Instead of spending the day in a haze of roast potatoes and chocolate, I'd trudged to work and sat bored at my desk, while the students were off on holiday. Paradoxically, though 25 December wasn't a national holiday, teachers were encouraged to take the day off and use their annual leave. I was determined, however, to save my annual holiday for upcoming escapes to Tokyo and Osaka. My reward was to sit in the staffroom practically alone, eating a cold *bento*. To make matters worse, after work I stumbled through a raging blizzard for a haircut that went horribly wrong, due to my inability to describe my desired hairstyle in Japanese. With nearly all my hair shaved off, it looked like the barber had used shears rather than a pair of scissors. I finished off my very merry Christmas by slipping on the icy roadside and tumbling into a pile of snow near my apartment. In the evening, I seethed with jealousy as I watched my family frolicking back home, pulling crackers and raising toasts with bountiful wine as I thawed out in my minuscule apartment.

Bastards.

When my second Christmas in Japan came around, I knew I had to do things right. I had a chance to one-up them.

I was about to join the estimated 3.6 million Japanese families who treat themselves to the nationwide tradition of spending their Christmas Day eating KFC.

It's the most wonderful time of the year.

In 1974, KFC Japan had the ingenious idea of filling the void that Japan faced every Christmas Day. The country had embraced the commercialization of Christmas with all the tinsel and fairy lights you could imagine, but on the big day itself there were no turkeys to tuck into. KFC launched the 'Kentucky for Christmas' campaign alongside a seasonal Christmas 'barrel' box stuffed full of chicken and promoted it to the masses as *the* way to celebrate Christmas. Just like Jesus would have wanted. The marketing paid off, and today the premium KFC Christmas menu can cost up to an astonishing 5,800 yen ($50), for a whole chicken, fillets in red wine sauce, fries and the all-important Christmas cake – in this case a vanilla and strawberry sponge.

'We should order the KFC soon,' Aika had warned, all the way back in October.

'Surely not! For KFC!?' I sneered, reeling in disgust at the idea of pre-ordering fast food months in advance.

What a fool I was.

When we did get round to ordering, in November, we'd missed the big-ticket item, the glorious full roasted chicken. It had long sold out.

And so for our Kentucky fried banquet we paid the unthinkable price of 4,500 yen ($40) for the second-best item: chicken fillets in a red wine sauce. Given the price tag and how far KFC had permeated Japanese culture, it must be good, right?

Hauling the immaculately branded Christmas barrel into the apartment on Christmas Day, with Colonel Sanders' huge face beaming from beneath his Santa hat, Aika tasked me with preparing the chicken. I tore into the box and found two pieces of rock-hard, semi-cooked chicken breasts smeared in something brown and wrapped in ghastly yellow plastic, and a bespoke and touching letter from the colonel himself.

'Merry Christmas! Put it in the microwave.'

What came out of the microwave five minutes later was a rubbery, steaming mess in a sweet red wine sauce that made me wish humanity had never developed tastebuds.

The Christmas cake was dry.

I wasn't impressed.

Aika loved it. Oblivious of a world of roast turkey, stuffing and crispy potatoes, this was all she'd known, growing up. As I chewed on a chicken leg and gazed into Colonel Sanders' eyes, I wondered what the man himself would have thought about conquering the Land of the Rising Sun with his secret recipe.

'This Christmas cake, it's like me!' joked Aika, taking a slice and helping herself to a thick dollop of cream and strawberries.

'No, no, no!' I laughed, shaking my head profusely. I got the joke.

There's a cruel, misogynistic saying in Japan, 'Women are like Christmas cake. Because after the twenty-fifth, nobody wants them.' It underpins the pressures faced by women in Japan to settle down and marry before turning twenty-six, or else go unwanted and for ever be alone. Awkwardly, Aika had just turned twenty-five.

We'd now been dating for nearly six months, and already scary words were starting to appear in conversation: 'marriage' and 'children'. Back home, the idea of bringing up these topics so early in would be unthinkable. Aika and I still barely knew each other.

We enjoyed each other's company, eating and drinking our way through Sakata and exploring further afield on weekends. Her self-deprecating humour struck a chord with me and she would always go out of her way to cheer me up, arriving at my apartment after a long day of work with a platter of sushi or whisking me away to a hidden *izakaya*. Every conversation between us presented a learning opportunity. Aika helped me through my Japanese language struggles, and I taught her about key British concepts like sarcasm and Greggs.

However, the tone was starting to shift and conversations about the future had begun to infiltrate and dominate our time together in a way that I wasn't willing to confront.

In our occasional arguments, I found myself in the baffling situation of arguing without knowing what we were actually talking about. Aika's English was slightly better than my Japanese, so we often spoke English together, but in the heat of an argument she'd often switch to Japanese and I wouldn't be able to keep up.

Even beyond the language barriers, cultural issues stood between us. Her parents seemed terrified to meet me.

I'd met Aika's mother once, by accident in a supermarket. Shopping for groceries after work, I turned into one of the aisles to find Aika examining jars alongside her mum in the pickled-food aisle.

'Well, hello there!' I said, catching them both by surprise.

Aika was was glad to see me, but her mum darted behind her as if I were a rabid dog on a rampage.

'This is my mum,' gestured Aika uncomfortably.

Her mother gave a sheepish nod and waved from behind her daughter.

Nothing about the interaction felt like we'd quite hit it off.

It turned out Aika's mum had never spoken to a foreigner before, something not unheard of in rural Japan. But the encounter reinforced the awkward reality that any future together would be a struggle on a lot of levels.

The relationship stumbled on for a few more months, but by summer of 2014 we had to accept that although we enjoyed each other's company, it was probably for the best that we parted ways.

Aika had been offered a job in Tokyo, and I encouraged her to take it. As much as I loved Sakata, I couldn't deny that decent paying work opportunities were few and far between. There was a reason all my best students fled to Sendai, Tokyo and Niigata after graduating.

As Aika left me behind for her new life in a distant city and I faced re-contracting for my fourth year in Yamagata as a teacher, I realized that I too had some important decisions to make.

20.

Saying Goodbye

One of the toughest decisions you have to make on the JET programme is whether to renew another year, and this question is asked of you just three months into the job, around late autumn. I'd always planned to stay a second year, given one year is nothing short of an extended holiday. When the time came to sign up for a third year, that decision was easy too. I was the happiest I'd ever been. Two years of furious Japanese studies meant that I was at last conversationally fluent, able to chat with students and colleagues in their native tongue. As a result, I'd grown more self-assured as a teacher and no longer felt like the awkward foreign guy people would give themselves whiplash just to avoid.

Thanks to winning the speech contest, I was brimming with confidence, and I had an action-packed weekly routine that had helped me integrate with the local community. After work on Mondays I volunteered at the *eikaiwa*, on Tuesdays I ran the school English club, on Wednesdays I'd meet with Itou sensei to study Japanese, on Thursdays I'd meet with Natsuki for yakitori, and on weekends I'd shoot YouTube videos around the Shonai plain. I'd gone from conspicuous foreigner to Sakata local all in the space of two years.

I recall opening the local newspaper one morning and seeing my face in no fewer than three articles: one with a victorious smirk as I clutched the speech contest trophy, another taken at the International Centre, where I'd run a speed-dating-style event where locals could practise their English with the local JETs, and the third at the *eikaiwa* I volunteered at.

It had taken two years to get here, but I felt I'd overcome almost every hurdle that had come my way. I'd finally settled into Japan, and life was good.

So when Nishiyama sensei approached me in the staffroom one day in December and plonked himself down in an empty chair beside my desk, he was taken by surprise by my answer to his question.

'You don't want to stay another year, Chris sensei?' He leaned forward to make sure he'd heard me correctly.

'I want to, but I know I shouldn't.'

I loved my life in Sakata and was happy that I still had nine months to go, but I worried that if I stayed beyond that my enjoyment would start to fade away.

Nishiyama seemed to understand.

'When that day comes, I'll be sorry to see you go, Chris sensei. It's been a pleasure working with you.'

Even though my life was perfect there and then, I'd started to grow restless. I'd loved getting to know my students and being able to sweep into my classes with new-found confidence, but that all ended every time I opened the same dodgy old textbooks. The gaping flaws in Japan's English education system had become clearer with each passing year. Students were tested into oblivion on vocabulary and grammar but never incentivized to learn conversational English – the actual fun part. What was the point in writing out complex English statements such as 'The elephant has a prosthetic leg' if you couldn't talk the basics in spoken English. It felt like the better I got at the job, the more I noticed the limitations. I could make no real impact.

Beyond my job satisfaction, or lack thereof, by now I'd seen almost every corner of Yamagata but barely scraped the surface of Japan's forty-five other prefectures. With only weekends and limited holidays to explore, it felt like I was chained to Sakata, and I wanted to get out and explore.

Overshadowing all this was my hobby, which had spiralled out of control. Every day, hundreds of people around the world were subscribing to the Abroad in Japan channel on YouTube. Somehow, I was on the cusp of 100,000 subscribers, and I was starting to feel like I was limiting my own potential. While other foreign YouTubers in Japan seemed to pump out videos, I could manage only one a month, given my tight schedule.

The channel had become so popular my students had discovered it. I was walking to class one morning carrying a pile of textbooks when two walked past and shouted, 'Hey YouTuber!' It caught me so off guard I tripped and fell into a heap on the floor. Sadly, the textbooks survived.

At first I liked the idea of having mini-celebrity status at school. I could delude myself that I was some kind of Indiana Jones figure. Teacher by day, camera-wielding adventurer by night.

Instead I just got taunted every day by students shouting 'YouTuber!' at me. It wasn't quite the red carpet I'd hoped for.

Trying to get the attention of forty students, many of whom didn't want to be there, felt almost trivial now that the most-watched video – on learning kanji – on Abroad in Japan had clocked up over 700,000 views.

It begged the question, why confine myself to teaching in a classroom when I had the means to teach thousands of viewers world-wide about Japan. YouTube was a game changer, and if I didn't jump on it soon I was in danger of missing the boat.

While I wondered what my next step should be, the months flew by. Before I knew it, it was the spring of 2015 and I had just four months until my contract ended. My anxiety levels were off the charts. I felt like I was strapped to a conveyor belt that led to an abyss.

At times of struggle there was only one man to turn to. Natsuki's questionable advice had seen me through many a dark time, if purely for entertainment value, like the time he'd spent four hours trying to convince me to open a British fish-and-chip shop in the middle of Sakata.

'I think maybe everybody want fish and chips!' he'd optimistically surmised.

'Er, I'm not so sure, mate,' I replied, imagining an insurmountable debt mountain that would no doubt overshadow this poorly thought-through idea.

Natsuki summoned me to Kichi Kichi one evening, where we devoured our usual platter of chicken skewers over beer and cigarettes. It was there that he whipped out a radical plan.

'I think, let's work together at my shop?'

'At your beauty salon?'

'Yeah. Let's making business together.'

On paper, it was a terrible idea. In reality, it was an even worse one.

'Natsuki, what the hell would I do at your beauty salon?'

'No problem. You can be cleaner.'

It's fun to think that, in an alternative reality, I may have said yes and turned my talents to sweeping hair in the salon. Who knows, together, Natsuki and I might have built a thriving barbershop chain that dominated Japan's west coast. Alas, it was not to be.

Truthfully, I'm not sure he wanted it to happen any more than I did, but I could see he didn't want to accept that there was nothing he could do to keep me in Sakata. As he puffed away on his cigarette, his next idea popped out.

'You should live in Tokyo. From Sakata, by plane is only one hour. I can visit.'

The idea of transitioning from my quaint countryside lifestyle to living in the world's largest city didn't overly appeal to me. It was less 'out of the frying pan into the fire' and more 'out of the frying pan into the sun'. It's true that Tokyo was where the opportunities were, especially for foreigners. I knew at least four JETs who had ended their contracts the year before and were now working as recruitment consultants in the big city. This wasn't quite what I had in mind.

A far more appealing option was to have the best of both worlds and move to neighbouring Sendai, the largest city in Tohoku. By the standard of Japan's megacities, it was tiny, with a paltry population of 1.3 million. But by British standards, it would be around the fifth largest city in the country. The only problem was, I didn't know a single person there. Natsuki was furiously trying to dissuade me.

'No, no, no. Sendai very shit. Very boring place.'

'But it's only a three-hour drive from here, mate.'

'No, no, no. I wanna go Tokyo. Many shopping.' At last, we'd got to the real reason: if I had to move somewhere, Natsuki wanted me to move to Tokyo. What a supportive friend.

I'd put the word out to my group of friends in Sakata that I was keen to move to Sendai. One of them knew of an English-speaking guy working in inbound tourism who might be worth chatting to and called him when we met up for dinner one evening. After a few words with my friend, he handed me the phone. The man on the line had a strong London accent.

'Is that Chris? All right, mate it's Ryotaro here. Listen, I've heard you're interested in moving to Sendai. I've seen your You-Tube channel and it'd be great to talk in person.'

A few days later I took the bus east to Sendai and found myself in a sushi restaurant with Ryotaro. Given the accent, I'd assumed the guy wasn't Japanese. But Ryotaro very much was.

'I studied at a university in Richmond, London, and the accent never went away!' he explained with a chuckle as we tucked into a plate of sashimi.

Where most Japanese strangers were reserved about and ambiguous in expressing their opinions, chatting with the refreshingly blunt Ryotaro felt like chatting to a fellow Brit. He'd mastered not just the English language but the Western way of thinking to go with it.

Having studied in Seattle and London and worked in Frankfurt and Sydney, all before the age of twenty-seven, Ryotaro had decided to return to Japan. He realized his knowledge of the world and Western ways of thinking would give him a major advantage in a land where just 23 per cent of the population have a passport and only 20 per cent have travelled overseas.

While his company focused on helping Japanese businesses learn how to deal with foreign customers, his real mission was to encourage inbound tourism to Tohoku in the wake of the 2011 earthquake and tsunami.

Impressed that I wanted to remain in Tohoku rather than flee to Tokyo, he sensed an opportunity.

'Look, I think maybe there could be many ways we could work together to promote Tohoku through Abroad in Japan. If you're serious about moving to Sendai, I could definitely see something happening. When you move here, let's meet again and I'll see what we can do.'

While I left Sendai without any firm offer, my conversation

with Ryotaro had not only opened up the possibility that we could work together but also given me a greater sense of purpose in aiming to put Tohoku on the map. That was all I needed to go all in and place my bets on Sendai.

When the time came to say my goodbyes to the school, the proceedings were more dramatic than I had envisioned.

My final speech took place on one of the hottest days of the year. Outdoors, it was 36°C. Indoors was even hotter, with the school gym we were crammed into a whopping 40°C.

I stood in front of 1,200 students and 120 teachers, a solitary fan on the stage to keep me cool, and delivered my farewell in Japanese.

I was a quivering, nervous wreck, but I needn't have worried. Half the audience were dozing off to sleep, it was so humid. At least I hope it was the heat, not the tedium of hearing my voice.

While the audience sat quietly sweating, I at least had the one fan. During my closing words, I witnessed at least two students with heatstroke being carried off on stretchers. If I'd ever needed an incentive to wrap up a speech fast, this was it. Lives were literally at stake.

I was given a hero's send-off on my last day at school. It was the summer holidays so the students had gone, but teachers from around the staffroom stopped what they were doing and joined in, while the legendary Chounan sensei graciously brought me bags of farewell gifts. One bag was full to the brim with goodbye letters written by students wishing me well and warning me not to revert to my poor-quality diet.

'Please do not become a big stomach, Chris sensei,' cautioned Yuko, a girl from the English club.

Awkwardly, at the school doors, the teachers halted in their tracks, unwilling to change their footwear to see me off into the car park. It was as if there was an invisible barrier as the teachers stayed at the door waving and I bowed repeatedly and walked towards my car.

Chounan stuffed my bags into the boot and slammed it shut theatrically.

'I'm trusting you with the drugs – don't fuck me over.'

I laughed and shook his hand.

'Thank you, Chounan sensei, I'll miss you most of all!'

He waved as I drove out of the car park, turning to look back at the school I'd likely never set foot inside again.

Saying goodbye to my apartment was especially hard.

As tiny and unimpressive as it was, I'd never been happier living alone, studying Japanese, scripting videos and falling asleep on my splendid futon, day in day out for three years. In a weird way, the apartment had taken on a life of its own, like a friend I could always rely on. No matter how bad my day had been, the moment I got home and plonked myself down on the carpet, I was in my own bubble, hidden away behind *shoji* sliding doors.

Slamming shut the heavy metal door one last time with a characteristic clank felt like the end of an era.

One of the hardest goodbyes was to Natsuki.

We'd gone for a last supper at an *izakaya* by Sakata station and, as we said our farewells in the dimly lit car park under the gentle hum of the train station sign, Natsuki broke down, believing we'd never meet again. He grasped my hand with both arms and wouldn't stop shaking it, as if unwilling to let me go, the tears running down his face.

'*Hontou ni arigatou*, Chris. Thank you so very much for everything.'

'Don't worry, mate, I'll be back,' I assured him as we had a final hug goodbye.

To anyone passing by, it might have looked like I was heading off to battle and, from the many dramatic goodbyes I'd faced throughout my last week, I'd begun to feel like this was the case.

At Shonai airport I was stunned to find that a dozen teachers and students had come to see me off at the departure lounge, among them Nishiyama sensei, who'd greeted me here the very first day I arrived.

As I stretched out my hand to say goodbye, he surprised me by diving in for a hug.

This was highly uncharacteristic given how reserved he'd been throughout our three years together.

'Thank you, Chris sensei, for making my job fun. I shall miss our classes together.'

To my surprise, Suzuki sensei had put in an appearance. Though we'd had a bumpy first year, barely teaching together, by the second year he'd started to approach me to join his classes and our relationship had greatly improved.

'I wish we could have had more chances to work together, Chris sensei. I want to wish you good luck for the future.'

As I shook the hands of colleagues and students who had made my three years in Sakata an absolute joy, I thanked them and said my goodbyes, feeling a perfect storm of profound sadness, excitement for the future, relief and regret whirl inside me.

As the plane started along the runway I looked over to the terminal building, and thank god I did. There on the rooftop the teachers and students who'd seen me off were standing and waving, particularly Nishiyama and Suzuki sensei, who practically chased the plane along the roof of the terminal, waving frantically with both hands all the while. For the first time, it truly hit home what an incredible life I was leaving behind.

Completely overwhelmed, I felt myself tearing up. What the hell was I doing? I had the perfect life, and I was throwing it all away. Maybe I could have stayed another year? Maybe I could have ended up working at Natsuki's salon or, hell, even set up Sakata's first fish-and-chip shop?

The towering volcano Mount Chokai came into view as the plane took off from the runway, as if it too was seeing me off. As the plane banked and made its way across the Shonai plain, I experienced some serious déja vu. The luscious green rice fields and hazy blue mountains looked exactly as they had when I'd arrived three years earlier. But I felt like a completely different person.

After three years of grappling with the Japanese language I was conversationally fluent, but these three years had taught me other things as well. The process of learning Japanese – the lack of comprehension, the struggle of trying to talk in gestures and the near-constant embarrassment – had taught me how to problem solve and become a better communicator. Two thousand hours of classroom experience, managing forty teenagers four times a day, had made me more confident in public speaking, and growing a YouTube channel from scratch had offered endless opportunities to flex my creative muscles. But my greatest achievement had been the lasting friendships I'd made across Yamagata and the feeling that I'd genuinely integrated into the community. A feat I couldn't have imagined when I was having my first awkward coffee at the airport.

Yamagata had treated me incredibly well. For the friendships I'd made and the sense of belonging I'd come to feel, it would forever be my spiritual home in Japan.

As the landscape and the life I'd come to know so well over the last three years disappeared from view, I wiped away my tears. I was in no hurry to be the weird British guy randomly sobbing over by the window.

21.

Starting Over

I'd always liked the idea of living in a hotel. Who wouldn't love the thrill of living out of a suitcase, returning to a room that was forever clean and tidy, mini bar restocked, never knowing who'd you run into in the lobby or where each day would lead.

What a load of bollocks.

My new life in Sendai had got off to the worst possible start. Without a job or a work visa, finding an apartment had proved impossible. Unlike Tokyo, where it was relatively easy to find a shared house, here in Sendai they seemed to be few and far between. For now, my only option was a business hotel. I'd booked into the cheapest one I could find, the Sendai Beverly Hotel. Despite the low price, the name had left me expecting some level of Hollywood glamour, even if they seemed to have missed out the all-important word 'hills'. This glamour was sorely absent.

The room I'd been given stank of a thousand cigarettes, and the walls were stained brown from years of smoke. The single bed had a decent mattress but a god-awful buckwheat pillow – a lumpy bag filled with the hard outer shells of buckwheat seeds – which made sleeping difficult.

Buckwheat pillows are one of Japan's worst inventions. They're as awful as they sound and I have endless hatred for anyone who says otherwise. If you want to give them a try, get a pillowcase, fill it with a thousand pistachio shells, then try to rest your head on it. One night of this torture and you'll be crying out for feathers.

Unfortunately, judging from my experience, about 50 per cent of Japanese inns use them, and roughly 30 per cent of Japanese business hotels. At the Sendai Beverly Hotel, I'd put folded bath towels on top in a desperate attempt to fall asleep.

After my first rudderless week, the excitement of moving to Sendai had evaporated. As I lay back on my crunchy pillow, inhaling the stale smell of nicotine-gone-by, my mountain of credit card debt piled higher than Mount Chokai. Why had I left Natsuki, Sakata and my comfortable life behind for this nightmare? The only person I knew in this city of over a million people was Ryotaro, and he was away on business for the month. Why hadn't I moved to Osaka? At least there, people would talk to me. Here, I hadn't had a single conversation in a week.

For the first time in my life, I felt truly alone. Without friends, colleagues, or even moody students to engage with, I felt completely at sea. It wasn't until I received a message from a friend in Sakata that I realized I'd done this all before. I'd been the town loner and had managed to overcome it. This town was ten times bigger than what I was used to, and it had been my decision to move here. It was up to me to dig myself out of this hole. And anyway, wallowing in self-pity was damn near impossible without a proper pillow.

Desperate to escape the confines of my room, I grabbed my coat and headed outside. It was January 2016 and I had been looking forward to a slightly milder winter than the ones I'd grown accustomed to in Yamagata. Sendai was on the east coast of Japan and rarely received snow, which was welcome news. However, this year, Mother Nature, in what felt like a rather personal attack, had decided to dump a foot of snow across the unprepared city, bringing life to a grinding halt. Many shops were shut, public transport was limited and the streets were uncharacteristically empty. Now *this* was the kind of snow response I remembered experiencing in the UK.

The neon lights of the shops and bars illuminated the white powder in a rainbow of colours across the streets. I enjoyed taking in the city while it looked like this, wandering the streets aimlessly. But ultimately, I was a rudderless ship.

Although it doesn't have any parks, Sendai is a very walkable city, full of wonderful coffee shops and tree-lined streets – its nickname is 'City of Trees'. Lovely as it is, a far more accurate name for Sendai would be the 'City of Tongue'.

Ambling through the town centre, I noticed that scarcely ten seconds went by before I stumbled across a restaurant serving something called *gyutan*. Every region and city in Japan has a *meibutsu*, a dish they're famous for. Kobe has wagyu beef, Hokkaido has snow crab and juicy mutton barbecue. Sendai had *gyutan* – literally, cow's tongue. Yay.

Having spent my first week in Sendai living off a diet of *onigiri* and my favourite Family Mart chicken, I figured it was time for a culinary adventure.

I spotted a restaurant with a stylish *noren* curtain out front called *Date no Gyutan*. I initially thought *gyutan* meant a romantic *date* night, which sounded pretty nice, until I saw the samurai figure of Date (pronounced *Da-tay* not 'date') Masamune out front. The sixteenth-century warlord after whom this restaurant was named had founded Sendai city.

Escaping from the snow, I slid the door open and immediately the sound of intense sizzling and the tantalizing aroma of what smelled like steak hit me. In the bright wooden interior with the classic long counter overlooking the kitchen, several customers were munching away as the chef calmly cooked dozens of tongues over a roaring charcoal grill.

Many of Japan's *meibutsu* dishes were established in the post-war era, when Japan was in the process of rebuilding both its cities and its sense of identity. In 1948, against a backdrop of food rationing and hunger, a yakitori restaurant in Sendai run by chef Sano Keishiro took the typically discarded cow tongue and developed a cooking technique that made it not only palatable but delicious. The recipe caught on fast and the previously wasted cut of beef became a local delicacy.

Having now lived in Japan for three years, I'd eaten all manner of questionable dishes. In the UK we're taught that the worst thing to put in your mouth is raw chicken. In Japan, it's a bloody treat. Chicken *sashimi* is served alongside soy sauce and ginger, and if you close your eyes and ignore your tastebuds, as you mash up the slimy meat in your mouth, it's sometimes possible not to be physically sick.

From *natto* (fermented soy beans) and squid guts, to *basashi* (raw horse) and deadly *fugu* (blowfish), eating Japanese cuisine can sometimes feel like a food challenge if you pick the wrong restaurant. The question was, how would Sendai's local dish compare?

For 1,500 yen, roughly $12, I ordered a plate of six slices of premium *gyutan*. They were flavoured with either miso or salt. In three short minutes, it arrived, the meticulously grilled slices of tongue, around 2 millimetres thick, served with a side dish of barley rice and a steaming bowl of oxtail soup.

As I raised the first slice with my chopsticks and inspected it for a moment, I noticed both the chef and the waitress watching me intently, waiting to see if I was about to make a mess of their restaurant.

Japanese people love witnessing foreigners trying their food. Their curiosity is almost childlike. For a moment, the joker in me wondered if I should fake my reaction, cry out in disgust and feign being physically sick all over the table.

But as I was new to the city and didn't want to make any enemies in my first week, I refrained.

I popped a slice of salted beef tongue into my mouth and instantly felt myself salivate at the juiciness of the meat. Chewier than regular beef, but just as meaty and flavourful, it felt like all the joy of eating a mini steak but without the sense of guilt that often accompanies it. I looked over at the waitress and chef and gave a nod and a thumbs-up, and they both laughed and went back to work.

I combined the next slice with a mouthful of the warm barley rice and a sip of oxtail soup. It was intensely salty, but I was surprised how good it was. I had a feeling I'd be eating a lot of *gyutan*. Perhaps Sendai would suit me after all.

It was a miracle. I'd found the perfect apartment.

Twenty minutes outside downtown Sendai and costing 60,000 yen a month, it was set across two floors. The kitchen and dining area were on the first floor, and a small staircase led to a double bed in a narrow attic space above. It was essentially one large room and, while it was far from spacious, it was modern and well lit, with double-height floor-to-ceiling windows.

It was everything I'd ever wanted. And there was no chance in hell I was getting it.

I was sitting inside a real estate agency optimistically branded as Happy Home Services – another ludicrous English name chosen for marketing purposes.

I was far from happy.

The real estate manager, a cheerful and well-mannered man in his early thirties, was clutching his phone, talking to the manager of the property I'd hoped to live in.

The rental process had been going well so far, and it looked like I would soon be living in my dream apartment. I was practically picking out curtains when Hiroshi delivered the bad news. He had contacted the owner, who'd been mortified at the prospect of a non-Japanese tenant living in their property. The decision was final. The answer was no.

'*Wakarimashita* – understood.' Hiroshi looked at me and gave a sympathetic shake of his head as he put the phone down. I was stuffed.

Finding an apartment as a foreign resident is perhaps the most stressful and alienating aspect of life in Japan. Not only is the process formidably expensive, with ridiculously high upfront costs that simply don't exist in most other countries, it's also one of the few areas of life in Japan where discrimination is openly allowed. The 'no foreigner' policy is ubiquitous and often the sticking point that leads many foreign nationals to leave the country. I'd met people who'd mastered the language, worked here for a decade and, in some cases, started families, only to bail on the country in the face of xenophobia. Japan isn't unique for it, but in a country where everyone is incredibly polite and cordial and society has an almost utopian atmosphere to it, it can take foreign residents by surprise when a situation such as this arises and breaks the perfect illusion.

For 265 years during the Edo era Japan's isolationist foreign policy, *Sakoku*, had closed the country off from the world.

Though it reopened in 1868, the sense of the country being in a closed-off bubble lingered. While Japan's isolation led to its unique sense of identity, every time I heard the word *gaijin* ('outsider') used when referring to non-Japanese it rammed home that an *us* and *them* mentality was still very prevalent.

I tried not to take it personally: I was far from an isolated case. In 2016, a study by the Ichhi Group real estate agency showed that 40 per cent of foreign respondents to a survey had been rejected for rental housing because they weren't Japanese. After all, why take a high-risk foreign tenant who might flee the country without paying rent, or someone who isn't used to Japanese customs, when you could wait a little while longer for a safer Japanese tenant?

Navigating the Japanese rental market was a minefield. Even if I had got my dream apartment, I would have practically gone bankrupt before I'd crossed the threshold. While the rent was a fairly reasonable 60,000 yen a month – paid upfront – there were the additional initial costs of the deposit (two months' rent) and the 'key money', a ridiculous one-off payment to the landlord to thank them for accepting you. Key money was equivalent to one month's rent. Throw in insurance and the agency fees, and I would have found myself parting with a whopping 280,000 yen just to get the bloody keys.

I'd been blissfully ignorant of all these rather expensive annoyances up until this point. On the JET programme, it's the responsibility of your school to arrange your accommodation, and I'd been lucky to live in a gloriously cheap government-subsidized apartment.

Unfortunately, being a YouTuber came with no such benefits. I was on my own.

'Sorry, Chris san. It might be very difficult to get regular accommodation. But I do know a company that might be able to help.' Hiroshi handed me a business card for Sendai Rentals, a company specializing in short-term apartments. I was grateful for this ray of hope, but things were still looking dire.

All the money I'd saved from my teaching job had gone already and I'd taken out a rapidly disappearing loan of £5,000 from a UK bank that was supposed to see me through my first three months in Sendai.

Despite Abroad in Japan having 100,000 subscribers, I was only pulling in roughly £500 a month from YouTube and, with my morale at an all-time low with trying to find an apartment, I'd lost all motivation to shoot any videos.

I felt like I was trapped on the first level of a crap video game, the only thing in my inventory being Family Mart chicken and the business card for Sendai Rentals. Well, it was something.

My extended stay at the Sendai Beverly Hotel hadn't gone unnoticed. Aimlessly sloping in and out of the lobby a few times a day, I'd got chatting to the staff there. I'd bonded with one of the chattier receptionists over our shared love for fast food. She tipped me off about an unusual McDonald's Japan food item: French fries served with chocolate sauce. Japan was famous for wheeling out unique and time-limited menu items that couldn't be found anywhere else on the planet. It was an easy target for a desperate YouTuber such as myself.

One of my first videos was of me trying McDonald's Japan's jewellery burgers, a premium trio of upmarket burgers containing rare cheese and truffles served in an over-the-top box and shaped to look like a crown. They weren't particularly good, but the video went down well with Western audiences.

As I hauled yet another brown McDonald's bag back to my hotel room, I unwrapped it to reveal a white box half printed in chocolate brown with the words 'Original Golden Crispy: McFry Potato Sauce'. A catchy name for sure.

It sounded promising, but the reality was unimpressive. I cracked open the box to find . . . regular French fries. Rummaging further, I found a plastic fork and a sachet of white and milk chocolate sauce buried at the bottom. That was it.

I split the sachet open, drizzled the chocolate over the fries and wondered how on earth I could possibly spin this into a YouTube video. Up to this point, my videos had been meticulously scripted and shot, planned frame by frame. Sitting in my smoky hotel room about to film myself eating a box of fries, it felt like the Abroad in Japan channel I'd staked my future on was over.

I edited the shitshow together into a two minutes and thirty-eight video and uploaded it, then collapsed on to my buckwheat pillow.

When I checked my phone the next morning I found I had been bombarded with messages. The McDonald's chocolate-fry video had become a smash hit overnight, clocking up a quarter of a million views.

Featured on YouTube trending, the internet hall of fame that was Reddit and numerous online publications, it seemed that lots of people were captivated by some chips drizzled in cheap chocolate. I watched, bemused, as no fewer than four American TV presenters reacted to my video live and debated the pros and cons of the dish.

Friends I hadn't spoken to in years popped up to say they'd seen it on Facebook. It was mad.

I felt like I was at the centre of the world. The tide was turning. And later that day, Ryotaro got back into contact, evidently impressed with my viral success.

'Hello, mate. Well done on the McDonald's video! That's

seriously crazy. Good news – I may have some videos for you to shoot later this month.'

My stupid McDonald's video had won him over. I'd proven myself and unlocked the next level in the video game. With Ryotaro's help, the Abroad in Japan channel was about to turn my fortunes around.

But not before a ridiculous project involving a staggering number of cats.

22.

Cat Nation

'OK, Chris, I want you to look over at the cat, then turn back to the camera with a sort of dumbstruck expression.'

I was standing awkwardly with a camera crew, watching about a dozen people queuing up eagerly to buy lottery tickets from a cat.

You can't make this shit up.

There's a Japanese idiom, *Neko ni koban*, 'like coins to a cat', which warns against offering things to those incapable of appreciating them. It was one of my all-time favourite idioms, but I thought these people might be taking it a little too literally.

Hachi was no normal cat, however. Hachi was a magic cat. Allegedly.

Despite our feline celebrity being a pure white American shorthair, she had a pair of strikingly large black eyebrows in the shape of the kanji for the number eight, *hachi* (八). It was almost as if they'd been squiggled on with a marker pen.

Eight is a lucky number in Japan, and Hachi's lottery stand had seen an unusually high number of winning tickets. Hachi was a real-life *maneki neko*, a lucky cat.

At first glance, it seemed like an unlikely location for a divine miracle – a gritty stand on a street corner in Mito city, 70 kilometres north of Tokyo. A bold sign had been stuck above the stand, boasting of the good fortune on offer: '1 million yen prize draw won 3 times this year!'

Unfortunately, Hachi wasn't doing any favours for good health, as half the people in the queue snapped up a pack of cigarettes alongside their lottery tickets.

Working between 1 p.m. and 6 p.m., Hachi was treated like an employee. The owner of the stand, Kaori Hasegawa, had been loaned the cat on weekdays by a friend who'd hoped she'd bring good fortune to him.

Looking at the audience crowding around the cat and taking photos, I found myself struggling not to laugh. Hachi sat upright on the counter, bored and unimpressed, like a queen unamused at the presence of fawning peasants.

With the cameraman ready to begin shooting, I moved over to the counter beside Hachi and turned to face the camera, speaking in a semi-serious presenter's voice.

'People come from all over Japan to meet Hachi, the lucky cat . . .' I gestured over to the shop front, now deserted. Hachi had got bored and wandered off, disappearing inside for a nap and ruining the segment. Typical cat.

'Could we bring Hachi back for a moment?' the producer asked Kaori san.

He shook his head solemnly. 'Hachi needs her beauty sleep.'
Bastard.

In late April my career was again in the hands of our whiskered friends. I'd spent the last week creeping through a graveyard in search of feral cats, sipping an abhorrent beverage branded as 'cat wine' and exploring a semi-abandoned island on Japan's Pacific coast inhabited almost exclusively by two hundred felines.

Two months earlier, I'd received an email from a wily Australian filmmaker called Tim Demalstro. He'd recently turned a decent profit on a Bitcoin documentary and wanted to invest his earnings into a follow-up project on Japan's crazy cat-obsessed culture. Having seen a few Abroad in Japan videos, he thought I'd be perfect for the job, with my knowledge of Japan and, I can only assume, my rugged good looks.

My 100,000 subscribers probably helped as well.

I had mixed feelings about presenting the documentary. Not only did I lack any professional experience, I wasn't convinced that viewers hoping to learn about cats in Japan would want to do so through the lens of a snarky, sarcastic, British dickhead. It felt like a mismatch.

To make matters worse, I don't even like cats.

Now this isn't to say that I actively dislike cats, but having a mild allergy has meant that I keep them at arm's length. In the past, in Natsuki's salon, the moment his Persian cat Rocker sauntered into the room, I'd flee, trying to avoid the instant itchy eyes and runny nose that always followed his presence.

But on our first video call Tim was adamant that I was the man for the job.

'Just act exactly how you would in your normal videos, mate. It'll work great!'

If I'd had any foresight, I'd have hired a manager to negotiate the contract and land me both a nice fee and a cut of the profits, especially if I was going to be promoting the documentary when it was released.

But I had neither a manager nor any foresight. In my desperation to get the job – *any job* – to help pay off my spiralling debt,

I'd suggested a ridiculously low fee, which Tim duly accepted. Looking back, I practically presented *Cat Nation* for free, and I have no one but myself to blame. At that point, if somebody had thrown coins at my feet and asked me to dance in the street, I'd have done it. YouTube was failing to pay the bills and my future in Japan was still hanging by a thread. Maybe Hachi would bring me good fortune.

There's no doubt Tim, despite my misgivings, was on to a winner from the get-go.

Japan's population of 8.9 million cats was about to overtake dogs as the most popular pet in the nation. Well-loved characters such as Hello Kitty and the round-faced blue cat Doraemon were a clear demonstration of how ubiquitous cats were in Japanese culture. But it was the many bizarre ways in which Japan's cat obsession had manifested itself that made the topic so wonderfully intriguing.

Though our journey would take us around the country, our first stop was a cat café in Shinjuku, Tokyo, where for just 1,000 yen customers could access a room drowning in no less than twenty-five cats and sip tea and coffee for an hour. It was most popular with young women, who'd turn up to play with the animals after school or work.

Japanese landlords often ban tenants from keeping pets, given the tiny apartments and the havoc claws would wreak on paper sliding doors and tatami flooring. Cat cafés were an ingenious solution to cater for the poor souls who longed for a cat but were cruelly forbidden from owning one.

While I enjoyed playing with the cats, after half an hour my allergies started to kick in. With my runny nose and my eyes watering uncontrollably, I retreated to the corner of the room, ordering a plate of pasta to devour as far from the cats as possible. As I sat down to tuck in, I realized the pasta had a bonus ingredient along with the tomatoes and sausages: a small pile of cat fur.

We hastily left for a nearby *sukiya* restaurant serving up beef bowls and I vowed never to order food in a cat café again.

It was a pleasure working with Tim and the cameraman, Cody. It soon felt more like working with friends than in a professional TV environment, and this helped put me at ease during the shoot. And though Tim had undertaken a decent amount of research and hired a local fixer to set up the interviews, it became clear that we were at the mercy of the weird and wacky subjects whose stories we were chasing.

One such subject was known only as Cat-man.

On most weekdays in Tokyo's eclectic shopping district, Harajuku, a middle-aged Japanese man, could be spotted pushing a stroller full of Persian cats. Nine of them. In a single stroller.

Our fixer had received a tip-off that Cat-man would be in the neighbourhood at around 11.30 a.m., so our team descended on the intersection where he was hotly anticipated to appear. Sure enough, at half past the hour, we saw a stern-looking figure with a shaved head and a blue chequered shirt emerging from an alley-way pushing a stroller.

The stroller was so small that at least four of the dozing cats were submerged beneath the fur of their neighbours. It was difficult to grasp where one cat ended and another began. Despite the flurry of commotion from excited onlookers, nearly all the cats were sound asleep.

Apparently, soon after our cat man, Masahiko Suga, had adopted the cats, they'd begun to wreak havoc on his home. Taking them for walks in a stroller helped calm them down.

It was certainly a baffling sight: how the cats remained put and so well behaved was a mystery. Rumours online started by angry cat lovers claimed that the cats had been drugged into a stupor and that Cat-man was exploiting the animals for attention and publicity.

I wasn't quite so sure what to make of it as I watched a small crowd encircle the stroller, but the production team had their opening shots: a pile of cats sitting peacefully in a stroller in Harajuku.

Our next encounter involved an e-commerce company called Foray that had taken the bold decision to let staff bring their pet cats into work. Their theory was that feline companionship would help de-stress the workers, an initiative that I imagined would be far cheaper than paying their employees overtime.

The image of kittens tumbling around in an office seemed rather lovely, but in reality it was nothing short of chaos.

Tucked away on the second floor of a small, nondescript building in Shibuya, the cramped office had two rows of desks facing each other. When we arrived, there were about eight staff working quietly at their desks, and half a dozen cats ambling around as if they owned the place.

We were met by Ken san, the cat-loving company manager who'd instigated the policy, who kindly gave us a tour.

The first thing that caught my eye was a computer keyboard with a half-chewed cable protruding from the back.

'Our pets can be very playful,' he chuckled, while I looked on, bemused, at a Siamese cat climbing around to the back of a computer in search of a chew toy.

He won't be laughing when Fluffy has 50,000 volts sent through him.

'Do the staff who don't bring in cats mind about this?' I asked.

'Our staff are nearly all female, and almost everyone brings their cat in,' the manager assured me. Gazing around at the workers, it seemed that, indeed, 90 per cent of the staff were female.

I was curious to know if there was anyone who resented the policy. Logic dictates that out of everyone in the room, *someone* was watching Mr Tiddles tearing through a month's work and trying not to lose it.

It certainly wasn't up my alley. The office smelled like the world's biggest litter tray.

Next up I had to try a range of 'cat-inspired' products, including an air freshener that supposedly smelled like a cat's forehead – whatever that smelled like. Filming in an Airbnb overlooking the majestic Sensoji Temple in Asakusa, I degraded myself by spraying the odour of a cat into my face. The concept of the spray had been to invoke the scent of cat at times of loneliness. Perhaps you're away on a business trip and longing to be reunited with your beloved pet. With this spray, it'll feel like they're right there with you.

The spray smelled like asbestos. A musty, shitty smell that invoked childhood memories of an awful village hall in rural England. I cursed the inventor of cat air freshener and hoped to god this smell would wash off.

Yet somehow, things were about to get worse.

Tell me, reader, have you ever sat down in the evening with a glass of red wine, looked over at your sober cat and thought, 'Oh gosh, little Mittens seems rather left out.'

Of course you have. Well, that, my friends, is where cat wine comes in. You need never drink alone again. With this groundbreaking new venture, you can take your cat along for the ride into flagrant alcoholism.

Presented in a 375ml bright green wine bottle covered in paw prints, the average non-Japanese shopper could easily mistake *Nyan Nyan Nubou* wine for regular wine. However, speakers of the language will note that *Nyan Nyan* is the Japanese sound for a cat meowing.

But as I took a sip of the appalling orange substance, the only sound to be heard was that of gagging as I instantly spat the so-called wine into the sink. It was as if somebody had combined cranberry juice with bleach. I doused my mouth with an entire tube of toothpaste to mask the flavour from hell and began to regret saying yes to this god-forsaken project.

For what was to be the most astonishing segment of the documentary, we hopped on a plane to Osaka and took a train 100 kilometres south to the remote town of Kinokawa in Wakayama prefecture, in search of a real-life rags-to-riches story.

Once upon a time, a stray cat called Tama grew up in the shadow of Kishi station, an unremarkable stop at the end of the rural Kishigawa line. Facing annual losses exceeding around $4 million, the railway line and its fourteen stops faced closure.

After a public outcry at the impending suspension of the rail service in 2004, the powers that be kept the Kishigawa line open but destaffed all the stations. Each town nominated an informal stationmaster to oversee the day-to-day management.

Local businessman and newly appointed stationmaster Toshiko Koyama befriended Tama on his regular trips to his local train station. Tama was a beautiful female calico, with an eye-catching coat of brown, black and white fur, and Toshiko soon made her the station mascot. By 2007, she had been awarded the formal title of stationmaster, and given the all-important role of greeting passengers as they passed through the station to board the train.

Instead of an annual salary, Tama was given a year's supply of cat food, a gold name tag and a bespoke stationmaster's hat. The hat had been specially commissioned and fitted like a charm, turning Tama into a local icon.

At this point, you'd be right in thinking that this story straddles the fine line between genius and insanity, but here's the kicker. Tama became so popular that folks were starting to go out of their way to visit Kishi station. There was a 10 per cent increase in visitors from 2006 to 2007: a whopping 55,000 additional passengers. Pretty soon, the media in Japan and around the world caught on and flocked to the station to hear the story. A study by Kansai University estimated that Tama's presence had contributed a bonkers 1.1 billion yen to the local economy.

We arrived in Wakayama after a long and complicated journey. Getting to Kishi station wasn't exactly easy, and that made the pilgrimage of tourists, many of them foreign, all the more astonishing.

But not as astonishing as the *Tama Densha*, a train built and branded in the image of Tama by the Wakayama Electric Railway.

The railway had hired Eiji Mitooka, an award-winning bullet-train designer, to create a cat-themed train. The train had a pearly white exterior adorned with paw prints, black whiskers and gigantic cat ears on the roof. The interior was full of playfully curved benches running the length of the carriage, a small library stacked with cat-related books and a wooden cabinet filled with figurines of Doraemon. Dotted around the carriage were 101 cartoon images of Tama cheekily licking her paws and flicking her tail. Riding the *Tama Densha* felt like a catnip-induced hallucination.

As our train pulled into the throne of Tama, otherwise known as Kishi station, I saw that the whole building had been designed to resemble the beloved cat stationmaster. The original dull, dilapidated structure had been updated in 2010 and the whole thing ingeniously converted into a cat's face, with two round windows as eyes, an arched doorway shaped like a nose and cat ears nestled in the eaves of the roof. No expense had been spared.

One Japanese economist described the influence of Tama as *Nekonomics*, a satirical reference to Prime Minister Shinzo Abe's economic policy, whimsically nicknamed *Abenomics*. But while Abenomics had been a mixed bag in its attempts to boost Japan's flagging economy, ironically, Tama the cat's impact had delivered substantial economic benefits to the local area. And other stations in Okayama and Fukushima had started acquiring their own cat stationmasters to get a piece of the action. It seems Tama was an influencer now too.

However, despite our long pilgrimage to meet the cat of the hour, we were one year too late. Tama had died of heart failure a year before, at the age of sixteen.

For her good service, she'd been memorialized at a Shinto shrine constructed on the platform at Kishi station. I stepped through the *torii* and across the rocks to the lavish wooden shrine erected in her memory, where an incense stick burned gently, and felt inspired, moved and a little bemused at the proceedings.

How had one cat had such a profound effect on the local economy? Did Dr Seuss have it right all along? Was it as simple as sticking a cat in a hat? What had been going through Tama's mind as she sat, day in, day out, watching hundreds of starstruck onlookers boarding the trains?

Feeling sad and a little pissed off that we'd travelled all this way to see the tomb of a deceased cat, imagine my surprise when on entering the station, to my amazement, sitting patiently on a pedestal was Tama herself! The stylish blue cap was perched on her head and a huge gold badge dangled from the collar. Over a dozen ecstatic fans were cajoling her into selfies and, I had to admit, it was pretty cute sight.

Closer inspection of the gold name badge revealed that this was in fact Nitama – Tama II, heir to the Kishigawa line empire. It answered the ultimate question: what happens when your legendary mascot dies after you've spent millions building a train line in their image?

Answer: You hastily prepare a similar-looking successor.

The branding geniuses at Kishi station had anticipated Tama's death and Nitama had been waiting in the wings for almost three years. The King Charles of the cat world.

As the befuddled cat looked around, taking no notice of her simpering audience, her eyes suddenly fixed on the patch of sunlight that lingered beyond the station exit. I wondered if our furry stationmaster longed to escape the lucrative circus it had inadvertently found itself ringleading.

Several months after we wrapped filming, and just as I was at long last overcoming the trauma of drinking cat wine, Tim sent me a copy of the finished documentary. It was called *Cat Nation: A Film about Japan's Crazy Cat Culture*. The quality of the footage was exceptional and the stories we'd covered were undoubtedly fascinating, but I was mortified by my performance.

Unsure of how to perform in front of the camera, I'd held back on a lot of my sarcastic humour, wary of offending the cat-obsessed viewership. On the few occasions I had been myself, I came across as abrasive and condescending. There was no way this was going to go down well with viewers hoping to enjoy a documentary about cute, cuddly animals.

'Tim, are you sure I don't seem like too much of a dick?' I nervously enquired on a video call.

'Not at all, mate! I think we've got a hit on our hands here. Distributors have shown a lot of interest,' he replied cheerfully, no doubt relieved that the project would soon bear fruit.

My sense of relief was outweighed by my annoyance at not having negotiated a good contract.

Distributors. Interest. Fuck. Why hadn't I negotiated a cut of the sales?

Cat Nation was released in 2017 and went on to be sold around the world in the most random places. One afternoon I received a flurry of messages from viewers in Sweden.

'Oh, wow, Chris. I saw you in a cat documentary on TV!
It was so random, but I loved it.'
'Dude, I was watching a show about a cat in Japan with
my wife, and your face popped up! What the hell?'

It seemed the show had appeared on Swedish television. Not
long after, I received a message from an old schoolfriend who'd
flown on Emirates, only to find me in a bizarre cat documentary
playing on the inflight entertainment.

'Was flying over the Himalayas today and your smug face
appeared. You were riding a cat train. Was so confusing,
man!'

At first I was grateful to receive the messages from bemused
viewers and friends, but when the documentary appeared on
Amazon Prime my worst fears were confirmed.

ONE STAR
'I had to stop watching halfway through,' began Jonathan.
'No respect for Japanese culture or cats. This guy doesn't
have a clue about them.'

ONE STAR
'Intolerable!' declared Steven. 'Didn't enjoy this moron
describing things as crazy, creepy or weird.'

ONE STAR
'Absolutely awful guy! If you don't enjoy Japanese customs,
leave the country!' sneered Natalia, as if a pile of cats stuffed
into a stroller was a Japanese tradition that hailed from the
Meiji era.

ONE STAR

'Lost my interest in 5 mins,' remarked Anonymous. 'Although
I laughed a lot at his tasteful clothes. Pay attention to what he
wears.'

It was true. I'd been wearing a tacky purple shirt throughout the
shoot and obscenely unflattering half-mast trousers. There were
no excuses.

Yet despite the outpouring of justifiable hate on Amazon and
my own personal disappointment at my performance, I didn't regret
taking part in *Cat Nation*. I'd discovered obscure corners of the
country and being a part of the production had given me the confidence to begin planning my own documentary projects. And
dare I say, I even grew to appreciate cats a bit more along the way.

23.

A Home at Last

It's not every day you get branded an 'alternative theorist'.

My stupid face was emblazoned across an online Australian article with the absurd headline 'How Jesus's brother did him the ultimate favour and took his place to be crucified, alternative theorist says.'

What sounded like a plot out of *The Da Vinci Code* had started out as a trip with Ryotaro to the far-northern region of Aomori, a prefecture famous for bluefin tuna, apples and dense snowfall. Yet we'd ended up going to the impossibly remote town of Shingo to gaze upon an impressive wooden cross protruding from a comically large mound of soil that claimed to be the true resting place of Jesus Christ. A tin containing coins and a post-card with manga fan art of Jesus sat on the mound, while an impressive Hebrew plaque donated by the Israeli ambassador stood nearby. It had been given as a token of friendship to the local area, though one wondered if they were simply humouring the townsfolk and their bold claims.

Apparently, rather than dying on the cross, Jesus had fled to Aomori and left his brother to take his place. Why his brother had been willing to sacrifice himself so readily we'll never know. But Jesus had allegedly spent his final days in north Japan, just 24 kilometres from the graves of Adam and Eve, who were, it was claimed, also entombed nearby.

As I gazed across the tranquil rice fields that rustled in the wind in the shadow of the huge wooden cross, I wondered whether Ryotaro and I had stumbled upon a conspiracy theory two thousand years in the making?

Or was it another desperate attempt to attract tourists to a dying village?

We'll never truly know. I'll let you decide.

By featuring Shingo in a video and telling the story, I was granted the title of 'alternative theorist'. It felt like a fitting successor to my previous title as a swear-word missionary, back in Sakata.

Shooting videos around Japan with the ever wily Ryotaro was certainly unpredictable. From nearly dying in a blizzard shooting a ski video atop one of Tohoku's tallest peaks to climbing up a cliff wearing jeans and without a harness to capture a shot of an old mountain shrine, things had almost gone spectacularly wrong on more than one occasion.

We were constantly at each other's throats, so our double act seemed more like sibling rivalry than friendship. But the banter and brinkmanship made each video more entertaining, and there was little doubt we made a great team.

In our first year we'd produced nine videos around Tohoku, covering everything from buttery wagyu beef to the cherry blossom season, doing our bit to put northern Japan on the map.

I'd always been shocked that in Japanese guidebooks Tokyo and Kyoto each have over a hundred pages devoted to them, while northern Japan's six huge prefectures are granted little more than four or five. Tourists were missing out on genuine wonders – the largest morning market in Japan in the port town of Hachinohe, Aomori; a delicious bowl of ramen in Kitakata, a town in Fukushima with more ramen shops per capita than anywhere else in the country; the magical hot-spring town of Ginzan in Yamagata.

With a slew of viral hits, we were having enormous fun exploring spectacular locations, encouraging viewers to break away from the ever popular 'Golden Route of Japan' that took tourists through Tokyo, Hakone and Kyoto and to take the more adventurous, uncharted journey through the north. But given the paltry 1 per cent of foreign tourists who visited Tohoku, in spite of the millions of views we'd racked up, we were facing an uphill battle.

Still, in my new role as an alternative theorist, I was certainly up for the challenge of turning things around. Especially now that life in Sendai itself had started to turn around.

One morning the doorbell of my new apartment rang.

I checked the video monitor screen and grew anxious when it revealed a police officer standing at my front door.

I'd only been living in this neighbourhood for three weeks. How had I already got entangled with the law? I composed myself and raced to the door, wondering what I'd done wrong. Perhaps it was a noise complaint because of the YouTube video I'd recorded with Natsuki the night before? Or maybe a department store I'd recently filmed without permission was exacting revenge?

As I swung open the door, the police officer – a mature man with a mop of grey hair, wearing the characteristic uniform of a pale blue shirt with matching navy suit – gave a deep bow and a warm smile. In clear and well-pronounced English, he said, 'I am Japanese policeman.'

'Uh, *konnichiwa!*' I gave an awkward smile and a slight nod.

'I would like to welcome you to the neighbourhood!' he said, switching back to Japanese. 'If you ever have any problems, please come see me at the *kōban!*'

Kōban are small neighbourhood police stations found on street corners in every town and city in Japan. At over six thousand locations, these police boxes are typically staffed by two or three officers at any one time. Often with a cosy interior consisting of desks and rudimentary tea-making facilities, they're an effective way of making the police more approachable. I'd only ever entered one once before, when I was lost in Tokyo, and the officers were more than happy to give me directions.

Relieved that I wasn't being deported for unknown crimes, I thanked the officer and he disappeared off down the corridor. What a nice, if slightly terrifying, welcome to the neighbourhood.

It was August, and after the turbulent start to my life in Sendai and several weeks on the road filming various cats with hats on, at last I had a place to call my own; a 2LDK *mansion* apartment twenty minutes from downtown Sendai and overlooking the Natori River that flowed through the city. It was a peaceful neighbourhood, save for the occasional flood-warning alarm being tested. Apart from the minor fear that the dam further upstream would burst and wash away half the city, life was great.

Bizarrely, larger apartment blocks in Japan are referred to as *mansions* (マンション), but do not have any of the characteristics of an actual mansion. The name was dreamed up in the 1950s by builders keen to promote the idea of multi-family residential living and, today, typically, any apartment block over two or three storeys high is called a *mansion*.

As the proud owner of a 2LDK, I reigned over a two-room apartment with a lounge, dining area and kitchen combined in one room (hence the LDK) and the bedroom as the other. At 80,000 yen a month, it was 10,000 yen more than the average Sendai apartment, but as I needed a room separate from my bedroom to film in, I viewed the second room as a studio and hoped the money would be worth it in the long term.

It was a huge step up from the hellhole I'd been living in during the months leading up to the summer. Having been turned down for the apartment of my dreams, I'd handed over ungodly sums of money to Sendai Rentals to have a roof over my head for the last six months in between my new accommodation and my life living out of hotels.

They had found me a modern apartment to live in temporarily. The short-term contract meant I avoided having to pay key money and a deposit and was billed 120,000 yen each month, an extraordinary amount given how tiny it was.

The estate agent, a young and chipper Japanese man who spoke English fluently, had shown me printouts of two apartment options around the city.

Option A was an apartment situated fairly centrally that seemed devoid of any light. It looked like an elongated prison cell, with metal bars on the glass windows and a cramped entranceway. The kitchen was no more than a gas hob and kettle and a door opposite led into a bathroom so small I wasn't sure I'd be able to sit on the toilet without my knees banging into the wall.

It looked like a screenshot of a holding cell in Guantanamo Bay.

'The metal bars are for peace of mind, given the room is on the ground floor,' explained the estate agent when I shook my head in a resounding no.

Option B looked like the Garden of Eden in comparison: a brightly lit studio apartment with light brown flooring and fresh white walls. There was one main room with a bed, a kitchen and a desk, and a shower and toilet in a separate room to the side. It was small, a 1LDK without the L or the D, but it looked like a decent short-term solution.

Life in the tiny apartment went well at first.

Though the monthly payments were extortionate, it still beat the bankruptcy-inducing stays at hotels and constantly moving my luggage and life from room to room. Best of all, I had a real pillow.

But after one month I was starting to lose my mind. While *mansion* apartments typically have walls made from concrete or metal, the two-storey apartment block was made from balsa wood. It wasn't just any balsa wood either.

It was the shit kind.

Sandwiched between three apartments, below and on both sides, I could hear practically every cough, snore or utterance. It was as if my neighbours were in the room with me. The first time I tried to tape something on to my wall it made a hollow noise and left me with a worrying realization that my private space wasn't so private after all.

At night, I would wake up at around 2 a.m. to a deafening snore, thinking someone was in my room, when in fact it was a man who lived next door. Our beds were both pressed up either side of the same wall, with barely two inches of balsa wood between us. We were practically in the same bed.

I'd hoped to shoot YouTube videos in the apartment but quickly grew self-conscious about talking loudly and bothering my neighbours. This meant I made no videos and wasn't getting the vital income I needed to live.

Japan's tiny apartments are beloved and often glorified online, effortlessly gaining millions of views, with viewers extolling the ingenuity of Japanese interior design and minimalism. You've not really lived in a Japanese micro-apartment until you've uploaded a video with a thumbnail of you in it with your arms outstretched, shocked at *just how small* it really is. And while these videos are often entertaining to watch, the reality is utter bollocks. Japanese real estate companies practically get away with murder, building increasingly small rooms that are tantamount to coffins. There's no way living in such a narrow space for extended periods of time can possibly be good for your mental health. Being in a constant state of self-consciousness and walking on eggshells in my own space and all the while dealing with my neighbour's noisy daily routines certainly didn't help my state of mind.

When Natsuki came to visit me for the first time, he was shocked by the lack of space.

'Kitchen very narrow!' he'd declared, mocking the fact that the sink was just one foot away from the end of my bed.

Being a YouTuber, naturally I made the obligatory tiny Japanese apartment video too, and it proved a hit on the channel. As hard as I endeavoured to put out unique and thoughtful content, the truth is, it's the crowd-pleasers that keep you afloat. After all, my media empire had been built off a video of McDonald's chocolate fries. My viewers particularly loved it when Natsuki was practising his English listening skills and misheard the words 'vacuum cleaner'.

'Eh! FUCKING? Cleaner?!' He reeled in shock.

'Vacuum, Natsuki! Vacuum!'

I'd spent three long months devising increasingly elaborate ways to block out the sound of my neighbours, from using earbuds and headphones to wrapping a towel around my ears and taking sleeping tablets. But at long last, with Ryotaro acting as guarantor, I'd been able to find a long-term apartment. Both my sanity and my future in Sendai were assured.

24.

Missiles Incoming

I'd been offered the opportunity to write an article for a Japanese magazine on a stunning UNESCO-protected forest called Shirakami Sanchi nestled in the mountains of Aomori. As the northernmost prefecture on Japan's main island of Honshu and one of the most isolated regions in the country, here I could relax and unwind while writing a mediocre article about some trees. Absolutely nothing could go wrong.

In the remote peace of the north, the only thing the locals of Aomori had to worry about were black bears. Or maybe it was the bears that had to worry. In the days leading up to my trip, a cheeky bear had wandered into a prized orchard and boldly approached an elderly farmer who was picking fruit. While in the UK the worst you'd come face to face with was a rabbit or perhaps a fox, in Japan the wildlife is rather more threatening. Bears are the tip of the iceberg in a land inhabited by wild boar, giant hornets and mischievous macaques rolling around in the snow. Rather than fleeing in terror, the farmer had squared up to the bear and punched it in the face. The bear recoiled in surprise and promptly fled, dashing back into the mountains of Shirakami

Sanchi. I almost felt sorry for the bear. However, attacks by bears had been on the rise in recent years. They had been emboldened by the dwindling populations of Japan's rural villages and so perhaps it was right to send a message to all of bear-kind.

My journey into the mountains would require me to waddle upstream for several hours, navigating perilous cliff edges and clambering over rocks to reach a secluded and dangerously inaccessible waterfall. A serious accident, and I would have been utterly stuffed, especially if I ran into the local wildlife. I certainly wouldn't be able to punch a bear in the face.

Despite the risks, I'd told myself that journeying into the wilderness to write an article that no one would ever read would be worth it for being able to delude myself, just for a short while, into thinking that I was essentially Bear Grylls.

The night before the trek was to begin, I and two local guides stayed in a run-down hotel in the nearby village of Nishimeya. Knowing I'd need a good night's sleep to prepare for the day-long jungle trek, my heart sank when I opened the door to my hotel room and discovered what may have been the world's worst bed. The springs were visibly broken and, judging by the sound it made when I sat on it, it had been assembled sometime before the fall of the Berlin Wall.

As an anxious person, if something is even slightly out of whack, sleep is simply off the cards. I'd seen it before, in my battles with the buckwheat pillow, and once again, as I tossed and turned on my Cold War-era bed, the springs digging into me like claws, any chance of a good night's sleep faded. By some miracle I managed to doze off at around 1 a.m., and I had to set off at 7.30 a.m. With six and a half hours' sleep, I'd be running up the mountains of Aomori.

But at 06.04 a.m. the world ended.

Or at least, it certainly felt like it.

I jerked awake and sat upright in bed. It's a strange sensation when your body takes over. Even though I was up, my brain hadn't switched on and my eyes were impossible to open, dried out from the relentlessly air-conditioned hotel room.

Next to my pillow my mobile phone was emitting a terrifyingly loud alert that I'd never heard before. It was somewhere between a burglar alarm and a foghorn, designed to be unmissable and to inflict a sense of urgency. It was accompanied by a message that I was struggling to read, due to the fact that I could barely open my eyes. At first I thought it was an earthquake alert, albeit a fairly large earthquake, given the alarm was blaring longer than usual. But then, outside my window, I heard something I'd never heard before. An air-raid siren.

To say I was shocked and disorientated would be an understatement. I'd jolted awake so suddenly that my body was trembling and my heart was racing to the point where I thought I was going to have a heart attack. To go from complete relaxation to having a gallon of adrenaline pumped through your body in under the space of a second is extremely intense.

I took a few deep breaths to try to slow down my heart rate, then stumbled towards the window to try to make out the words being spoken over the siren.

I swung the window open, the sticky summer air instantly misting my dry, air-conditioned face, and peered out across the village. From the third floor, I had a sweeping view of the area. Despite the blaring overhead, I could see no signs of life and no explanation as to what on earth was going on. It made the whole experience even more unsettling, like the opening seconds of a disaster movie. Then, suddenly, the siren was replaced by an ominous voice.

'Missile launched. Missile launched. A missile launch has been detected. Take cover in a reinforced building.'

A missile? Holy crap, where from?!

For a brief moment, a swell of terror overcame me. Was this a full nuclear exchange between NATO and Russia? Had there been a major incident?

As I stood looking out across the sleepy town, it dawned on me that the end of the world could be unfolding right now. And I was here. Impossibly far away from my friends and my family.

My eyes darted up frantically to survey the sky for any traces of a missile, half expecting an inbound object to pierce through the thick morning clouds and crash-land directly in front of me.

Of course, it would happen here. The one place in the world where nothing has ever happened.

The air-raid siren continued to wail, and a lone car appeared, slowly making its way out of town.

But then I heard a word in the air-raid siren that I'd missed before. The alert was of course in Japanese and there'd been one word I couldn't make out.

Kitachousen . . .

I knew that word, but I used it so rarely I'd forgotten what it meant. What was it?

I opened the dictionary on my phone and typed it in.

North Korea.

Of course it bloody is.

The idea that a shoddy North Korean ICBM could fall from the sky at any minute and bomb one of Japan's most rural villages seemed both absurd and highly unlikely. During my time in Japan, the spectre of North Korea's missile tests had loomed large over everyday life. North Korea was like the Bogeyman, a constant thorn in the side of a relatively peaceful region. Along Japan's west coastline in particular the country was reviled; over a dozen Japanese citizens had been abducted from rural beaches in the seventies and taken to Korea to teach Japanese. Relations between the two countries had been damaged irreparably.

My first thoughts were, if North Korea had fired a missile, it was likely to be a test. But what if it had gone off course and was on its way to Aomori? I'd been following North Korea's antics for seven years at this point and assumed that the state had no intention of hitting Japan with a missile, which would in all likelihood kick off the biggest East Asian conflict since the Korean War.

I peeked out into the corridor to see if there were any fleeing guests. I was met with absolute silence.

At this point, panic and confusion turned to anger and a very British brand of incredulity. It was six o'clock in the morning, for god's sake. How could North Korea be so selfish? How dare they wake everyone up at such a stupid time?

There are moments that forever define us, and I was about to stumble into mine.

I whipped out the only camera I had on me at the time – my iPhone – and hit record.

'It's 6 a.m., and I've just been rudely awoken by an air-raid siren for a missile from North Korea. I don't know if it's real or not, but it's not a very nice way to wake up in the morning.'

In an alternative universe, it's strange to think those could have been my last words. The words of an idiot.

But instead, without warning, the siren stopped and, assuming the situation had passed, I made my way back into bed with a sigh of relief. Fortunately, I was in that crucial period where it's still easy to drift back to sleep. No sooner had my head hit the pillow and my spine the broken springs, I was out like a light.

Five minutes later, all hell broke loose again. This time, not only did my phone go off and the air-raid siren resume, but the TV switched itself on, adding a new dimension to the situation. The room was now haunted.

I glared at the TV. It had switched on to breaking news, and a reporter was announcing the North Korean missile launch.

Clearly, it was some kind of emergency system rather than a mischievous poltergeist. The news report delivered the worrying headline that North Korea had launched its first ever intercontinental ballistic missile, capable of reaching North America.

Despite the worrying developments, I felt confident that it was just another chapter in North Korea's constant sabre-rattling. Angry again, I grabbed my phone and filmed myself in bed.

'Just back in bed. The phone went off again. Now I'm really angry.'

I was fully awake, and furious. I recalled watching a recent video in which a bunch of YouTubers travelled to North Korea and filmed videos of themselves having fun at a water park in Pyongyang. Somehow, they had managed to overlook the staggering human rights issues and ongoing nuclear weapon development in the country.

'This is what annoys me about all the people who go to North Korea on holiday because it's so different and unique to see a culture that's so weird and strange, like the 1960s. Fuck off. Every time you're going to North Korea, you're funding a regime that has thousands of people locked away in detention camps and fires missiles stupidly and randomly at six o'clock in the morning.'

It was a bizarre, politically charged monologue to deliver at six in the morning, and had I known what would happen to the video in the days ahead, I probably would have worn a T-shirt. Still, at least the alarm had died out.

Before uploading the video to YouTube, I checked the news to make sure no one had been hurt. It turned out the missile had flown directly over the village, albeit several hundred kilometres above us, before plopping down in the East Pacific. Thankfully, nobody had been harmed.

I opened YouTube, Twitter and Facebook and hit the upload

button, and then, for the third time that morning, I went back to sleep for all of twenty minutes, before it was time to leave.

The day-long trek through Shirakami Sanchi's forests and streams was spectacular. Wading through the river, water flooded my boots, and heavy rainfall soaked everything else, but the warm, humid weather made it just about bearable and after a four-hour-long expedition we made it to one of Japan's most stunning waterfalls. Standing in the pool beneath, the spray of fresh mountain water cleansing my exhausted, sweaty face, I tried to keep my mind on the article, but my thoughts were consumed by the morning's unusual events.

I'd asked my two guides if they'd heard it. To my surprise, both of them had slept right through it, simply brushing off the end of the world.

'*Taihen desu ne!* It's terrible, isn't it?' one of them remarked in a blasé fashion.

I was starting to wonder if the event had been overblown. Did anyone really care?

Having spent the day trekking through a rainforest, half expecting a bear to finish me off where the ICBM had failed, I collapsed into the back of the car as we began our drive out of Aomori.

One benefit to having been in the middle of nowhere was the absence of a phone signal. We'd spent the last day completely cut off, an experience that's hard to come by in the modern world. But as we returned towards civilization and my phone latched on to a signal, it began to vibrate.

At first I thought it was another missile warning, because it started making yet another weird noise. Then I realized the phone was simply struggling with the sheer number of notifications it had to process.

The message ring tone rang out over and over, each new

notification burying the last. The phone was buzzing off the hook, relentlessly delivering messages, emails and missed calls.

What on earth was going on?

I opened YouTube to see that my hastily shot ranty cluster-fuck of a video had been watched by a million people. My jaw dropped. While I'd been paddling around in the mountains, I'd become an internet sensation. And that was just the tip of the iceberg.

On Facebook, the video had been shared by almost every media outlet imaginable. It had garnered an astonishing 20 million views. The equivalent to a third of the population of the UK had watched it.

My inbox was bursting with messages from mainstream media outlets; everyone from the British broadcaster ITV to the World Economic Forum had slipped into my inbox, keen for me to explain the geopolitical situation in Japan. Friends and ex-girlfriends I hadn't spoken to in a decade popped up saying they'd seen the video. On some Facebook pages the hate comments were out of control, with viewers angry that I'd chosen to be sarcastic during such an event.

The North Korean missile story was dominating headlines worldwide and my video was some of the only footage of the event that existed online. As I sat in the back seat of the car clutching my phone, for the first time in my career I truly came to appreciate the power of the internet. It was utterly terrifying that a poorly shot video could find its way to millions of people around the planet in just a matter of hours.

Despite being one of the worst videos I'd ever uploaded, the three-minute video of me slouched topless in bed was the beginning of a very strange month indeed, and a turning point in my life in Japan.

25.

Ground Zero

One of the most unusual aspects of living in Japan is knowing that despite the country being one of the safest on the planet, with low rates of homicide and violent crime the envy of the world, the country lives in the shadow of so many existential threats. While North Korea remains a constant thorn in the side of peace, the real danger lies beneath.

At 14.46 JST on 11 March 2011, just 72 kilometres east of Tohoku, a horrifying earthquake of magnitude 9.1 unleashed destruction across the country. The most powerful earthquake ever recorded in Japan, millions of people from Tokyo to Aomori felt the ground shake like never before, crumbling homes, shattering glass and causing skyscrapers to wobble like jelly. The colossal Shinjuku Mitsui Building, towering 200 metres above central Tokyo, had, astonishingly, swayed up to two metres.

Far worse was to come for those living and working along the Pacific coastline. Tsunami sirens screeched from remote fishing villages in Iwate to sprawling cities in Miyagi and Fukushima, warning the locals to move to higher ground fast.

The sea receded ominously and then a large, frothing wave

appeared on the horizon. It gathered in size and scale then smashed into over 250 kilometres of coastline. In the space of seconds, calm gave way to chaos, with cars and entire homes swept away as if they were made of paper.

A 14-metre wave had swept inside the Fukushima Daiichi nuclear plant and damaged the emergency diesel generator. There was a catastrophic meltdown which resulted in the worst nuclear disaster since Chernobyl in 1986.

In the space of one afternoon amidst the earthquake and tsunami, an estimated 19,759 people were dead, 6,242 were injured, and almost 250 kilometres of coastline was turned into a wasteland, waves coming a shocking 10 kilometres inland in some regions.

In Fukushima, huge swathes of land were now uninhabitable due to radioactive contamination, and 135,000 people were evacuated from the plains surrounding the Daichi plant. In the panic, foreign governments advised nationals to avoid travelling to north-east Japan, and hundreds fled the country, fearing the worst.

At an estimated cost of $235 billion to the Japanese economy, the World Bank assessed the Tohoku earthquake to be the costliest natural disaster in history at the time. But for a generation of locals living amid the ruins of the Pacific coastline, the damage cut far deeper than economic losses. Almost everyone had been affected or knew somebody who'd suffered the loss of a loved one. The situation could not have been more dire.

Six years had passed since the disaster and, having been incredibly lucky to call Tohoku my home for half a decade now, I'd wanted to produce a documentary video about it, and meet the locals who'd been rebuilding their lives in the shadow of the tsunami.

It was a daunting prospect to go from sitting on the floor of my apartment making videos mocking Japanese television to doing serious interviews with people who'd lost everything. Never had I felt so out of my depth.

At the same time, I felt I owed it to Tohoku. The last five years had been the best of my life, and now, with my channel having one of the biggest followings of foreign YouTubers in Japan, I was uniquely placed to cover the story and do what I could to put the region back on the map.

The tsunami-struck coastline and the deaths of over 19,000 people seemed to have been forgotten by the mainstream media. While the world knew about the Fukushima nuclear disaster, there had been little coverage of the people who had suffered and the towns that had been annihilated. Producing the documentary felt like a way of confronting that.

Through the videos I'd produced with Ryotaro travelling around Tohoku, we'd been able to show that, far from being a dystopian wasteland, it was very much business as usual in northern Japan. It was incredible to see the transformation. From the rubble, the reconstruction effort had transformed the landscape, reshaping the land and raising vast concrete walls to protect the coastline and rebuilding towns from scratch.

One such town was Onagawa (女川町). The town closest to the epicentre of the earthquake, 827 people had died there and 70 per cent of the buildings were destroyed. Incredibly, despite its close proximity to the earthquake, the Onagawa nuclear plant had survived the tsunami: 14-metre-high concrete seawalls had prevented severe flooding. At the stricken Fukushima Daiichi plant, seawalls were a mere 5.7 metres high, a catastrophic decision that had contributed to the disaster.

Ryotaro's help had been invaluable in producing the documentary; he set up interviews with key people along the coastline, including the mayor of Onagawa, Yoshiaki Suda.

When we arrived in the sleepy fishing town on a sunny November morning a cool sea breeze was blowing through the bay, and fishing boats chugging into port with the oysters and salmon the region was famous for.

Along the waterfront, the first thing that caught my eye was a destroyed concrete building, jarring and somewhat out of place, given the rest of Onagawa had been so impressively rebuilt. Almost all other traces of destruction had been removed from the landscape.

We met Mayor Suda, a tall, imposing figure whose stern expression gave way to a smile as he welcomed us. He noticed that my eyes were fixed on the ruined concrete building.

'This area has seen many tsunamis over the centuries. But the people forget. We wanted to leave something as a reminder and a warning to future generations.'

While other towns along Japan's coast had wanted all traces removed, the locals here had voted to keep it as a powerful reminder of the ever-present dangers that lurk beneath the earth.

One of the boldest decisions Mayor Suda took was empowering the young people in the area to influence the redesign of the town. The town elders were left out of the consultation process.

'If we're to keep the younger generations here in Onagawa, it's them we need to appeal to. We need to listen to their ideas.'

Inspiringly, entrepreneurs and local businesses descended upon the town to get stuck in to the reconstruction process and revive the local economy. One of these was a luxury guitar company called Glide Garage founded by craftsman Yosuke Kajiya. He pioneered a guitar called the Questrel, the first guitar in the world to be made without screws or nails, instead employing traditional Japanese carpentry techniques used in building temples and shrines. The guitar was a hit, selling at an eye-watering $7,000, and proceeds went towards the recovery effort. Yosuke had been drawn to Onagawa after taking part in the recovery efforts. Befriending the locals and inspired by the town's reconstruction, he'd relocated 1,000 kilometres north from his native home of Tanegashima to start his business. He'd given a heartwarming motive for the relocation: 'When you're producing something, the positive atmosphere of your surroundings is reflected in the things you create.'

Next door to his premises, a local cardboard company had built an impressive to-scale replica of a Lamborghini – out of cardboard. Cleverly branded as the *Danborghini*, a play on the Japanese word *danbo*, for 'cardboard', it had attracted national press coverage and the approval of the emperor himself, who'd inspected it on a visit to the tsunami-stricken coastline. The PR helped cast Onagawa in a positive light, less a victim of the disaster and more a phoenix rising from the ashes.

Up and down the coast I found stories of ingenuity in the face of immense adversity. Farmers along the Miyagi coastline had lost their livelihood overnight, when the saltwater swept across their fields, robbing the soil of essential nutrients. The fields could no longer produce rice and other crops.

Unwilling to let this beat them, one hour south of Sendai in the town of Yamamoto, farmers had banded together to start a new type of farm.

Ryotaro and I were delighted to visit Miyagi Ichigo World, literally 'Strawberry World', to taste the award-winning polished strawberries that now sell for up to $20 per berry. Yes, you read that correctly. Twenty dollars for a single strawberry.

This may sound extreme, but they were relatively affordable by the standards of luxury fruit.

Japan boasts the world's most expensive fruit to date in the form of the Yubari King melon. A record 5 million yen was spent on a pair of Yubari melons in an auction in 2019. It wasn't necessarily about size, though the melons were larger than average. It came down to the flawlessness of the outer skin; cultivated to be so meticulously round and smooth, it was almost as if the gods had handcrafted the fruit. And don't even get me started on the grapes; a bunch of Japanese Ruby Roman grapes sold for an astonishing $12,000 at an auction in 2020.

I hope the winning bidder ate them slowly. That's $400 a grape.

It's not uncommon for these budget-busting fruits to be given as gifts on special occasions or as *omiyage* souvenirs, and the Miyagi Ichigo strawberries were no exception.

As I sunk my teeth into one, I could almost understand the ludicrous price. It's worth noting that the strawberries were the size of apples and utterly perfect in appearance. Strikingly red, and quite literally polished to glimmer in the sunlight, they looked more like the plastic food replicas you'd find displayed in the window of a restaurant.

But it was the taste that made it all make sense. The moment I pierced the thick, fleshy skin, the juices flooded my mouth. They were sweet, flavourful and frighteningly addictive, and I vowed to stay away from trying more, lest I pick up an expensive fruit addiction.

As I asked the manager, Takao Ono, how many of the strawberries he got through in a week, he responded, 'Too many!' in a way that evoked a serious amount of envy from me. I was in the wrong business.

The farmers of Yamamoto chose strawberries because of the conditions required for growing the fruit. Typically grown in carefully controlled conditions, Sendai's mild annual climate provided the ideal weather, and the sprawling land that had once been used for rice had a purpose once more. The polished strawberries were finding customers everywhere from Tokyo to Saudi

Arabia and creating a fantastic export opportunity for the Tohoku economy. It was a great example of innovation in the face of the worst possible situation.

But of all the stories we covered, none was more moving than that of Ichiyo Kanno, a woman living on the outskirts of Kessennuma fishing port who'd suffered a terrible loss.

Ryotaro and I had been in town to cover the K-Port café, a restaurant started by world-renowned actor Ken Watanabe to help revitalize the area. During the recovery efforts in 2011, as one of the most recognizable faces in Japan, he helped raise awareness world-wide by shining a light on communities affected by the disaster. Despite having no former affiliation with Kessennuma, he adopted the town as his second home, forging friendships and launching the K-Port café to encourage a sense of community spirit. While we didn't meet the man himself, his staff gave us a tour, sharing his story. They even showed us a book containing the letters Ken would send daily to the café when he wasn't able to visit in person.

While shooting footage in the town, Ryotaro had been networking furiously and had discovered the story of Ichiyo Kanno, the owner of a local *minshuku* bed and breakfast called the Tsunakan Inn.

Situated on a secluded peninsula in an already inaccessible region of Tohoku, the Tsunakan Inn was separated from the sea by a towering 6-metre wall of concrete. Many of the locals up and down the coastline had protested against it, lamenting that as well as blocking the stunning coastal views, the wall couldn't possibly hold back the formidable power of a tsunami. For the most part, the tsunami of 11 March had swept right over the seawalls in ports up and down the country.

Knocking on the door of the inn, we were met with a loud burst of welcome as Ichiyo threw open the doors to greet us.

With light brown hair and the widest smile I'd seen in Japan, Ichiyo was bursting with energy. In her fifties, she had the personality and demeanour of someone twenty years younger, and I took an instant liking to her. As the owner and hostess of the Tsunakan, being a people person was an essential requirement. While she was open about her lack of English, she tried her best to speak it and to bridge the language barrier with foreign guests, with her excitable hand gestures and basic spoken English.

'Please, please! Let's eat!' she laughed, sitting Ryotaro and me down at her dining table to treat us to a delicious meal of local fish and oysters that had been caught earlier that day by her neighbours.

Before the tsunami, Ichiyo's husband had been a local fisherman, and in the late morning, when he returned from work, she'd prepare the catch of the day in her kitchen. When the tsunami swept through her village, it destroyed her home. The destruction was devastating, but she channelled her boundless energy and positivity into rebuilding the local community alongside her husband. Photos of Ichiyo and her husband proudly leading the local community could be seen around her newly rebuilt home, framed newspaper cuttings charting their successes. It had all culminated with the couple reopening their home as a *minshuku*, welcoming guests travelling up to Kessennuma and turning Ichiyo into something of a local celebrity around town.

But just as her life had started to regain some semblance of normality and the village's fortunes had been turned around, the sea took from her once again. On a morning fishing trip out into the Pacific Ocean, her husband, eldest daughter and son-in-law lost their lives when their boat overturned. Consumed with grief, she closed her business for several months.

When I met her in 2018, she'd said that the Tsunakan gave her a sense of purpose, taking her mind off her suffering. As we sat down to shoot the documentary, it tore me apart to interview the nicest woman I'd ever met on an aspect of her life that had inflicted so much pain.

'The secret to getting through the pain is I don't look back,' she told me. 'If I ever look back at what happened, it'll be when I'm seventy or eighty. I don't want to dwell on the past, nor do I expect too much from the future. If I can get by now, if I can live in the moment, I can keep going.'

Poignantly, Ichiyo tried to make her peace with the sea that had rewarded her family with a thriving fishing business yet also destroyed her home and taken the lives of her loved ones.

'The sea has given us so many things. but it's wrong to always take from it. Sometimes I have to give back. It sounds almost wrong, I know. But I have to believe that if there are positives, there will always be negatives. I have to believe the world is balanced like that. It's hard to go on if I don't tell myself that.'

I felt both shaken and inspired by her words. She was so outwardly positive and selflessly focused on bringing other people joy. Spending time with Ichiyo and Yoshiaki Suda had demonstrated to me the triumph of the human spirit.

Until the tsunami documentary, I'd never felt proud of any of my videos. But when I released it, the outpouring of comments from viewers around the world inspired by the stories of Ichiyo Kanno and the reconstruction of Onagawa made me understand the power and satisfaction that comes from sharing important stories with the world. The video featured in an article in the *Nikkei Financial Times*, one of Japan's most respected newspapers, and the then CEO of YouTube, Susan Wojcicki, endorsed it on Twitter. I felt like I was really making waves.

But most importantly, in the years since the release of the documentary, many Abroad in Japan viewers have made the long journey 400 kilometres north to the city of Kessenuma to stay at

Ichiyo's inn. It remains one of the proudest chapters of my career.

Amidst shooting the tsunami documentary, I'd become a Z-list celebrity. A month had passed since the North Korean missile incident and friends had jokingly started referring to me as 'bleary-eyed Broad' after a piece on Australian 9 News mocked my exasperated early-morning video.

Meanwhile, I'd been brought in for an interview in a sinister edition of the UK's ITV *Tonight* titled 'ITV Tonight: Trump vs North Korea'. There was a potential conflict between North Korea and the West, and having been woken up by an air-raid siren apparently qualified me as a boots-on-the-ground geopolitical expert on the subject.

After a bold segment hypothesizing an all-out nuclear war between Kim Jong Un and Donald Trump, the show cut to a stern presenter having a cappuccino in a London coffee shop looking at my dopey face on the laptop screen as we chatted casually on Google Hangout about the end of the world.

'Chris, how did it feel, being woken up by an air-raid siren?'

'Not overly great.'

'And what's the general atmosphere in Japan?'

'It's tense. This is all we need right now.'

Groundbreaking TV at its finest.

My viral video had also attracted notice in Japan. One evening I was hunched over my laptop editing the tsunami documentary when I answered my phone to an overexcited Ryotaro.

'Oh my fucking god, mate, you've won an award! You're one of the finalists of Shingo Ryuugoutaishou!'

'Wow, that's amazing!' I exclaimed. 'What the bloody hell is it?

He told me. Japan holds an annual event called 'The Words of the Year', where they take a look back at the past year and highlight new words and terminology that have surfaced then crown one of them *the* word of the year.

Candidates for 2017 included *Insuta-bae* (インスタ映え), meaning to look sharp on Instagram, *handosupina* (ハンドスピナー), referring to the fidget spinner that was unfathomably popular at the time, and *Yuchuba* (ユーチューバー), meaning YouTuber.

It was a prestigious list indeed.

I wasn't representing the word 'YouTuber'. It turned out my missile video had promoted Japan's new alert service for disaster warnings, J-Alert.

It had been J-Alert that had scared me to death the morning of the North Korean missile launch.

'They want you to come to Tokyo for the award ceremony,' said Ryotaro. 'It will be broadcast on national TV. It's one of the biggest events of the year.'

'Honestly, Ryotaro, I think I'm good, mate.'

'This is a once-in-a-lifetime fucking chance. You have to do it.'

I reluctantly gave in, suspecting that Ryotaro was cheekily hoping to ride off the back of the PR. Especially as he'd insisted that he should join me on stage to collect the award. Regardless, I was grateful for the company.

The award ceremony was to take place at the Imperial Hotel. It was built in the early twentieth century to cater to Western visitors and is often regarded as one of Tokyo's three great hotels, the other two being the Okura and the New Otani. The original palatial building had been built by iconic architect Frank Lloyd Wright in the 1920s, but after being bombed in the Second World War and controversially demolished in 1967, the luxurious five-star hotel had been rebuilt into the world's ugliest building.

I met Ryotaro in the shadow of the thirty-one-storey concrete monstrosity. The exterior was grey and dull, as if it was sucking up the daylight, but the lobby was significantly more glamorous, the old money of Tokyo's wealthiest on full display. Its external appearance may have been an atrocity, but the allure of the Imperial Hotel was undiminished. Looking around at the lavishly dressed guests, I could hardly complain. If it had been good enough for Marilyn Monroe and Queen Elizabeth II, it was good enough for Ryotaro and me.

Checking into our dated twin room and with hours to spare, I set about ironing my tattered shirt while Ryotaro took selfies of us two and sent them to his Japanese friends, who were hotly anticipating our TV appearance.

It was a strange feeling knowing that millions of people across Japan would likely see my face, and yet I felt no real excitement. Perhaps the same way a Japanese person would feel about getting to appearing on *Britain's Got Talent*. If you're unaware of what you're appearing on, it's hard to gauge how big a deal it is.

In the early evening we ventured down into the cavernous ballroom where the award ceremony was being held. This room was typically used for hosting weddings with up to three thousand guests.

As we entered, I realized the scale of what was about to happen. In front of the stage was a wall of at least 150 photographers, some standing and holding cameras, others using tripods. Sitting between the photographers and the stage was a wall of journalists tapping away on a sea of laptops, ready to live-post about the event online. It was bigger than a White House press conference.

I'd never seen anything like it and, all of a sudden, I realized how fucked I was.

The idea of standing in front of a hundred cameras and being broadcast on TV and online to millions was beginning to seem very unappealing.

'Are you sure you can't just do it alone, Ryotaro?' I asked as I paced restlessly backstage.

But now we were behind the curtains and the event had begun. I couldn't stop the image of me walking out and falling flat on my face playing out in my mind on repeat.

'No, you *have* to do it. It's too late now.'

'You bastard.'

With the amount of public speaking I'd done in my time in Japan, from teaching to speech competitions, and even presenting a TED talk on life in Japan earlier that year, I was truly confident that I'd never feel nervous about talking in front of a crowd again.

Sadly, that turned out to be bollocks.

This event was on another level. The whole thing was being live-streamed on Japanese television and online to an audience of hundreds of thousands, and as the only foreigner appearing in the show, I didn't want to blunder my big moment while stumbling around on stage like a headless chicken. It didn't help that a group of incredibly popular Instagram girls representing the word *Insutabae* went on before us. As I watched them leave the stage to rapturous cheers and applause, I felt the pressure piling on.

'The next word of the year is . . . J-ALERT!' shouted the presenter, to a drum roll.

A harried stagehand gestured for me to stand up and prepare to burst through the curtain, but not before sticking a comically large rosette on my chest.

'Good luck!' Ryotaro gave a double thumbs-up.

'I hate you,' I spat out as I left.

To the sound of a tacky cover of the *Mission Impossible* theme tune the presenter continued, 'And here is the foreign man who helped put J-Alert on the map. Chris Broad!'

With that, the *Mission Impossible* theme crescendoed and the curtain opened to reveal me clumsily walking out, blinded by the flashing of a hundred cameras. It was a miracle I didn't tumble off the stage.

A woman in a red-and-black chequered kimono raced forward with my award: oddly, a clock presented in a polished wooden box. She bowed and I graciously accepted it, while my benevolent translator, Ryotaro, was ushered on to the stage behind me.

'Chris san, 2.3 million people watched your video online. How did it feel being viewed by so many people around the world?' asked the presenter.

I wasn't quite sure what to say or how long I should speak. I got a sense that everyone was eager for the next person, as if I'd won the Best Lighting Award at the Oscars and the crowd was eagerly awaiting prizes for the A-list celebrities.

'Honestly, it was strange going on TV and being featured in the media as some kind of specialist on North Korea and Japan, when in reality I'm just a YouTuber who got woken up.'

Ryotaro translated it and the room went quiet. Maybe I'd said too much.

'And what did your mum think about it all?' the presenter enquired.

As a twenty-seven-year-old man, it was an odd question. All of a sudden, I felt like I'd won a competition for the best crayon drawing.

'She thought it was crazy,' I replied. The audience remained awkwardly silent. A tumble off the stage felt quite appealing now.

'Thank you, Chris san!' And with that, Ryotaro and I were escorted down the stairs to a table at the front, to sit among the photographers.

I wasn't sure how it had gone. Ryotaro seemed pleased, though, as his phone alerts had started to pop off.

About an hour later the winning word of the year was announced. *Insutabae* took the crown.

I wasn't quite sure how I felt about losing. It wasn't as if I'd been trying to win the damn contest. I'd only learned about its existence several days earlier. On the other hand, I felt like the threat of nuclear conflict and the prospect of World War Three was a more pressing issue than Instagram selfies, however sharp they are.

Either way, Ryotaro had enjoyed his five minutes of fame and I was glad I could share this moment with him. Seeing his huge smile had made it all worthwhile.

26.

Seeking Redemption in a Lost Year

Everything was going wrong.

On paper, I'd just completed the adventure of a lifetime, cycling for forty-six days straight, covering 2,000 kilometres across Japan, and vlogging the entire journey.

I'd called the series Journey Across Japan; a twenty-eight-episode series stretching from Yamagata in the rural north to the bustling city of Kagoshima, which nestled alongside Sakurajima, Japan's most active volcano, at the southern tip of Kyushu.

It had been the trip of a lifetime and a victorious response to finally hitting the unthinkable milestone of 1 million subscribers on YouTube. It felt like a lifetime since the early days, when I'd rubbed my hands with glee at 250 views for my first video. Together with Natsuki and Ryotaro, we'd built the largest Japan travel channel on YouTube, and I felt immensely proud. Journey Across Japan was supposed to be the victory lap.

Instead it'd nearly been my demise.

To pull it off, I'd assembled a fantastic support team of camera crew and producers. But wanting to control the production process, I'd decided that I and I alone would edit the videos. And I'd promised my viewers that the videos would be coming out daily.

You can probably see where this is going.

To this day, I don't understand what I was thinking.

When it came to Abroad in Japan, I'd always been a control freak, in charge of every aspect of the production process, delivering the videos to the highest standard without cutting corners. It worked when I was delivering a video every couple of weeks. But to somehow upload daily while cycling six hours a day, presenting and filming all the while, would require a fundamental shift in time and space. Even if I'd had a dedicated editor, it wouldn't have been enough, and here I was, scrambling to edit videos until 3 a.m., before setting off, haggard, several hours later on my bike.

Remarkably, I'd somehow pulled it off for the first five videos. But after a week I was a shell of my former self, both physically and mentally.

By the end of the trip I was so ill that the last three videos weren't usable: I was unable to string a sentence together on camera. My pale skin was covered in rashes and lumps so bulbous they looked like they were about to explode.

But it was the online backlash that hit me hard.

'So disappointed. He said the series would be daily.'
'Very let down. Was really looking forward to the videos.'
'Got bored and forgot about Journey Across Japan while waiting for the episodes.'

The comments were in their hundreds. Brutal, but fair.

I'd made a promise I couldn't keep and suffered the consequences of immense guilt and personal disappointment.

Then, just to kick me while I was already down, I received tragic news from a friend in Sakata. Itou sensei had passed away.

I only found out a day before his funeral, while filming at the opposite end of Japan. I crunched the numbers and tried to find a way, but I wasn't able to make it back in time.

Having returned to Sakata only a handful of times in the last year, we hadn't been able to meet up recently and I felt deeply remorseful that I hadn't been more proactive in keeping up with such a good mentor and friend.

Nevertheless, my feelings of guilt at not being able to attend Itou's funeral or meet in the year leading up to his passing were outweighed by the immense gratitude I felt at getting to know such a wonderful man and hearing his amazing story.

Together, we'd won the speech contest – at least, the second time around – and he'd experienced a degree of mini stardom through his breakout appearance on the infamous 'Teaching swear-words to Japanese People' YouTube video.

But it was the memories of spending our Wednesdays together at the International Centre, tucked away in a classroom, sipping green tea and hearing his stories as we laughed the hours away, that I would revisit on a bad day.

For most of 2019, I sought to pick up the pieces and finish the twenty-eight episodes of Journey Across Japan, spending January to August stuck in a room editing the past. The series had wrapped filming and the trip had ended in November 2018, and it wasn't until 5 August 2019 that I finished the last episode, wondering if anybody still cared.

Alone indoors, editing endless videos alone and reading negative comments from disappointed viewers, I spent many months feeling lost. At no other point had I felt so close to giving up. I considered quitting YouTube and leaving Japan altogether.

But it turned out that the cure wouldn't be to flee from work.

It would be to race towards it head on, with two wildly different documentaries that would take me from the glamorous dressing room of Japan's biggest rock star to the exclusion zone of the world's second worst nuclear disaster.

Nobody does celebrity culture quite like Japan.

As I stood outside the bustling Zepp Tokyo, a concert hall overlooking Tokyo Bay, I watched crowds of fans swarming the tables buying merchandise, CDs, shirts and even credit cards endorsed and emblazoned with the face of enigmatic rockstar Hyde. As frontman for L'Arc en Ciel, a legendary Japanese rock band that has sold over 40 million records, Hyde had godlike status within his home country. He was also the first Japanese act to perform a solo show at Madison Square Garden in New York. Hell, in Osaka, they'd themed a train in his honour, with his handsome face circled by striking blonde hair gazing out across commuters. Take that, Hachi the cat.

But most exciting for me, it was Hyde's voice I'd heard all those years ago, tucked away in my first Japanese apartment watching the anime GTO: Great Teacher Onizuka. The theme tune, 'Driver's High', which kicked off each episode was performed by Hyde and his band. My past self, tucked under my *kotatsu* watching GTO, would never have believed what was about to happen.

I'd been granted a full week with Hyde, to film a documentary on his life and career. Usually this would be reserved for prime-time Japanese television, so it was an extraordinary opportunity for a YouTube channel, and practically unheard of in Japan's tightly choreographed world of celebrity. As I fought my way through the crowd to get inside the venue, I couldn't believe my luck.

I met Hyde several days before we started shooting, at a

kushiyaki restaurant hidden away in west Tokyo. *Kushiyaki* has all the magic of yakitori skewers, in a vastly more unhealthy form. Fish, meat and vegetables are placed on a skewer, dipped into a deep-fat fryer and served with sharp, tangy Worcestershire sauce. Wonderful.

Arriving at the restaurant early, I met Hyde's international manager, an affable American called Jason who'd contacted me after watching a few Abroad in Japan videos, wondering if we might be able to collaborate on a documentary.

It'd be a win-win. I'd get to spend a week getting to know a Japanese living legend and Hyde would receive exposure overseas. Hyde was keen to perform more widely outside Japan.

After having a few *kushiyaki* skewers and drinks with Jason, a hooded figure emerged from the shadowy doorway, accompanied by someone else. Hyde's bleached hair protruded from his hoodie, and he had an almost angelic face, with a youthful complexion of a man half his age. He certainly had the aura of a rockstar.

He wandered over and pulled down his hood.

'Nice to meet you, Chris,' he greeted me in a soft voice. We shook hands and he sat down to join us.

Hyde was calm, cool and collected and we found common ground in our love of eighties music, particularly Depeche Mode and Duran Duran, whose song 'Ordinary World' he'd recently covered.

His chosen name soon seemed completely appropriate. Like a real-life Jekyll and Hyde, I witnessed his softly spoken, calm manner vapourize the moment he got on the stage. He launched the show by shouting, 'Are you fucking ready?' to the screaming crowd, and his set was electric, as if he was possessed by an evil spirit. One minute Hyde would be singing from a giant speaker at the side of the stage, the next he'd be flinging himself into the crowd, his legendary showmanship matching his powerful vocals.

It was fascinating to see the fans meet him afterwards. I witnessed a group of girls spontaneously burst into tears the moment they met him backstage. I'd never seen anything like it. The closest I'd got to that was the occasional viewer who bumped into me in the streets of Tokyo and asked for a selfie. Hyde's screaming, crying fans were on another level.

Throughout my week with Hyde, Natsuki had been pestering me to join the shoot in Tokyo, and I'd reluctantly caved in to his demands. I told him he was free to attend the concert, but there'd be no way he could meet the man himself.

Secretly, though, I was scheming for Natsuki to bump into Hyde backstage after the gig. And sure enough, after an impressive two-hour set, Hyde came barrelling down the corridor to high-five a visibly shocked Natsuki.

'Wow, so fucking good!' screamed Natsuki, startling the weary rockstar.

It was the interaction I never knew I needed to see, and it was glorious.

While I was cutting together the Hyde documentary, Ryotaro suggested an equally challenging documentary project. Off the back of our successful tsunami documentary, he said, we should think about covering the Fukushima disaster.

No news story had dominated my time in Japan quite as much as this. Oddly, though I lived just 100 kilometres north of the reactor, in Sendai, I found that most of the residents of Miyagi prefecture felt detached from it. It was a situation unfolding 'over the border', in Fukushima prefecture, despite Sendai being closer to the reactor than much of Fukushima itself.

As we drove along the highway into the Fukushima exclusion

zone, we were met with the sinister sight of colossal trucks filled with bags of contaminated soil stretching down the road before us. (355,000 trucks were used in the clean-up operation.) Along the roadside, Geiger counters began to spring up, indicating a level of 2.7 microsieverts per hour (mSv/hr), far higher than the global average of 0.17–0.39 mSv/hr, but still less than a passenger would experience on a flight (3–9 mSv/hr). So, Fukushima was now deemed safe to live, but certain areas were still exposing returning residents to higher than average levels of background radiation.

A lot of the terror surrounding radiation is the psychological uncertainty it can bring. When the alert was raised after the meltdown at the Daiichi reactor, 300,000 people were evacuated and scattered across Fukushima prefecture, leaving their homes and possessions behind. As our car made its way through the worst-affected towns of Tomioka and Futaba, we saw villages that had been eerily reclaimed by nature and were now buried beneath foliage. A shrine had semi-collapsed, the structure leaning sideways. Windows in homes and offices were shattered, and a local pharmacy was boarded up and sealed off, a 'contaminated' sign ominously placed out front. It was a real-life post-apocalyptic setting, with piles of green bags full of contaminated soil stacked high on the outskirts of every village.

A survey by the newspaper *Mainichi Shinbun* found that the trauma caused to locals by displacement had led to the deaths of 1,600 evacuees in the year since the disaster, more than the number of deaths in Fukushima caused by the tsunami. And worse still was the stigma associated with the evacuees who arrived in towns and cities across Tohoku.

'People said they're infected; you'll catch it. Don't get married to women from Fukushima. Many people endured this kind of rhetoric,' recalled Masami Yoshizawa, a farmer who lives just 14 kilometres from the reactor.

He'd been told to slaughter his three hundred contaminated cows by the local government but had ignored the advice and had chosen to keep the animals alive, funded by donations from around the world. A resilient man in his later years, the gateway to his property, Hope Farm, was adorned with cow skulls. It was as if they were telling visitors of the fate the herd had faced. And the stench of cow manure and pineapples – a cheap and abundant source of food for the cows – was no less welcoming. Wandering around the farm without feeling queasy was no easy feat.

Masami's story was one of resilience and defiance. He was appalled that Fukushima had suffered so greatly and been left behind by the government.

While I sympathized with Masami and felt I couldn't begin to comprehend all that he'd gone through, everything I witnessed indicated that the Japanese government were doing their best to contain the horrific situation, overseeing a $29 billion clean-up operation to remove 14 million cubic metres of contaminated topsoil. Rice fields that could no longer be used to grow rice had been converted into a solar-energy farms; many abandoned buildings were being bulldozed and removed. And after eight years, with the government's encouragement, some locals were starting to move back to the area.

I interviewed horticulturist Katsumi Arakawa in a blossoming greenhouse. He'd returned to the exclusion zone to start his business growing and selling flowers. 'I'd be lying if I said I wasn't worried about being close to the reactor. But when it comes to everyday life, there's nothing particularly frightening about it.' The idea of never being able to return home was far worse than living in an area with marginally higher background radiation.

Witnessing the scale of the clean-up and meeting some of the hopeful locals gave me a sense of optimism for the future of the region, just as the tsunami documentary had done over a year before. It also helped me put my own trivial concerns into perspective. How the hell could I feel sorry for myself when 300,000 people had been forced to leave their homes and livelihoods behind in an instant, not knowing when they'd return or how much radiation they'd been exposed to.

Working on the documentaries had brought a degree of clarity and salvation to my life. I remembered that my work could have a positive impact, through sharing the stories from the disaster with millions of people around the world.

As for Journey Across Japan, it wasn't until a full year after the series was finished that it gained recognition, against the backdrop of the terrible circumstances.

During Covid, when everyone was in lockdown and many people were trapped inside, losing their minds, I received a ton of messages and emails from viewers around the world who'd binge-watched the series as a means of escaping their homes. For many, it was the closest thing they could get to travelling around Japan.

In spite of its calamitous production, Journey Across Japan went on to become the most watched Japan travel series on YouTube.

For all the trouble I'd had filming and editing it in those two years, hearing about the positive impact of the series made me feel it had all been worth it. It had taken two years, but at last I felt vindicated for undertaking the project that nearly broke me.

27.

Disappearing Kyoto

Japan was changing. In the year 2000, Japan had 4 million overseas visitors. By 2018, that number had exploded to 31 million. Every major city in the country was receiving a face lift, the gritty backstreets of Shinjuku and Shibuya rapidly gentrified, with gargantuan hotels to cater for foreign tourists. Remarkably, even Japan's lenient smoking regulations had been torn up; with the exception of small *izakaya* pubs, smoking indoors was banned. Where once people could smoke wandering the city streets, now there were designated areas. It was a far cry from my early years, when entering every bar or restaurant meant descending into a cloud of tobacco.

In a country that had just faced two 'lost' decades of economic growth after the bursting of the real-estate bubble in the early 90s, and a devastating tsunami and nuclear disaster in 2011, tourism had turned things around for Japan. The build-up to the Tokyo 2020 Olympics had created a sense of momentum, particularly after the country had successfully hosted the 2019 Rugby World Cup. In 2020 the eyes of the world would focus on Japan.

And then, after almost a decade of anticipation, the opportunities were cruelly snatched away. In March 2020, the country shut its border in the face of Covid. Tourists were not able to travel to Japan for two and a half years.

Living in Japan had always felt like being in a bubble, between the language, the culture and the country's tendency to hold the rest of the world at arm's length. But now, with the gates in and out of Japan effectively sealed and the stark warning, in the early months of the pandemic, that permanent foreign residents would not be able to return to Japan should they leave, the bubble was completely sealed.

In some respects, no country was better equipped to handle Covid than Japan, given the widespread use of facemasks in daily life, an etiquette that shied away from physical contact and one of the world's lowest obesity rates. Testament to this was the fact that despite 30 per cent of the population being over sixty years old and therefore more susceptible to the virus, the number of Covid-related deaths in Japan was less than a third of the US figure.

With the doors to Japan firmly shut and the anticipated 35 million tourists kept out, nowhere in the country was transformed quite as dramatically as Kyoto. I'd always had a love-hate relationship with the city. On my first trip there with George, after surviving our climb of Mount Fuji, we'd stayed for several days and been somewhat underwhelmed. We'd expected an ancient city, steeped in tradition. Instead, as we wandered out of the hideous monolith that was Kyoto station and into the shadow of the steel eyesore of Kyoto Tower, there was nothing to suggest the city was any different from Tokyo.

As we made our way out of the downtown area, Kyoto's beauty began to reveal itself. Immaculate temples and traditional wooden buildings stood at every corner. However, when we visited Kinkaku-ji temple, the glamorous golden pavilion pasted on the covers of every guidebook to Japan, we had to queue for half an hour and found ourselves being crammed into the grounds with a huge crowd of onlookers, the deafening sound of iPhone camera shutters on a constant loop. The gold-leafed pavilion was undoubtedly striking, but the original structure had burnt down in 1950, and although it had been faithfully reconstructed and renewed, it looked as if it had been built yesterday. As we snaked along the designated path around the pavilion, amidst the noisy crowd battling it out for selfies, George wasn't overly impressed.

'Crikey, was that it?' he lamented, as we followed the path back out towards the exit, feeling emptier than when we'd walked in.

By day two, as we battled our way through the crowds leading up to Kiyomizudera temple, one of Kyoto's famous attractions, it felt like we were exploring the city because we felt we *had* to. It was regarded as Japan's cultural capital, with no less than seventeen UNESCO World Heritage Sites to gaze upon. We dragged ourselves to as many as we could manage.

There were pleasant moments, wandering through the tranquil Arashiyama bamboo forest and ascending the steps beneath the ten thousand *torii* of the Fushimi Inari shrine. We both agreed that the Philosopher's Path, a hidden stone track along a canal in Kyoto's Higashiyama district, was a highlight. Free from any clear attractions or photo opportunities, the path was devoid of tourists, allowing us to contemplate the beauty of the city as we strolled past traditional homes, encountering a kind old man making boats from fallen leaves and sailing them downstream.

But the problem was undeniable: Kyoto was a victim of its own success. While Tokyo was so big it could soak up millions of tourists, Kyoto was bursting at the seams. An incredible city had been reduced to an overcrowded theme park.

At one point, as George and I ambled through Gion, the geisha district, we saw almost a dozen tourists harassing a lone geisha as she tried to make her way down the street. She wore a striking blue kimono and we watched as tourists blocked her path to snap selfies. She continued walking calmly on, as though the tourists simply weren't there. It was a sad sight. Excessive tourism in Kyoto had sapped away its old-world charm.

Suddenly bereft of millions of tourists, a new problem had presented itself for Kyoto.

Bankruptcy. The prolonged decline in tourism had led to a deficit of $440 million, on top of an already mounting debt pile of $7.5 billion. Tourists weren't solely to blame for this. The city's star attractions – two thousand Buddhist temples and shrines – are exempt from tax. Any attempts by the local government to change this policy were hit with staunch resistance.

Worst of all, the stunning *machiya* wooden townhouses that were at the heart and soul of the city's architectural identity were facing their own crisis.

It was November 2020, and I'd been invited to Kyoto to produce a documentary on *machiya* by Koji Maeda. Koji was a Tokyo entrepreneur who'd fallen in love with Kyoto on a trip and decided to start a business renovating *machiya*. It was a trip that would fundamentally reshape my views on Kyoto and lead me to fall in love with a city I'd neglected for almost a decade spent living in Japan.

Riding the *shinkansen* bullet train was always a joy. Gliding across the Japanese countryside and barrelling through cities at 320 km/h felt like the ultimate travel cheat code. Taking in the views from a throne-like reclining chair while munching on skewers of yakitori, the *shinkansen* makes a mockery of British public transport. And with the many tunnels, the tracks make a mockery of Japan's vast mountain ranges, though admittedly at an environmental cost. To make all this possible the landscape is blighted by an elevated concrete track from Hakodate to Fukuoka.

Many of the villages and the towns in between reap no benefits; instead, they have to live with the train's deafening roar as over a thousand passengers shoot past in an instant.

Dozing off after a mountain of chicken, I was abruptly awoken by the sound of a jingle warning passengers of our imminent arrival. If I'd stayed asleep, I would have woken up in a disorientated mess in Hiroshima two hours later.

Arriving at Kyoto station, I noticed a difference straight away. I couldn't spot a single foreign face. Scanning from the platforms and the ticket gates to the entrance, I realized I was the only non-Japanese commuter. While in towns like Sakata, tourists were always a rarity, in normal circumstances Kyoto would be overrun with visitors from across the globe. Not now.

At the taxi ranks, the taxis with English-speaking drivers, specially provided to cater for the crowds of foreigners, sat in a quiet queue, the drivers looking bored. Seeing my face, the driver at the front of the queue perked up. I'd intended to hop into a regular taxi, but once we'd made eye contact I felt I had little choice but to get in.

'Kyoto is so empty these days,' he said as we drove along the banks of the Kamo river. 'It's like a different city.'

'How do people feel about it being so quiet?' I asked, anticipating a gleeful response. I imagined Kyoto usually felt overburdened by the hordes of tourists.

'It's nice at times. But we worry about the local businesses. So many are closing.'

It seemed that, by the time we'd all got through the pandemic, Kyoto would likely be a very different city indeed.

It was a sunny afternoon and I decided to visit Kiyomizudera temple before my evening meeting. Without the crowds, I could finally appreciate the architecture of the temple without fear of being knocked over or swept away.

I strolled in the shadow of the five-storey Yasaka pagoda, perhaps the most photographed pagoda in Japan. A handful of Japanese girls wearing lavish kimonos were taking selfies, but then they scurried away, leaving me alone. A few years ago, this would have been unimaginable. Gardens, temples, alleyways lay empty to explore and get lost in.

As I relaxed on a bench in Maruyama park – Kyoto's most popular *hanami* cherry-blossom-viewing spot in spring – I watched a Japanese family wander across a wooden bridge that stretched over a pond, searching the surface of the water for koi carp as the cool autumn breeze rustled through the trees. At that moment, I started to wish I'd put Kyoto on my JET application all those years ago. A few peaceful moments alone was all it took to make me appreciate this ancient city's ever-lasting allure.

There are around 40,000 wooden *machiya* in Kyoto. Poke your head down any alleyway in the city and the odds are you'll spot one of these traditional townhouses. One giveaway is often the *kōshi* lattices shuttering the windows, for added privacy and discretion but still allowing light in. Each design has a meaning: windows covered from top to bottom indicate a liquor store, while *kōshi* that use slimmer pieces of wood signify a kimono or textile shop.

Machiya are sometimes referred to as *unagi no nedoko*, literally, 'eel's nest'. Thankfully, the houses aren't littered with eels; it's a reference to the long, narrow, often deceptive layout of a *machiya*. In the Edo era, properties were taxed according to their street frontage, so they were extended ever backwards. Sliding open the front doors, if the townhouse sold goods, you'd immediately enter into the shop space, and a further door would take you into a large living room concealed within, often described as the *kakureya*, or 'hidden space'.

Due to the lack of windows and the labyrinthine rooms, *machiya* feel incredibly cosy, but far from being dark or cramped, the home is built around a small courtyard, or *tsuboniwa*. It's not just for aesthetics; the *tsuboniwa* allows a space for reflection and improves airflow through the interior, something that is desperately needed in Kyoto's humid summer months.

Built of natural materials, from the wooden beams and paper sliding doors to the tatami mats, the inside of a *machiya* has an atmosphere of unmatched calm, and the wooden surfaces provide a soft, warm illumination to each room.

You might think that the locals of Kyoto would be keen to protect the *machiya*. But as Maeda san showed me around one that he was renovating, to my surprise, he revealed that the locals were complicit in their destruction.

'People in Kyoto often don't feel comfortable in *machiya*. In summer, they're too hot; in the winter, too cold. As they are made out of wood, they can be vulnerable to fire, so it's common for people to demolish them to build a modern home.'

The sad reality is that maintaining *machiya* is quite a financial burden. While many of them are being renovated and rented out to tourists, which should keep the townhouses alive in some form, the future isn't looking good. Between 1993 and 2003, 13 per cent of Kyoto's *machiya* were demolished. At the current rate of eight hundred townhouses lost every year, by 2066 they could all be gone, taking Kyoto's history with them.

Retreating from my interview with Maeda san to a townhouse he'd let me stay in for the night, I slipped into the *hinoki* cypress-wood bath. I'd had a long day of travel and filming. Gazing upon the quaint courtyard garden, the cool night air blowing in my face, I felt gloomy at the speed at which Kyoto was changing and disappointed that I'd written off the city for so long. It's sad it took a global pandemic to help me appreciate what makes Kyoto so special and what it stands to lose.

28.

'This is My Dream'

For almost a decade after starting my YouTube channel, I'd often joke that the day Japanese movie star Ken Watanabe appeared on one of my videos would be the day I'd leave the country. If I hit that seemingly impossible goal, my Japan bucketlist would be completed.

'You're not gonna believe this. Ken Watanabe is interested in featuring on Abroad in Japan.'

I suppose I'd better pack my bags.

Perhaps Japan's greatest living actor, and certainly the most recognizable, Ken Watanabe had an enviable career that had seen him nominated for an Academy Award for his role in *The Last Samurai*. His powerful performance as a warlord alongside Tom Cruise was legendary. He'd gone on to feature in Clint Eastwood's *Letters from Iwo Jima*, Christopher Nolan's *Inception* and the Hollywood reboot of *Godzilla*. In 2015, his Broadway debut in *The King and I* led to a nomination for a Tony Award – a first for a Japanese actor.

Against the backdrop of his trailblazing acting career, I'd discovered one of his biggest roles had been offscreen, helping a destroyed town recover in the aftermath of the Tohoku tsunami.

In 2011, while taking part in the recovery efforts along the coastline, his journey had taken him to the fishing port of Kessennuma, one of the worst affected towns, whereover 1,400 people had lost their lives and 8,400 homes has been destroyed.

After striking up friendships with the locals, Ken adopted Kessenuma as a second home and immersed himself in the port's long-term revitalization. He built the K Port, a café in the heart of the town, and became a 'mental pillar for the local community', in the words of a local business leader.

In a world where celebrities are constantly seeking PR opportunities to boost their image, Ken's motives were genuine. He was still involved in the town ten years after the tsunami, and giving the people in it a sense of pride and the confidence to move on.

'Many people were in a hopeless situation after the tsunami,' explained Ryuji Ando, owner of the town's vibrant fish market. 'Ken Watanabe was a huge moral support for us. He really is samurai!'

In 2017, while filming my documentary on the tsunami with Ryotaro, we'd shot a scene at Ken's café and had left feeling inspired by the story of Japan's biggest movie star quietly helping to rebuild a town in northern Japan. It was a beautiful story that demanded to be told, especially as so few people inside and outside Japan were aware of the impact he'd had.

Having dedicated the last five years to producing videos showcasing Tohoku, the Abroad in Japan channel seemed a natural fit for him, but it felt like an impossible goal.

One day I was out gorging on sushi in Tokyo with my good friend Yasu, a Japanese entrepreneur working in media, when he proposed something truly radical.

'I mean, why don't we just send Ken and his team a letter?'

'Ha. A letter! It'll end up in the bin,' I scoffed, my cynical British mindset getting the better of me.

'I'm serious, Chris. You've already done the work to get there by covering his café, and you've shown you can work with a Japanese celebrity like Hyde. We should send a proposal.'

Even with the success of the Abroad in Japan channel, working with celebrities always seemed somewhat out of reach. We'd been lucky to work with Hyde, but it had taken substantial negotiations to make it happen – and Hyde's team had approached *me*. That was half the battle won – they'd opened the door for us from the outset.

The idea of interviewing Ken Watanabe had started almost as a joke in my first year as a YouTuber. It seemed so unattainable as I sat watching him in movies from the tatami floor of my tiny Sakata apartment, or spotted him on giant billboards in Osaka. Natsuki would frequently tease me about it over our Thursday-night yakitori dinners: 'You still haven't met Ken then?'

Ryotaro and I had come close during our documentary shoot. We discovered a week after filming at K-Port that Ken had spontaneously arrived in the town to work at his restaurant.

Meanwhile, every time a viewer ran into him, they'd send me a photo. After Ken began performing on stage at London's West End in *The King and I*, I received numerous smug messages from cheeky viewers who'd bagged selfies with Ken and sent them over. Even Ichiyo Kanno had joked, as we interviewed her at her inn in Kesennuma, that I was sitting in the very seat where Ken Watanabe had sat and enjoyed dinner.

We'd always been so close, yet so far, and Yasu was claiming that this whole time we could have simply sent a bloody letter?

If any other person had proposed it, I would have shot it down. But like all good entrepreneurs, Yasu was ruthlessly persistent. 'We've got nothing to lose. Best case they read the proposal and say yes, worst case they ignore it.'

I reluctantly agreed, and Yasu put together a slick proposal and sent it, hand delivered, to Ken's management agency.

A few days later, I was off shooting a video in Asakusa with Ryotaro when I got a phone call from an ecstatic Yasu. Ken was very much interested.

'His manager said we could join Ken for a week up in Kesennuma and shoot while he's in town for an event he's taking part in.'

'Jesus, a whole week! This can't be right, Yasu. If this happens, I'll eat my fucking hat.'

Less than one month later, I was sitting in Ken's café, stirring my coffee and watching the boats sail through Kesennuma's harbour.

'Have you eaten it yet?' cracked Yasu.

'Even if I had a hat, mate, I'd be too bloody anxious to eat anything right now.'

I hadn't slept a wink. I was about to meet the man who, unbeknownst to him, had loomed over my time in Japan. Terrifying was an understatement.

Not too dissimilar from the movie *Inception*, I felt immersed in a waking dream. Maybe it was the adrenaline. Maybe it was the lack of sleep. Probably the latter.

As an inconspicuous Toyota rolled into the car park, I spotted the staff perk up, and several tables of customers began muttering excitedly. Having kept away for several months because of Covid, like a king returning to his kingdom, Ken had arrived.

I've never been truly starstruck before. But seeing his face as he emerged from the car, a face I'd seen on cinema screens, billboards and TVs, I felt an absolute rush of excitement.

A tall figure, casually yet impeccably dressed in a dark T-shirt and grey hooded coat, he walked into the café with a beaming smile and shouted, '*Hisashiburi!* Long time no see!' to the staff. He was given a hero's welcome. A handful of fans who seemed to have been aware of his impending visit rushed over with a notebook, and he graciously gave autographs and took photos while I sat gobsmacked in my chair, taking a jittery sip of coffee.

After a few minutes touring the room and catching up with familiar faces, his manager ushered him over to the quiet corner in which I perched with my film crew.

'Chris, it's very nice to meet you,' he said, and we fist-bumped each other – Covid rules. 'Now, would you like some pizza?'

You don't say no to pizza with Ken Watanabe.

And so it came to be that in my first minutes with Ken we sat in his café and chatted. We shared a stone-baked pizza, and he proudly explained that it was made from scratch in the café.

'I'm nervous about all this. It's pretty scary,' I muttered at the start of our interview.

'Why?' he replied, in a voice so deep and booming it sounded almost ironically terrifying.

Spending a week with Ken was even more inspiring than I could have imagined. Everywhere we went, the locals were delighted to see him wandering through the town, and so proud. Over dinner at a local restaurant, a customer came over and got on his knees to thank Ken. I soon learned that he worked at a local school and Ken had donated musical instruments so the students could play in their free time. The owner of a local brewery graciously gifted Ken a few bottles of his award-winning sake.

I got a real sense of the humanity underpinning his support for the town as we strolled across the port and Ken recalled the day he first arrived.

'Standing here now, we can hear boats, cars, people talking nearby. But when I stood here on that day, there was absolutely nothing. There were no sounds at all. It felt as though the town wasn't breathing.'

The transformation was undeniable. If you stood in downtown Kesennuma today and watched the boats sailing in and out of the port, the customers buying the catch of the day and sipping coffee at the K Port café, you'd find little evidence to suggest the town had so recently been destroyed.

At the end of our time together, I mentioned to Ken how I'd often joked about leaving Japan the day I met him. But, I said, it felt so unbelievable, it was likely just a dream anyway.

'So if it's real you'll leave Japan?' Ken remarked with surprise.

'Absolutely,' I assured him.

'OK then, let's see.' And just like that, he pulled out the spinner from *Inception* to determine if we were in reality or not.

'This is my dream,' he remarked wistfully as the spinner spun its way across the table, and my week with Japan's most successful actor came to an end.

I don't think Ken ever realized how much of a big deal it was to meet him and spend a week working so closely together. The most important thing was to hear his story and tell it to the world, but for me personally it was a symbol of how far I'd come on my journey in Japan.

I left Kesennuma feeling uncharacteristically optimistic. Perhaps, above all, I had learned that if you're willing to wait around long enough, sometimes even the craziest dreams in life may end up becoming reality.

29.

Fear and Earthquakes

For ten years, I'd lived in Japan without ever experiencing a major earthquake.

Though my life in Tohoku had been lived out in the aftermath of the devastating 2011 earthquake and tsunami and the spectre of the Fukushima nuclear disaster, Japan had moved on. Sendai was prone to monthly minor earthquakes, but they lasted no longer than ten seconds. By the time you'd noticed the sound of windowpanes gently clattering or a wooden cabinet creaking it was already over.

Rather than fearing this shaking of the earth, I'd found the experience oddly fascinating. After all, the only time I'd felt my house shake in the UK was when my friend Dave fell down the stairs. This type of natural phenomenon barely ever happened where I was from. I'd taken geology for granted in school geography lessons, but the idea of a tectonic plate half the size of the Pacific Ocean moving beneath my feet had made me appreciate just how fascinating it was.

Then, one afternoon in March 2022, that appreciation turned to horror. A horror that morphed into full-blown fear.

It was 16 March at 11.36 p.m. and I'd just returned to my apartment block after a fine yakitori dinner with Natsuki, who'd made the three-hour voyage east to Sendai for a long-awaited catch-up.

Living over a dozen storeys high with my girlfriend, Sharla, I'd taken the lift up, entered the apartment and plonked myself down on the sofa with a glass of water, pointlessly trying to avert the inevitable hangover the following morning.

My phone let out the ear-piercing sound of an earthquake alarm. I nearly spilled my water as I jumped in surprise. The noise brought back traumatic memories of the air-raid siren that had woken me up so abruptly five years previously.

The Japan Meteorological Agency had developed an earthquake alarm that was able to pick up the initial seismic shockwaves that arrive just moments before the main event, providing crucial seconds of time to prepare. In my case, I used those seconds to sit there dumbstruck. In my dopey, semi-drunken state, I wasn't quite sure what to do when I heard a deep rumbling noise fill the room. When you're a dozen storeys up in the air, hearing this noise, like the building is being demolished with you trapped inside it, emanating from all sides is pretty alarming.

In three seconds, the room had gone from being peaceful and stationary to rocking like a ship caught in a storm. Modern Japanese buildings are built to sway in an earthquake, rather than trembling and shaking, which is far more likely to cause structural damage. Many people use an ingenious device called a seismic damper, in effect, a gigantic pendulum mounted in the roof of the building to help offset the swaying and reduce the movement of the buildings.

As the intensity grew and the swaying gave way to more shaking than I'd ever experienced, I started to worry. Books rocked and fell from the shelf, and Sharla's pet cat, Maro, leapt from a chair and ran from room to room, unsure how to escape his collapsing world.

After a tense ten seconds, it all died down and I was relieved that one of the worst earthquakes I'd experienced was over.

I plonked myself down on the sofa and caught my breath.

'Well, that wasn't fun,' I remarked to Sharla, as she tried to calm down poor Maro, who was shaking in fear.

Then, out of nowhere, the room jolted upwards, taking the sofa with it, almost as if a bomb had gone off below. At first I thought the building was collapsing. The deep rumbling had been replaced by the sound of glasses and crockery being flung across the kitchen and smashing on to the floor. This was no run-of-the-mill earthquake. The others I'd experienced had started gradually and worsened over the course of several seconds before gently abating. This time, however, the earthquake was unpredictable, hitting peaks and troughs with an intensity I'd never experienced before.

Maro ran around erratically, diving for the window, hoping to get out, while a nearby bookshelf rocked precariously as if it was about to collapse. The rumbling, the smashing and the clattering of windows combined with a shaking so intense I was almost unable to stand up triggered a panic attack that made me want to get out, just like Maro. I felt trapped and longed to be outdoors.

Watching the concrete walls shake as if they were built out of Lego, I started to consider the worst. Was this the big one? The follow-up to the 2011 disaster scientists had theorized about? Surely the building wasn't designed for this level of stress?

Standard procedure during an earthquake is to get under a table or stand in a doorway, in case chunks of the ceiling break away and fall on you. But as the longest thirty seconds of my life dragged on, I found myself holding on to my bookcase for dear life, believing for the first time that I might actually be about to die.

After an eternity, the shaking and the banging died out and the sounds of dozens of fire alarms rang out across Sendai city. The cool spring night had been transformed into what sounded like a war zone.

My first thought was to flee, in case round three was just around the corner.

We put Maro inside his box and made for the stairs. Unsurprisingly, the lifts were out of service, not that I wanted to go anywhere near one, in the circumstances.

In hindsight, we should have stayed in our apartment. Standing outside a building isn't a great idea, in case loose objects or tiles fall and hit you. But in the throes of a full-blown panic attack, I needed air. My fight-or-flight response was firmly locked in flight mode.

Reaching the lobby, I saw that a few other residents of the block had had the same idea, either choosing to wait it out on the ground floor or dashing out of the building to find an open space. Everyone's face was as ashen as mine no doubt was.

Soon sirens from the emergency services filled the air, and an ambulance pulled up across the road and two medics dashed through the doors of a neighbouring apartment block.

Not long after, my phone flooded with notifications and messages from concerned friends and family. News reports had pinpointed the epicentre to nearby Fukushima prefecture, just south of Sendai.

It wasn't long before Natsuki came running down the street from his hotel.

'Woah, fuck! Very scary!' he shouted. Incredibly, despite the situation, hearing Natsuki's animated voice brought some comfort. It was odd, because it was usually Natsuki invoking the chaos.

'My hotel room, water everywhere. Oh my god.'

Apparently, Natsuki's hotel had flooded after a pipe burst. But he was safe, and that was all that mattered. He was shaken, but he'd been able to run out of the building with his cigarettes so, as far as he was concerned, all was well.

The earthquake clocked in at a magnitude of 7.4. It was the largest since 2011 and was later reported as an aftershock of the earthquake that had taken place a decade earlier. Three people died and 247 were injured. In many ways, it was remarkable that the damage wasn't more severe, given that thousands of buildings across north Japan experienced such intense shaking.

As for me, I was profoundly scared. For the first time, an earthquake had put me in my place. No longer was I fascinated with the Earth's workings beneath my feet. The ever-present threat felt more acute. I spent the next few days living in fear, afraid to take the lift and wondering if at any given moment my apartment would turn into a glorified bouncy castle. The extent of the damage wasn't terrible; apart from all my kitchenware, which was now a mosaic, most things seemed unscathed.

The Abroad in Japan studio wasn't so lucky.

Months earlier, I'd inaugurated my first studio space with a professional-grade film set, built to resemble an 80s ramen shop. I'd collaborated with local designers to create a space I was truly proud of. While the studio was a dream come true, it was constructed inside a building from the 1970s that had been erected without modern-day earthquake protection.

The next morning, Natsuki and I opened the door to find that not only had half the set collapsed but a pipe had burst in the room above us, flooding the studio and turning the shattered crockery from the ramen shop into a ceramic, pulpy mess. A half broken *maneki neko*, a lucky cat, lay among it all, its beckoning paw protruding from the rubble.

It was disheartening to see the brand-new set, built with love and care, so cruelly destroyed so early on.

For all the terror it had inflicted, the 2022 Fukushima earthquake (as it came to be known) had shown how good Japan was at adapting to the chaos Mother Nature dealt out so ruthlessly. I'd come across it before, when meeting survivors of the 2011 tsunami – Japanese people have an unbreakable spirit and a stoic mindset that I've come to respect and admire greatly. People dusted themselves off and got back to work the next day as if nothing had happened.

I wish I could say some of that strength and resolve had rubbed off on me, but for the longest time after the earthquake I was unsure whether it was time to leave Sendai. It wasn't because I felt it was time to move on to greater things, or because I was tired of the city.

It was because of fear. Fear of experiencing another earthquake of similar magnitude, which, unfortunately, is what seismologists are predicting off the coast of Miyagi prefecture in the near future.

Yet I've remained in the city I love for over half a decade now. Allowing myself to be driven away from my home by fear just wasn't an acceptable outcome. When I leave, it'll be on my own terms, not Mother Nature's.

After the earthquake, I received messages and emails from viewers who also felt uncomfortable about living in Japan because of the earthquakes. I imagine my panic-stricken videos online hadn't helped in the hours after the event. But to avoid Japan due to earthquakes would be to avoid the sea for fear of sharks, or aeroplanes for fear of crashing. As they say, 'to live in fear is to never live at all'.

Epilogue

I often wonder what would happen if Natsuki transported back to the year 2008 and told my past self that he was my best friend sent from the future. A future where I'd spent my twenties living in rural Japan as an English teacher and Youtuber.

I likely would have laughed as this cocksure Japanese man finished his peculiar description of my future in between drags on his Marlboro cigarette. Then, after he'd finished smoking, I'd have called the police to have him taken away.

Nothing about the first eighteen years of my life hinted that I would live and work in Japan. While some people move here after years of dreaming and painstaking planning, it was a twist of fate that set me on my course all those years ago. It scares me to think about how close I came to missing all of this.

You might have picked up over the course of this book that I'm quite an anxious person. I'm not entirely sure why that is. Maybe I got it from one of my parents. Or maybe it was growing up with asthma, waking up in the middle of the night with the feeling that I was being suffocated by an invisible ghost. Perhaps it's the lofty expectations I set for myself and the fear I'd never meet them. But at every step of this journey, anxiety has loomed over me.

In the months after I learned I was moving to Japan, I began having aggressive panic attacks on a regular basis. I recall one particular occasion in the kitchen of my shared house at university. I was chatting with a friend about their drunken night out, tuning out of the conversation a little bit, and felt an immense sense of dread sweep over me. It was as if something terrible was about to happen. Like a monster was about to burst in through a window. It felt like if I got up and opened the door, I'd fall into an empty void of nothingness.

And as quickly as it came, it went away. All within about twenty seconds. It was so fleeting that my friend didn't notice, caught up in their story of projectile vomiting on a wall.

At first I thought I might have had a mini stroke or a heart attack. Searching online didn't do me any favours. I realized, on a subconscious level, that it was the thought of leaving my world behind to live in a country where I knew nothing and no one.

Back then, leaving scared the hell out of me. What scares me now is the thought that if I'd given in to that anxiety, none of this would have happened. If I hadn't forced myself to go outside of my comfort zone, I would never have left the UK.

Now I ask myself one simple question whenever a big decision presents itself. No matter how much something terrifies me, I ask myself, *If I walk away, will I live to regret this?*

After all this time, not a single day has gone by that I've regretted moving to Japan.

Even in the bad days, when I was being rejected by landlords or crawling around looking for cats, when forty students gawped at me with apathy or I got booted out of a love hotel. I don't regret any of it.

Living in Japan has challenged me every step of the way to become a stronger person. More resilient, more open-minded – and more overweight, thanks to the greasy wonders of Family Mart fried chicken.

Two thousand hours in a classroom, over 250 videos and 47 prefectures visited, it's been a wild ride. And while I might have enjoyed a degree of fame from YouTube and the mind-boggling 400 million views the Abroad in Japan channel has racked up over the years, YouTube has been a means to an end to discover Japan in a way that I'd never dreamed was possible. I feel incredibly grateful to have taken millions of people along for the ride, through this crazy journey uncovering the country.

You might think it would be the blockbuster moments that stand out when I look back. Appearing on Japanese national TV and being rudely awoken by a North Korean missile. Sharing a pizza with Ken Watanabe or shivering on the summit of Mount Fuji at dawn. Giving Itou sensei a victorious hug after winning the impossible speech contest will always be a favourite memory and producing a documentary on a terrible event and the inspirational people I met doing it.

These are certainly all moments I'll treasure until the day I die. But the truth is, the really special memories I return to on a bad day are often the most unremarkable. Sitting alone on a remote beach after finishing work, gazing across the sea at a dormant volcano, deeply grateful that fate brought me here. Watching the snowfall billow across the window of the yakitori restaurant as Natsuki and I ride out the bitter cold and tuck into yet another plate of greasy grilled chicken. Disappearing into the mountains on a weekend jaunt, driving my rickety Toyota Starlet in circles and chancing upon a crumbling *torii* at the entrance of a forgotten hamlet.

The thrill of living in Japan is not quite knowing what surprise lies in store for you next. And if being here for ten years has taught me anything, it's that there's always one more wild discovery waiting for you, just around the corner, in the Land of the Rising Sun.

Acknowledgements

Writing this book has felt like a time-travelling experience. For the many months spent working on it, I've constantly cast my mind back to moments and memories I had long thought lost, returning to the present eternally grateful to the many people who've helped me along my journey.

Firstly I would like to thank the teachers and staff of Sakata Senior High who put up with me for three years, practically babysitting me in my first few months of life in Japan.

I'm particularly thankful to Natsuki Aso for finding me on the streets of Sakata and taking me under his wing all those years ago and joining me through the highs and lows of my decade spent in Japan. I feel incredibly lucky to have him as a best friend throughout it all.

To the evil mastermind Ryotaro Sakurai, I also wanted to say thank you for giving me a sense of purpose in my life in Tohoku, promoting Japan's most underrated region through our many videos and trips together. Our chaotic adventures, lost in the mountains of north Japan, are amongst my fondest memories of all.

I'm also incredibly lucky to work closely with longtime friends David Parish and Ellen Kavanagh, as well as my sister Emma Broad on the Abroad in Japan team. Thanks for standing by me through thick and thin over the years!

I can't possibly get away without acknowledging my partner and best friend Sharla, who has supported me throughout the years, first as a friend and fellow vlogger and now as a partner and fiance. I feel incredibly lucky to have had her by my side.

I'd also like to thank my parents Sally and Richard, for letting me flee to the far side of the world so recklessly unprepared and somehow never doubting me along the way.

A special thanks to Sharika Teelwah at Transworld Publishers for making this book possible every step of the way. Her attention to detail and sharp sense of humour turned editing this book into a joy over the many months spent writing it. Thanks too, to Sarah Day, Viv Thompson, Rosie Ainsworth and Hana Sparkes for helping to bring this book into the world.

Lastly, I have to say a huge thank you to everyone who's been a part of Abroad in Japan over the years. What started out as me in a tiny apartment complaining about culture shock and illegible phone bills has evolved into something I couldn't possibly have imagined, but I'm constantly amazed at how many viewers have stuck around all of this time. Whether you're a viewer who has been around since day one, for half a decade or even just a few months, thank you for watching the crazy things I create and being a part of this journey uncovering Japan. To share in the experience of discovering a culture and continuously humiliating myself in front of the whole world has been an utterly surreal adventure that I wouldn't change for the world.

ABOUT THE AUTHOR

Chris Broad is a British filmmaker and founder of the Abroad in Japan YouTube channel, one of the largest foreign YouTube channels in Japan with over 2.5 million subscribers and 400 million views. Over ten years and two hundred videos, Chris has visited all of Japan's forty-seven prefectures, focusing Abroad in Japan on travel, food and culture. He has also covered contemporary issues through documentaries on the Fukushima nuclear disaster and the Tohoku earthquake and tsunami. His experiences have made him a sought-after voice on life inside Japan and he has been featured on the BBC, TEDx, NHK and the *Japan Times*.